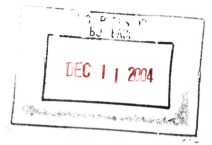

DIGITAL MARKETING STRATEGY

Text and Cases

Glen L. Urban
Professor of Management
MIT Sloan School of Management
Massachusetts Institute of Technology

PEARSON
Prentice
Hall

Upper Saddle River, New Jersey 07458

Library of Congress Cataloging-in-Publication Data

Urban, Glen L.
  Digital marketing strategy / Glen L. Urban. -- 1st ed.
    p. cm.
  Includes bibliographical references and index.
  ISBN 0-13-183177-1 (case)
  1. Marketing--Management. 2. Electronic commerce--Management. 3. Internet
marketing. 4. Consumer behavior. 5. Strategic planning. I. Title.

HF5415.13.U735 2003
658.8'4--dc21   2003 048729

Senior Editor: Wendy Craven
Editor-in-Chief: Jeff Shelstad
Assistant Editor: Melissa Pellerano
Editorial Assistant: Danielle Serra
Media Project Manager: Anthony Palmiotto
Marketing Manager: Michelle O'Brien
Marketing Assistant: Amanda Fisher
Managing Editor (Production): John Roberts
Production Editor: Maureen Wilson
Permissions Supervisor: Suzanne Grappi
Manufacturing Buyer: Michelle Klein
Cover Design: Kiwi Design
Cover Illustration/Photo: PhotoDisc
Composition/Full-Service Project Management: Carlisle Communications, Ltd.
Printer/Binder: Phoenix

Credits and acknowledgments borrowed from other sources and reproduced, with permission, in this textbook appear on appropriate page within text.

10 9 8 7 6 5 4 3 2
ISBN 0-13-183177-1

To Andrea—my trusted advisor and partner

Brief Contents

Contents

Preface

This book began in 1999 as the impact of the Internet was becoming clear. I initiated a course on Internet marketing strategy with the intent of inserting the Internet's potential within a framework of strategic marketing. Although initially some argued that the Internet was a revolution and that "old" marketing would be replaced with new concepts and methods, it soon became clear that the Internet would not be a substitute but rather a complement to existing strategic marketing practices. I remember in 1999, after I gave a lecture stressing the fundamental concept of understanding customer needs and building a viable business model, a student raised her hand and said, "Professor Urban, you do not get it! It's all about the new game, seizing the high ground and capturing eyeballs." I responded that that may be true but that it was my feeling that fundamentals would rule and that she should "stay tuned" to developments over the next year. To her credit, at the end of 1999 when it was evident that the dot-coms were in trouble, this student e-mailed me, saying, "Well, that was not such a bad course! Could you send me the lecture notes again?"

We have gone from the optimism of 1999 to a crash of expectations about the Internet in 2001. If the Internet was too hyped and expectations were too high, now the opposite has occurred. Students' expectations are unrealistically low. However, all measures of digital impact are up—even on-line retailing is up over 25 percent per year for the past three years and up even when traditional retail sales were often flat. In 2002, after the same general lecture on customer needs and business models, a hand went up in the classroom, and I thought, "Oh no, not again!" But this time the student wanted to know why I did not teach these fundamental ideas to those who jumped into Internet start-ups and dramatically failed. Students are now open to learning the essential principles of marketing within a technological environment. They have a more realistic view of both the potential and the limitations of digital technologies.

Large companies were not fooled by the hype and crash of dot-coms. Since 2000, they have consistently allocated more resources to utilizing the Internet and other digital technologies. The impact has been to improve the efficiency and effectiveness of marketing. Digital technologies have become a powerful method of improving marketing practice in a multichannel environment.

As I began the course in 1999, I found a shortage of up-to-date cases on digital marketing and few texts that stressed a strategic perspective of utilizing the new technologies. Therefore, I set out, with the help of my teaching assistants, to write a set of new cases. Fourteen cases were created, and nine are included in this book. I have abstracted the text notes from my lectures and from the comments of guest speakers and managers directly involved in the cases.

The structure of the book draws on the strategic framework from *Advanced Marketing Strategy* by Glen Urban and Steve Star, but the digital focus and cases are all new. During the past four years, I was codirector of the eBusiness Center at The Massachusetts Institute of Technology (MIT), so I benefited from discussions with our sponsors, who include Hewlett Packard, Intel, General Motors, British Telecom, United Parcel Service, Mastercard, Merrill Lynch, Cisco, Dell, Price waterhouseCoopers, and the Interpublic Group. This center contained few dot-com companies, but the major gains from the Internet have accrued to existing firms. Although some new companies like eBay, Travelocity, and Amazon have been successful, the majority of gains have occurred in the improvement of marketing in large established companies.

This book discusses the concepts of understanding customer needs and behavior, formulating a strategy to fill needs, implementing effectively and efficiently, and building a trusting relationship with customers. I present brief textual descriptions of the critical concepts in each area and then follow each chapter with a case chapter. I include cases that discuss the issues in large companies like Dell as well as small start-ups like MotherNature. Some cases deal with high-tech products (e.g., InSite Marketing Technology), and others stress the use of new high-tech marketing methods to sell established products (e.g., Citibank). Some are global (e.g., Terra Lycos), and I consider products (e.g., OSRAM) as well as services (e.g., Travelocity). I span the functions of marketing from new product design (MarketSoft) to physical distribution (Logistics.com).

The goal of the book is to prepare the student to be an effective innovator and change agent by utilizing new digital technologies strategically to contribute to the firm's sales growth, profitability, and stock price. The technologies are pervasive in marketing and equip students to make valuable contributions to new product design, product management, advertising and public relations, selling, pricing, distribution, customer service, job opportunities as vice president of marketing and sales. With these skills, the student should be well qualified for the best jobs in established, emerging, and start-up companies. I cannot imagine marketing managers of the future not being skilled in digital marketing tools.

This text can be used for a range of courses. One is in a dedicated digital marketing course. Increasingly, digital technologies are being internalized into the basic marketing course, so this text can be used in marketing strategy or marketing high-tech products. I am even using the cases and much of the text from this book in my New Product Development course at MIT. Finally, this text can be useful in executive education courses that stress state-of-the-art marketing topics like trust-based marketing and emerging market research methods. A teacher's manual is available to aid professors in utilizing and customizing the case and text pedagogy.

The future will continue to change rapidly as new digital technologies emerge and the marketing environment morphs. This book's use of a fundamental strategic structure will, I hope, allow students and managers to use this book as a learning platform. The future is full of potential for existing and new firms, and if this text trains managers who can successfully innovate with new digital technologies, I will consider it a success.

Acknowledgments

Many people have helped me in writing the text and cases. First, my teaching assistants over the years helped to create, revise, and update the cases for this book and material for sidebars. Various teams worked on the case material over the three years from 2000 to 2002. They are listed alphabetically here, and I am very appreciative of their contributions: Gulsun Bozkurt, Esther Chang, Ben Gibbons, Maria Jackson, Kristen Koehler, Susan Lee, Shyan Lim, Srinath Narayanan, Sebastian Pereira, Fernando Ramirez, Shiva Ravikumar, Jessica Santiago, Telmo Valido, and Keith Waxelman.

Most of the case discussions involved company managers, and I want to express my appreciation to the various executives who came to my class over the years. Thanks to Ross Blair of Experion Systems, Joel Book of Prime Response, Jose Carrete of Terra/Lycos, Denise Champagne of OSRAM/Sylvania, Howard Citron of Semisales.com, Key Compton of Solbright, Sam Decker of Dell, Greg Erman MarketSoft, Gabriela Ferreres of Terra/Lycos, Yong Kang of Kozmos, Mike Kozub MarketSoft, Richard Last of J. C. Penney, Mark Lopez of Terra/Lycos, Steffania Nappi of Insite Marketing Technology, Mark Parsells of CitiBank, Greg Schmidt of OSRAM/Sylvania, Yossi Sheffi Logistics.com, Carol Snyder of Travelocity, Mike Stacy of Travelocity, Jeff Steinberg of MotherNature.com, and Julio Vaca of Terra/Lycos.

The cases were edited by Andrea Meyer and Dana Meyer of Working Knowledge. In addition, their contributions went beyond the cases to the text. They integrated my text notes within detailed chapter outlines to produce effective text copy and exceeded the usual writer's function by adding new ideas or finding sidebar material to serve as exemplars of the strategic concepts. A special thanks to them.

I would like to formally thank the eBusiness Center at MIT, which supplied financial support for the case writing and book integration as well as numerous industry contacts that have helped make the book managerially relevant.

Finally, I would like to thank my administrative assistant, Sandra Crawford-Jenkins, who was invaluable in proofreading, generating graphic material for the book, and obtaining permissions.

CHAPTER 1

Introduction

The Internet and digital technology have changed how marketing is done. While the underlying principles of marketing remain the same, digital technologies provide new ways to improve the efficiency and effectiveness of strategic marketing activities. This book teaches new tools that make marketing more productive. It also describes how the Internet is changing consumer behavior and increasing consumer power. These new phenomena threaten the prevailing practices of many businesses. In the travel industry, travel agents are being supplanted by consumers who research and book their own travel on-line. In the health care industry, patients come to doctors armed with the latest information on maladies and demanding the latest drug by name.

Along with the threat to existing practices, however, come new opportunities. The Internet lets companies establish relationships directly with customers, offering customized service without high costs. Companies can deliver highly targeted, individualized promotions, and they can deliver them quickly. The digital era brings new strategic choices and possibilities. One of the most exciting new strategic choices is a trust-based marketing strategy. We explain and explore this new strategic choice in chapters 5 and 15.

Marketing strategy requires defining the market domain in which the company will compete. It also requires determining the core benefit that customers will get from the firm's products and services. Recognizing customer needs and filling them better than the competition is the heart of successful marketing strategy. Companies that satisfy customer needs without overspending company resources achieve financial goals.

Marketing is the great matchmaker between the company and its customers, matching customer needs with company products and services. But marketing is more than making the customer want to buy a company's offerings. Hype and buzz may create short-term revenues but are not a basis for long-term competitive advantage. Marketing's most important role is to help make a company's offerings something that customers want to buy. The customer comes first in marketing. Marketing guides the generation and deployment of resources for new product development, for communication, and for the distribution functions of the firm. Marketing begins and ends with the customer—from understanding needs and behavior to building a relationship based on trust and customer satisfaction.

Digital marketing uses the Internet and information technology to extend and improve traditional marketing functions. Digital technology includes customer relationship management software, sales force automation, wireless technology, marketing automation software, and decision support systems. Highly connected information systems are helping companies offer new levels of personalization. Extensive data on every transaction means that companies can now do campaign management. Companies can objectively assess the return on investment of their marketing efforts. In short, digital technologies make marketing more effective because they allow for individual attention, better campaign management, and better product and marketing design and execution. New technology can now even take on the role of a trusted adviser who helps customers make purchase decisions in the way that they prefer to make decisions. As we will see in chapter 6, companies are creating electronic advisers that enter into consultative discussions with customers.

The "digital" behind digital marketing represents a number of technological trends. First, the rise of pervasive computing and networking has brought new ways for customers and companies to connect. Companies and consumers can communicate through a range of connected devices, such as PCs (at home or at work), digital set-top boxes, Internet-enabled game machines, cell phones, and two-way pagers, and they can communicate by voice, text, data, images, streaming video, and so on. The coming years will no doubt bring new devices and device standards. The point is not the exact nature of the devices but the fact that there are increasingly greater levels of connection and communication.

> In the coming decade, the number of businesses and consumers connected to the Internet will easily surpass one billion. Internet trade between businesses rose 73 percent in 2001 to $496 billion.
>
> *Source:* Robert Hof, "How E-Biz Rose, Fell and Will Rise Again," Special Report: The Future of E-Business, *BusinessWeek*, May 13, 2002, 64–72.

Digital technology also includes the enterprise software systems that accelerate the efficient execution of routine business processes. Marketing-specific software systems (e.g., customer relationship management and sales force automation) combine with other business software systems (e.g., enterprise resource planning, decision support, and groupware for knowledge work) to improve marketing-related business processes. Moreover, the same enterprise tools that help a company execute marketing functions within the company help it perform marketing-related functions with its industrial customers and suppliers. Business-to-business integration helps companies understand their customers (and their customer's customers) and fulfill their customer needs more rapidly and efficiently.

Why Digital Marketing Is Important

Digital marketing is important because it revolutionizes almost all aspects of marketing. Digital technology (1) introduces an entirely new channel to sell and market products, (2) allows new pricing options and individual promotions to customer, (3) enables new hot media communication, (4) offers opportunities to find new product needs and launch new products, and (5) supports improved distribution and service. Even more important, the Internet has changed the balance of power. Across industries, consumers are gaining the upper hand. Customer power in this Internet era is driven by three factors: more options, more information, and simpler transactions. The Internet provides a new channel for buying products and services, giving customers more options when buying a given product or service. The Internet also gives customers more information because it makes it easy for customers to learn about products and services, to compare offerings between companies, and to read third-party evaluations of product/service performance. Finally, the Internet simplifies transactions, making transactions easier or more convenient to execute. Consumers have more power when they can more easily find, select, and buy competing product or service offerings.

> With digital technology, the opportunity for direct promotion to customers allows customers to opt into a mailing list rather than one being pushed on them. For example, JC Penney has five million customers who have opted to be on JC Penney's list to receive promotions and product information.

Digital marketing is not just about bits and bites—marketing managers have to think strategically about what products and services to offer, how to segment the market, which segments to pursue, how to position their products, how to implement their strategies, and how to ensure customer loyalty. Consider these examples:

• **United Parcel Service (UPS)** reinvented itself from a package delivery provider to a total service provider that not only moves packages but also handles the information and funds flow associated with shipping. The economy runs on three flows: a flow of goods and services, a flow of information, and a flow of money. UPS was traditionally a mover of packages, supporting the flow of goods. With the rise of the Internet, UPS added many more services related to the flow of information, such as shipping tools, tracking tools, and e-commerce tools. The company foresaw e-business driving the convergence of the three flows, combining ordering on-line, tracking purchases on-line, and paying on-line. As a result, UPS started offering a range of e-commerce and fulfillment services. E-commerce support includes on-line tools that help integrate a business with shipping services from UPS. Fulfillment services go beyond just package delivery to include managing inventory, pick-and-pack, returns processing, and so on. For example, UPS software can help e-businesses set up complex returns processes that automate the routing and tracking of returns. In short, UPS made a strategic shift around digital technology.

• **BT,** formerly the government-owned telephone monopoly known as British Telecom, restructured around high-growth, customer-facing markets such as wireless, Internet, and business services. BT made a strategic decision to reorganize from being a commodity mover of bits to becoming a diversified provider of high-value services. The fundamentals of its new strategy are customer satisfaction, financial discipline, value-added solutions for corporate clients, and a clear strategy for each customer group. For example, BT Ignite, a £4.5 billion subsidiary and one of four BT divisions, is focused on a wide range of business Internet services. BT Ignite's services range from business consulting to Web hosting to managed network services. A broad portfolio of skills and services means that BT Ignite can handle the broad range of needs of corporate customers.

*   **Hewlett-Packard (HP),** traditionally a manufacturer of products and supplies, is expanding to provide a broad array of services. Although still the world leader in printers and printing supplies, HP saw the opportunity that providing services brings. HP Services provides consulting, outsourcing, and support IT services. Even during 2001, a year marred by economic downturn and the 9/11 tragedy, the HP Services division grew 15 percent, outperforming the market in each segment of the services business. In the area of printing, HP is focusing on the opportunities brought by digital technology. Digital imaging solutions—encompassing photo printers, software, computing infrastructure, and an understanding of networking—use HP's existing depth and breadth of its printing product line to leverage into this area.

These kinds of strategic changes indicate the opportunities that managers have. But making changes is risky, as the lessons from the Internet bubble illustrate.

Lessons from the Internet Bubble

The first generation of digital marketing has passed into history, and a second generation is now being born. The first generation was marked by high hopes, a landgrab for potential market opportunities, and an infatuation with Internet technology rather than customer needs. As excitement about the possibilities promised by the Internet's disruptive technology mounted, dot-com prices rose to unsustainable levels. A crash inevitably followed, and digital marketing is now positioned for a second generation that will deliver real benefits and returns. We have learned valuable lessons from the failures. The Internet will not be a revolution that replaces existing marketing. Rather, it will be a new channel and a set of methods to improve the efficiency and productivity of marketing. Digital technology will improve how we design, communicate, promote, price, and distribute our products. Although there will be opportunities for new firms, the chief beneficiaries of digital marketing will be existing companies. In many of these companies, the Internet will transform how marketing is done.

However, the experience of the early days of the Internet shows us that a focus on digital technology alone is risky. Evidence points to the failed assumptions about how the Internet will change business.

The early exponential growth rate of the Internet led many to assume that the trend could only continue and transform the economy. On-line retailers assumed that everyone would buy everything over the Internet. Dot-coms believed that a clever domain name, a few product pictures, and a flashy banner ad were enough to generate an unending stream of orders. Many also assumed that companies would abandon old buying and selling processes to move to pure information-mediated business-to-business exchanges. The assumption that bits would replace atoms led many to predict the rise of brutal price competition via on-line price comparators.

Internet companies assumed that balancing revenues and costs was no longer important. Indeed, some companies even bragged about not having profits. Companies ignored fundamental business principles as they flipped from strategy to strategy. Companies assumed that being fast and first was all that mattered. A massive influx of capital from venture capitalists (and exuberant stock prices) led companies to think that they had bottomless wells of equity. The start-ups assumed that hype and buzz in the form of Super Bowl ads and free giveaways would be the key to success.

Throughout this exciting period, pundits assumed that traditional companies would go the way of the dinosaurs: The fast-moving new would replace the slow-moving old. Traditional companies were believed to be too stodgy to innovate. Even those within traditional companies assumed that they had to create a separate company with younger management in order to join the bandwagon. The belief that the new economy did not follow all the old rules of business was pervasive, but it was mistaken.

What's Working and What's Not

What's Working

Large-Volume Branded Sites   Some companies did manage to create a brand and a solid customer base. Broader business-to-consumer companies, such as Amazon, continue to do well, providing customers with deep sources of information, reviews, and ratings of products.

Transaction Fee Models   eBay thrives with over 42 million registered users. eBay holds no inventory but helps buyers and sellers find each other and transact sales. Sellers pay eBay a listing fee and a transaction fee for each transaction made on the site. Over $30 million worth of goods is transacted on the site every day by individuals, small businesses, manufacturers, and retailers. eBay facilitated $9.3 billion in gross merchandise sales in thousands of categories around the world. eBay's net revenues for 2001 were $749 million.

Clicks and Mortar   Traditional retailers, such as Barnes & Noble, that have successfully added on-line functionality to their operations are on solid footing. Some companies tried stand-alone e-business divisions but learned that combined clicks-and-mortar operations were better. When Citibank merged its e-Citi division back into Citibank operations, the on-line customer base rose 80 percent to 10 million customers. The reason for the dramatic rise was that after the operations were merged, e-Citi customers could use Citibank teller machines. Companies discovered that customers want more channels, not just to shift from old channels to a new Internet-enabled channel.

Infrastructure   Companies that provide the technical infrastructure for e-business (such as Dell, Microsoft, and Intel) reaped great rewards as both consumers and business jumped on the Web. The Internet also created a myriad of small success stories as manufacturers found new suppliers, new prices, and new ways to connect.

What's Not Working

Pure-Play Business to Consumer   Many pure-play business-to-consumer companies discovered that bits do not easily translate into dollars. Creating value, attracting customers, and fulfilling expectations is hard. The cost of acquiring customers rose as the novelty of banner ads wore off and Web users stopped clicking on them. Many narrowly focused and undifferentiated on-line retailers found that getting customers was expensive.

The Advertising Model   Companies also discovered that simply selling banner ads on their Web site was not enough to make money. Productpedia, a company that provided product information, may have enjoyed $1 million in ad revenue per year, but it also suffered from $5 million in costs. Companies learned that running a business is much harder than creating a business model on a napkin and getting buzz. Convincing customers to actually buy is much harder than declaring that your business will grab some share of the huge e-business pie. Fulfillment and service are essential business competencies that are much harder than putting up a Web site. Business models that require 200 percent growth are not sustainable.

Exchanges   Business-to-business exchanges that did not reflect the in-depth personal relationship between channel partners and offered little solution/decision content failed. Many exchange companies discovered that what they did was not valuable enough. For example, the Internet may be a perfect infrastructure for connecting truckers to loads, but some fifty such exchanges found that providing this simple service was not enough. The value proposition to the customer was insufficient. Customers wanted more encompassing services, such as those offered by Logistics.com. As we will see in chapter 14, Logistics.com targets the tougher (and more valuable) problem of managing complex transportation networks and fleets of trucks. Logistics.com survives where the simple exchanges failed.

Lesson: Fundamentals, Operations, and Finance Are Essential

The era of unfocused experimentation and speed to market above all else is over. To succeed, managers must understand the fundamentals and then run their businesses on the basis of those fundamentals. Three lessons learned from the Internet bubble show the three key aspects of business fundamentals.

Lesson 1: Deliver Fundamental Value
Companies must look harder at the value that they create for their customers. That is, companies need to create and articulate strong customer benefit propositions. The rise in customer power—and the ease with which customers can click to a company's competitors—leads to a new emphasis on the customer. Marketing and front-end systems are the means for both understanding and delivering value. Fortunately, digital technology helps companies to both understand their customers and match customers to the company's products and services. Companies also need a business model that reflects value delivered.

Lesson 2: Create Operational Excellence
Promises made by the front-office must be promises kept by the back-office. Crafting and articulating a customer value proposition is necessary but not sufficient. Companies must also achieve operational excellence in delivering on their promises. Operational excellence includes many dimensions, such as quality, reliability, cycle time, and cost efficiency. These operational variables underpin elements of the customer value proposition and the company's business model. Companies need to understand which elements of operational excellence are truly valued by their customers and how competition is defined by operational excellence. Digital technology, especially enterprise and supply chain management systems, helps companies achieve new levels of operational excellence with reasonable costs.

Lesson 3: Build Financial Sustainability
Revenues must exceed costs and deliver acceptable returns to investors. Although companies need to survive the quarter to survive the long term, an excessive focus on

short-term financial performance is detrimental to long-term success. Companies must take care that cutting corners does not lead to cutting customers. Marketing plays a crucial role in helping understand the impact of financially motivated decisions (pricing, promotions, and cost-modulating product features) on customers, customer buying, and customer loyalty. Digital technology helps companies analyze customer data and understand the relationship between financial inputs (costs and investments) and financial outputs (revenues and profits). Digital technology also helps companies operate more cost efficiently through both operational improvements and low-cost customer channels.

Ultimately, the dot-com bubble proved that the Internet and digital technologies do not replace the old economy; rather, they augment it. Companies now have new channels for interacting with customers, new low-cost means for servicing customers, and new ways to understand their customers. Yet these new ways fit within the traditional approaches to strategy and tactics. The fundamentals of business have not changed, but companies now have new opportunities to execute those fundamentals more efficiently and effectively.

Objectives of This Book

In this book, you will learn how digital technology can improve marketing strategy formulation and execution. The book teaches a strategic approach to marketing that uses the following flow of four principles: understand customer needs, formulate a strategy, implement the strategy, and build trusting relationship with customers (see figure 1.1). By following this four-step flow approach, you will learn techniques to build profitable growth that leads to long-term success. The book will teach methods to help you fulfill customer needs when you develop new products. It will also show you ways to use

FIGURE 1.1   **The Four-Step Flow Diagram**

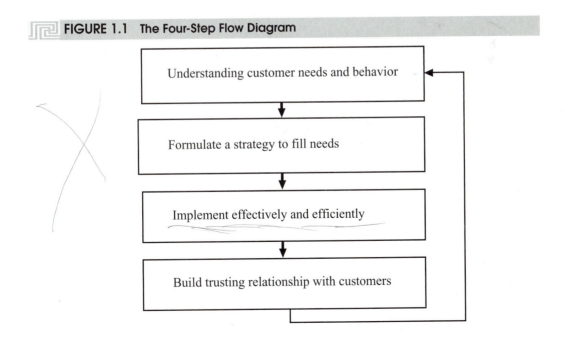

technology to sell to customers in the ways suited to how those customers make purchase decisions. Although the Internet brings new marketing tactics, new threats, and new opportunities, we find that the fundamental theories of marketing remain useful in developing a response to the threats and opportunities created by the Internet. In this book, we show how the Internet can improve each step in the marketing strategy process.

The concept of good marketing strategy is easy: identify customer needs, fulfill them with good products and services, and build a trust-based relationship with your customers. Executing the concept is harder. It requires both art and science, both creativity and technology.

Finally, this book will help you in your career. The continuing strong growth in business-to-consumer and business-to-business Internet sales means that digital strategies represent important career opportunities. Anyone pursuing a career in marketing will have to know these digital strategies. We hope that by the end of the book, we will have trained you in the tools you need to be successful in your career, be it in advertising, product development, public relations, and so on.

Structure of the Book: Alternating Concepts and Cases

This book features alternating chapters of conceptual material and case studies—odd-numbered chapters explain concepts, and even-numbered chapters provide cases that illustrate these concepts. Separating the cases from the concept chapters gives instructors the opportunity to assign cases at different points in the curriculum, substitute an individual case, or assign two cases together.

After this introductory chapter and its associated case study (Mothernature.com), we explain how customers make decisions (chapter 3). The customer decision process is affected by the way the mind works. For example, limitations of short-term memory and information processing lead customers to use heuristics that simplify decision making. Next, we provide five methods for identifying customer needs, from simplest to most advanced. Understanding customer needs is essential to designing successful new products and strategies.

In chapter 3, you will learn the following:

- How customers make buying decisions: the customer decision process both for individual consumers and industrial buyers
- Market research methods to understand customer needs, including digitally based market research techniques, such as on-line focus groups, virtual concept tests, and Web-based conjoint analysis

Chapter 4 uses the case of Dell Computer Corporation to illustrate the tools that companies can use for understanding customer behavior on the Internet. The case also illustrates the complex nature of customer decision-making processes in on-line buying.

Having learned about customer needs, chapter 5 covers the marketing manager's next step of formulating a strategy to fill those needs. Formulating a strategy begins with assessing your company's strengths and weaknesses and balancing them against threats and opportunities. Having assessed strengths, weaknesses, threats, and opportunities, you begin formulating strategy by mapping customer needs onto threats and opportunities. One of the new threats/opportunities facing companies in the digital era is the rise of consumer power. We describe this rise and compare it to Douglas McGregor's Theory X and Theory Y of management. The marketing analogues of McGregor's theories X and Y are Theory P and Theory T (Push-based marketing and Trust-based marketing, respectively). With this foundation, we proceed to describe the fundamental strategic choices available to marketing managers today, from push-based marketing to trust-based marketing. We supply a weights-and-balance tool to help managers determine which strategy to use. We conclude with a deeper look at trust-based marketing, examining what trust is, how the Internet enables trust building, and what benefits companies can expect from trust-based strategies.

Chapter 5 will help you do the following:

- Learn to conduct a thorough analysis of your firm's resources as well as the external environment and then develop a marketing strategy based on your firm's strongest advantages
- Assess your company's strengths and weaknesses relative to the competition
- Evaluate threats and opportunities facing your firm
- Learn about the growing threat/opportunity of consumer power
- Understand the new demands of marketing: Theory T marketing
- Choose the appropriate marketing strategy for your firm, understanding when to use push-based and trust-based strategies
- Understand what trust is and how the Internet enables trust building
- Grasp the benefits of trust-based strategies

Chapter 6 expands on the theme of trust-based marketing with the case of Insite Marketing Technology, a provider of software and services for trust-based marketing.

Having determined the strategic approach you will use, chapter 7 discusses how to determine which customers to target and how to position your product/service relative to the competition. This chapter explains why segmentation is important and how digital technologies change the dynamics of traditional segmentation strategies. We describe the four most common bases for segmentation (demographics, attitudes, importances, and usage) and detail the analytical support tools available. We then move on to discuss product positioning and the use of perceptual maps and conjoint analysis to support positioning processes.

In chapter 7, you will learn the following:

- Why segmentation is important
- How digital technologies change segmentation strategies
- The four most common bases of segmentation
- Analytical support for segmentation
- How to position your product, using tools like perceptual maps and Web-based conjoint analysis

Chapter 8's case study of TerraLycos presents some of the key issues of segmentation and positioning within the context of a global merger between two Internet companies.

Chapter 9 presents the key role of marketing in new product development. To stay competitive, firms must maintain a steady stream of profitable new products. Yet one-third of products fail in the marketplace after introduction, and many more fail before they are even introduced. In chapter 9, we discuss why new products fail and how to avoid those failures. We look at the structured process for product development and the use of new methodologies, such as Information Acceleration and Listening In, to improve premarket forecasting of products. Finally, we discuss the life cycle of products and what marketing managers need to do at each stage of the life cycle.

In chapter 9, you will learn the following:

- Why products fail
- How to prevent new product failures
- A structured approach to product development
- Proactive and reactive product development strategies and when to use which
- How to use two new digital market research methodologies—Information Acceleration and Listening In—to improve new product success (Information Acceleration is used in premarket forecasting of radically new products, while Listening In identifies the potential for unmet needs.)
- How the diffusion of innovation works
- The four stages of a product life cycle and which actions to take at which phase

Chapter 10's case study of Marketsoft illustrates how a company follows a customer needs-focused product development strategy. After its initial success, Marketsoft wants to expand its product line and address the rise of competition.

Chapter 11 addresses how to communicate the benefits of your product to your target customers once you have targeted your market and uniquely positioned your product. Communication takes the form of advertising and selling. In chapter 11, we describe how to evaluate advertising options. You will learn to assess the return on investment of advertising and use decision support models. Two approaches to selling (push-based and trust-based selling) are described. The chapter concludes with a look at multichannel communication.

In chapter 11, you will learn the following:

- How to evaluate media copy (weighing objectives and rating alternatives)
- Understand the return on investment of advertising
- How new media raise complexity and how automated work flow makes it manageable
- Two approaches to selling
- How to coordinate selling with your overall marketing strategy
- Multichannel communication strategies

Chapter 12's case study of OSRAM SYLVANIA provides an example of relationship selling and how the Web is changing selling to long-standing business-to-business customers.

Chapter 13 moves beyond communication, addressing how implementing your marketing strategy requires effective pricing and distribution. In this chapter, we discuss the role of incentive sites, business-to-business exchanges, and reverse auctions. Then we describe distribution, examining both physical distribution as well as new channels of distribution offered by digital technology.

In chapter 13, you will learn the following:

- New pricing strategies enabled by the Internet
- Why business-to-business exchanges failed

- The role of reverse auctions
- Why eBay is so successful
- How new digital technologies facilitate distribution—both physical distribution as well as channels of distribution

Chapter 14 describes Logistics.com as an example of the new mechanisms for service distribution and innovative pricing opportunities offered by the Internet.

Chapter 15 amplifies on the development of longer-term customer relationships and how such relationships build stable, increasing revenues and profits. Now that you understand customer needs, have built a strategy around those needs, and have implemented it through effective new product development, communication, pricing, and distribution, the final step is to build an enduring relationship with the customer. The most enduring relationships are based on trust.

In chapter 15, you will learn the following:

- That trust is a process
- How to cross-sell and grow customer relationships
- How to build loyalty and community
- Methods to encourage constant innovation

Chapter 16 examines Travelocity's strategic options in creating a loyalty program for frequent buyers of travel services.

Chapter 17 takes a look forward at the future of digital technology and consumer responses. We examine the structural changes taking place in marketing and their implications for managers.

In this final chapter, you will learn the following:

- The future of digital technology
- The future of consumer response
- Structural changes underlying marketing and their implications for managers.

Chapter 18, the final case of this book, illustrates the impact of digital technologies by describing the efforts of Citibank to capitalize on digital technology while leveraging existing assets.

Features of the Book

This book is structured to balance theoretical frameworks with practical details. To maximize comprehension, this book features the following:

- An organization around an easy-to-understand flow diagram for formulating marketing strategies
- Short chapters on well-defined aspects of digital marketing
- In-depth case studies to illustrate the real-world issues of digital marketing
- Numerous sidebars that highlight the technological impact of strategic concepts

Audience for the Book

Anyone pursuing a career in marketing needs to understand how to use the Internet to create effective marketing strategies. This book is intended for students and practitioners who wish to expand their understanding of marketing and the role that digital technology plays in making marketing more effective. The book is ideal for undergraduate marketing majors and MBA students who have taken a basic marketing course and are looking for in-depth exposure to advanced marketing strategies. Executive training programs and corporate training departments can also use this book to help executives understand how to leverage digital marketing.

Practitioners, marketing professionals, and consultants can use this book to advance their professional knowledge, gain insight from the case study company examples, and develop new digital marketing strategies for their companies or clients.

MotherNature.com Case Introduction

The MotherNature.com case illustrates the importance of understanding what needs your product fulfills, what the lifetime value of a customer is, and how to communicate with your customers.

REFERENCES

Brynolfsson, Erik, and Glen L. Urban. 2001. *Strategies for eBusiness Success.* San Francisco: Jossey-Bass.

Urban, Glen L., and John R. Hauser. 1993. *Design and Marketing of New Products.* Upper Saddle River, N.J.: Prentice Hall.

Urban, Glen L., and Steven H. Star. 1991. *Advanced Marketing Strategy.* Upper Saddle River, N.J.: Prentice Hall.

MotherNature.com

Introduction

In early March 2000, Jeffrey Steinberg was reevaluating his marketing plan for MotherNature.com, deciding how best to attract visitors to the company's Web site and convert them into lifetime customers. Steinberg, the chief marketing officer, had joined MotherNature.com in February 1999. MotherNature.com was an early entrant into the on-line health products market. During the first 13 months of Steinberg's tenure, the company was successful in raising capital, building a well-known on-line brand, and recruiting a solid management team. In March 2000, MotherNature.com is one of the front-runners to capitalize on the burgeoning on-line health market.

During the Christmas season of 1999, e-commerce sites had begun to fulfill expectations for exponential sales growth (expectations that had long fueled exuberant investing in Web-based ventures). Despite improved sales figures, however, dot-com stock prices fell during the first quarter of 2000. Firms in the health-related market as well as firms in other industries, including Amazon.com, Buy.com, and Pets.com, saw their stock prices drop (see figure 2.1). Like its counterparts at these firms, management at MotherNature.com began turning its attention to long-term prospects and profitability. As part of planning the transition from start-up to going concern, Steinberg focused his marketing efforts on three areas:

- Attracting and retaining on-line customers
- Crafting a marketing plan with a high return on marketing investment (ROMI)
- Creating, using, and modifying models to quantify customer lifetime value (CLTC)

Company Overview

MotherNature.com is a leading on-line retail store and information site for vitamins, supplements, and minerals (VSM) and other natural and healthy-living products. Through its combination of content and commerce, MotherNature.com is poised as the

FIGURE 2.1

Comparison of On-Line Health Care Firm Stock Performance

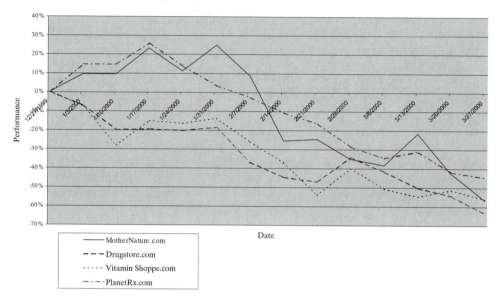

Comparison of Major e-Commerce Firm Stock Performance

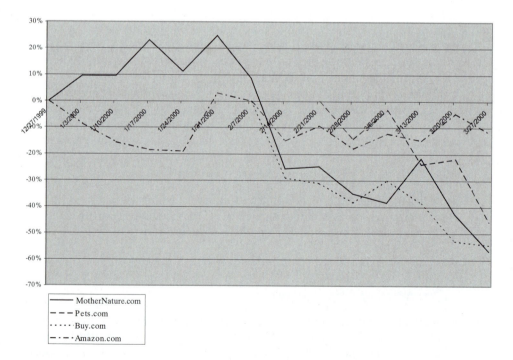

preferred destination for consumers interested in such products. Headquartered in Concord, Massachusetts, the company had recently opened a large distribution center in Springfield, Massachusetts.

History

MotherNature.com was founded in December 1995 under the name Mother Nature's General Store. During the first three years, the founders established distribution channels and an Internet presence. They opened the first customer service and distribution center, developed relationships with suppliers of vitamins and other natural health and beauty products, established a private label for these products, and developed and maintained the Web site.

In 1998, the company focused its efforts on growth and becoming the market leader in the natural health and beauty products space. To achieve this goal, the founders would need a significant amount of additional venture capital as well as a seasoned and respected management team. With the additional funds and talent, the firm would expand its business, improve the Web site's infrastructure and technology, and promote the brand. In June 1998, the company changed its name to MotherNature.com and raised $7 million in its first round of venture financing. In July 1998, Michael Barach joined MotherNature.com as the chief executive officer. Barach, who held graduate degrees from both Harvard Business School and Harvard Law School, was previously a partner at Bessemer Venture Partners and specialized in e-commerce.

During 1999, MotherNature.com continued to add to its successes of the previous year. In February, Steinberg joined the firm. In May, the company closed one of 1999's largest venture rounds, raising $42 million from such venture capital firms as CMGI, Morgenthaler, North Castle Partners, BancBoston Ventures, and Bessemer Venture Partners. By September, MotherNature.com had over 160 employees. At the end of 1999, MotherNature.com went public, raising an additional $53 million by selling 4.1 million shares at $13 per share. By March 2000, MotherNature.com was well funded and at the early ramp-up stage for a planned exponential growth curve.

The Opportunity

MotherNature.com positioned itself at the nexus of two major growth trends: the growth in the VSM market (driven by health-conscious aging baby boomers) and the growth in the on-line market (driven by adoption of the Internet by consumers). The following paragraph is from the MotherNature.com IPO prospectus:

> The vitamins, supplements and minerals market is projected to grow as the "baby boomer" population becomes increasingly concerned with aging and disease, preventative health care and natural products. Sales of vitamins, supplements and minerals totaled approximately $8.9 billion in 1998 and are forecasted to grow at a compound annual rate of 13.3% to $16.6 billion in 2003, according to Packaged Facts, a consumer products market research firm. Research studies have indicated that the percentage of U.S. adults who take vitamins has increased from 43% in 1993, to 56% in 1998, according to Packaged Facts. We believe there is also a large market opportunity for us in other natural

product categories beyond vitamins, supplements and minerals, including personal care products, household products, non-perishable foods, organic coffees and teas, sports nutrition, cosmetics, baby care products and pet care products.

In mid-1999, Jupiter Communications predicted that the on-line health care market would reach about $1.7 billion by 2003. Jupiter also predicted that the on-line market specific to vitamins and herbal supplements would reach $434 million in that same period. Several conditions made the on-line market for VSM players particularly favorable, making sales for VSM products likely to migrate to the Web more rapidly than other health care products. First, purchase via mail-order catalogs was prevalent in the VSM market, making purchase via the Web a natural progression. Second, VSM products do not serve immediate needs (as opposed to prescription drugs), and therefore delivery speed is less important to customers. Third, VSM products have high value density, making them economical to ship (compared to fifty-pound bags of dog food, furniture, or toilet paper). Finally, VSM products are likely to be purchased repeatedly, also making on-line purchasing compelling. Overall, MotherNature.com felt it could grab a profitable slice of the large and growing on-line health care market.

Against the backdrop of this opportunity, however, were the rising costs of customer acquisition during the 1999–2000 time frame. The combination of a gold-rush mentality and increasingly jaded on-line consumers led to two results, respectively: rising on-line advertising rates (in terms of dollars per million impressions) and falling customer response rates (in terms of click-through rates on banner ads). Millions of dollars of venture capital flooded into nascent e-commerce companies, and these companies rapidly burned through their investors' cash in a desperate bid to get big fast. In resorting to money-losing ploys to grab market share, on-line companies were paying increasing sums to get customers. Steinberg knew that his marketing efforts needed to create customers whose lifetime stream of repeat purchases would offset high customer acquisition costs.

Strategy

In its IPO prospectus, MotherNature.com outlined the following core elements of the company's strategy:

- **Advertising:** Promote the memorable MotherNature.com brand name through an aggressive advertising campaign, including a national television campaign
- **Brand:** Establish MotherNature.com as the trusted authority for VSM and other natural and healthy-living products through marketing efforts and informative, authoritative content
- **Repeat Customers:** Capitalize on the inherent need to replenish VSM by promoting repeat and complementary product purchases
- **Affiliates:** Enlist and provide financial incentives for other businesses in the healthy-living industry, such as health care providers and health clubs, to refer their customers to the MotherNature.com site
- **Service:** Provide quality customer service and rapid product delivery through MotherNature.com's in-house order fulfillment facility, which is being expanded in order to increase inventory levels of popular products
- **Global Growth:** Expand the company's international presence in order to establish MotherNature.com as a global brand

🔲 Central Marketing Issues

Marketing played a crucial role in many elements of the company's strategy. As a start-up, MotherNature.com was creating a customer base in the new, untried channel of on-line commerce. Accordingly, MotherNature.com planned to spend the majority of investor money on marketing-related expenses.

Attracting, Converting, and Retaining On-Line Customers

MotherNature.com sees its marketing efforts as a three-stage process. First, Mother Nature.com will attract new prospective customers to its Web site. As head of marketing, Steinberg is choosing among a myriad of possible outlets for finding prospective customers and for building a general awareness of MotherNature.com. His choices include a range of on-line and off-line approaches. Off-line approaches could include advertising (in a range of both local and national media), special promotional events (that garner free press coverage), direct-mail campaigns, and so on. On-line approaches could include banner ads, on-line affiliates programs, on-line couponing, permission-based e-mail marketing, and so on.

Second, MotherNature.com will convert the new prospects attracted to the Web site into customers. MotherNature.com is considering issues of pricing, site design, and the use of value-added information (e.g., on-line content on health-related topics) to convert visitors into shoppers and shoppers into customers. Site design is especially important to the company as a means of creating a trusted brand. The look and feel of the site is a major part of the company's brand-building effort. MotherNature.com wants to promote commerce without being excessively materialistic.

Third, MotherNature.com will work to retain customers and gain a lifetime stream of repeat orders. Having paid a high price to acquire a customer, the company wants to retain that customer. The company will encourage customers to replenish products and to increase MotherNature.com's wallet share of the customer's health care product needs. MotherNature.com is considering tactics involving e-mail, updated content, cross-selling promotions, and on-line offers to encourage buyers to return.

Achieving High Return on Marketing Investment

Although tallied as an expense on an income statement, marketing can be considered an investment—a means of creating assets in the form of lifetime customers that create a future stream of profits. Thus, embedded in all of MotherNature.com's decisions on a marketing plan is the broader issue of return on investment. Will MotherNature.com's investments in marketing yield a high return in terms of ongoing, paying customer relationships? MotherNature.com is using the ROMI (return on marketing investment) model to help answer this question.

ROMI is a framework for understanding the financial impact of marketing to determine which marketing investments yield a high return. The ROMI equation has two conceptual quantities: the amount of investment in marketing and the amount of financial return created by that marketing investment. The return side of ROMI is the incremental income (not just the incremental revenues) ascribed to the marketing investment. Return is expressed in terms of contribution margin (product revenues minus the direct costs of those product sales). Thus, a marketing investment that increases sales of extremely profitable products will have a high, positive ROMI. By contrast, a marketing effort that increases sales of a money-losing product will have a negative ROMI.

For a start-up company like MotherNature.com, the return side of the ROMI model encompasses the total future stream of contribution margin (product sales minus cost of goods sold) from new customers. Start-up companies have a negligible initial customer base, as virtually all customers are new customers. Therefore, the return side of ROMI for MotherNature.com is simply a function of the total stream of gross income. Because MotherNature.com expects customers to return repeatedly to buy a continuing supply of health products, Steinberg is using customer lifetime value (CLTV) to compute ROMI.

Quantifying CLTV

For MotherNature.com, the stream of contribution margin (the return side of ROMI) is defined by the lifetime of repeat sales generated by a satisfied customer. This implies computing the CLTV, which assesses the value of a customer as an asset in terms of the future net income from that customer. Thus, CLTV models include terms such as average order size, gross margins, order frequency, retention rates, and the expected duration of the customer relationship.

Table 2.1 is a spreadsheet, provided by Jeffrey Steinberg as a sample model for quantifying CLTV and ROMI. This spreadsheet has shaded line-item entries for crucial parameters such as market size, customer behavior, and financial margins. The spreadsheet contains hypothetical, numerical inputs (not necessarily reflective of MotherNature.com's business) that illustrate the expected ROMI based on a set of assumed inputs. This spreadsheet has the following four sections:

- **Annual New Customer Arrivals:** The expected number of new customers based on market size and conversion rates
- **Total Marketing Cost per Retained Customer:** The investment needed to create a "lifetime" customer
- **Customer Expenditure to Offset Marketing Expense:** The required number and frequency of purchases required to offset marketing costs
- **Market Response Forecast and Forecasted Returns:** The expected ROMI based on forecast order size and forecast numbers of repeat purchases

Issues with ROMI and CLTV

Although conceptually simple, ROMI and CLTV raise complex issues. First, any given marketing effort can have complex and contrary effects on CLTV and ROMI. For example, a graphically rich Web site design might delight first-time visitors but frustrate repeat buyers. (This increases customer conversion but decreases retention.) Or decreasing the prices on key products might increase conversion and repeat buying (increasing ROMI) but reduce gross margins (reducing ROMI). In developing a marketing plan, Steinberg is considering the multifaceted impact of various marketing tactics on the key parameters of the LCTV and ROMI models.

Second, a company can compute ROMI for individual marketing activities. This helps a company learn from its marketing efforts and invest more in marketing tactics that generate a high ROMI while ending marketing efforts that have low or negative ROMI. In practice, however, computing an accurate value of ROMI for individual

Line Item	Value	Notes
Target Market Size	40,000,000	Input; estimated market size
Marketing Expense—Building Traffic to Site	$ 25,000,000	Input; Mothernature.com Sales and Marketing Expenditures (first 9 mos. 1999)
Attraction Rate	10.00%	Input; Fraction of Target Market Size coming to site for total marketing expense
Number of New Visitors to Site	4,000,000	Target Market Size* Attraction Rate
Cost per Click	$ 6.25	Marketing Expense/Number of New Visitors
Conversion Rate	1.70%	Input; percentage of new visitors expected to make purchases
Number of Customers (Buyers)	68,000	Conversion rate* Number of New Visitors
Cost per Acquired Customer (CPAC)	$ 368	Cost per Click/Conversion Rate
Retention Rate	25.00%	Input; Function of the number of customers who remain buyer on a site
Cost per Retained Customer (CPRC)	$ 1,471	CPAC/Retention Rate
Customer Expenditure to Offset Marketing Expense		*What you must sell to get your break-even return*
Operational Margin (%)	60.00%	Input; Function of (Revenue − COGS)/COGS
Customer Expenditure to Offset Marketing Expense	$ 2,451	CPRC/Operational Margin %
Average Customer Order Size	$ 50	Input; Historical data
Number of Purchases Required to Meet Customer Expenditures	49	Customer Expenditure/Average Customer Order Size
Number of Purchases Made Per Year	8	Input; Historical data
Duration of Customer Relationship (Years)	6	Number of Purchases Required/Number of Purchases per Year
Market Response Forecast and Forecasted Returns		*Rate of Return given assumptions on attraction and retention rates*
Average Customer Order Size	$ 50.00	Input from Average Customer Order Size (above)
Operational Margin (%)	60.00%	Input from Operation Margin (above)
Average Order Contribution ($)	$30.00	Average Customer Order Size* Operational Margin
Number of Purchases	6	Input; Based on Repeat Orders
Total Contribution ($)	$ 180	Average Order Contribution $* Number of Orders
Customer Lifetime Value Based on CPRC (no PV)	*$ (1,291)*	*Total Contribution—CPRC*
Customer-Level ROMI	*−87.76%*	*Customer Lifetime Value/CPRC*

Note: These data are for instructional purposes only and are not actual marketing data of MotherNature.com.

marketing activities is difficult because it implies measuring the individual contribution of each marketing activity on incremental changes in sales and income. Attributing financial returns to individual marketing efforts can be difficult, especially within holistic multifaceted marketing campaigns. Moreover, marketing efforts can have delayed or indirect benefits (such as greater brand awareness and increases in visits or time spent on the site) that are underappreciated by strict financial metrics such as ROMI.

Finally, ROMI helps companies understand only the quantitative impact of marketing investments. ROMI does not address the qualitative impacts of marketing, such as brand image, customer perception, and overall reputation. MotherNature.com seeks a trust-oriented, nature-oriented brand image. This implies certain trade-offs that are either out of the scope of ROMI or even contrary to creating a high ROMI. For example, MotherNature.com must balance its reputation as a trusted repository of health information and "green" products with its need to offer promotions and sell its products.

Prior Marketing Efforts

Through December 1999, MotherNature.com's marketing efforts had taken several forms. First, the company had tried a range of off-line (traditional) advertising through print, radio, and television. Specifically, the company targeted major urban centers such as Boston, New York, and San Francisco through each of the previously mentioned media. Radio ads featured the voice of actress Blythe Danner as "Mother Nature." Television advertising for MotherNature.com aired during traditionally highly rated events, such as the Emmy Awards and the U.S. Open tennis tournament.

Second, on-line advertising (prior to December 1999) consisted primarily of search engine keywords, permission-based marketing, and e-mails through incentive programs such as Mypoints, Netcentives, and Coolsavings. MotherNature.com also provided incentives for health care providers and health clubs to promote VSM products and refer patients and members to the Web site. Other marketing efforts included targeted newsletters and direct mail, special offers, and public relations events. On April 15 (tax day), MotherNature.com sponsored "Stress Relief for a Taxing Day" in Boston, New York, and San Francisco. MotherNature.com handed out samples of Kava Kava (a private-label product that works as a natural stress reliever) to tax-return filers at selected post offices in those cities.

Mothernature.com had also focused on the customer experience. The company made extensive use of data mining techniques and had full-time employees analyzing information about their customers' habits, preferences, and site usage. In addition, the company periodically observed users on the site in an effort to better understand the customer experience. Twelve Internet novices examined the site critically every three months. Analysts considered MotherNature.com's deep customer knowledge to be among the most sophisticated in comparable e-commerce firms. As a result of these efforts, the site ultimately offered four ways to shop (product category, lifestyle, medical problem, and brand). In addition, a simpler site was added for novice visitors. Conversion rates increased tenfold from 0.2 to 2 percent (1 percent for first-time visitors).

In March 2000, MotherNature.com was seeking to convert its war chest of $34 million in cash into a customer base that will underpin the company's future profitability (see table 2.2 for financial status). Because MotherNature.com is planning

TABLE 2.2   MotherNature.com, Inc., Balance Sheets

(in thousands, except share and per share data)
(unaudited)

	December 31, 1999	March 31, 2000
ASSETS		
CURRENT ASSETS:		
Cash and cash equivalents	$ 44,152	$ 34,710
Accounts receivable	183	246
Inventories	2,251	1,864
Prepaid advertising and other expenses	7,593	2,367
Total current assets	54,179	39,187
Property and equipment, net	2,194	1,936
Intangible assets	14,908	13,252
Other assets	93	81
Total assets	$ 71,374	$ 54,456
LIABILITIES AND SHAREHOLDERS' EQUITY		
CURRENT LIABILITIES:		
Accounts payable	$ 1,925	$ 1,304
Accrued expenses	3,018	2,446
Accrued compensation	364	989
Other current liabilities	29	24
Current portion of capital lease obligations	68	69
Current portion of notes payable	16	9
Total current liabilities	5,420	4,841
Long-term portion of capital lease obligations	226	209
Other liabilities	32	39
SHAREHOLDERS' EQUITY:		
Common stock, $0.01 par value:		
Authorized 93,300,000 shares; issued and outstanding 15,118,198 and 15,119,556 shares at December 31, 1999 and March 31, 2000, respectively	151	151
Additional paid-in-capital	133,784	133,432
Deferred compensation	(1,879)	(1,390)
Accumulated deficit	(66,360)	(82,826)
Total shareholders' equity	65,696	49,367
Total liabilities and shareholders' equity	$ 71,374	$ 54,456

(Continued)

21

TABLE 2.2   CONTINUED

STATEMENTS OF OPERATIONS
(in thousands, except share and per share data)
(unaudited)

	Three Months Ended March 31,	
	1999	*2000*
Net sales	$ 251	$ 4,079
Cost of sales	224	2,911
Gross profit	27	1,168
Operating expenses		
Selling and marketing	2,553	13,644
Product development	880	1,748
General and administrative	647	2,720
Total operating expenses	4,080	18,112
Operating loss	(4,053)	(16,944)
Interest income	72	497
Interest expense	(9)	(19)
Net loss	$ (3,990)	$ (16,466)
Basic and diluted net loss per common share	$ (5.82)	$ (1.09)
Shares used to compute basic and diluted net loss per common share	685,656	15,118,578
Pro forma basic and diluted net loss per common share	$ (0.58)	$ (1.09)
Shares used to compute pro forma basic and diluted net loss per common share	6,894,362	15,118,578

to invest the bulk of its investors' dollars in marketing, it wants to ensure that those investments have a high return. Steinberg must decide how to market the company and convert the growing pool of on-line users into loyal customers of MotherNature.com.

QUESTIONS

1. In the battle of Green ($) vs. Green (environmentally friendly), how can MotherNature.com strike a balance that will maintain its image as a trusted brand while actively seeking customers and strategic partners to help it grow? What must the company *not* do? In this context, what kinds of marketing programs would help MotherNature.com beat its competitors? What innovative strategies (promotions, alliances, Web site modifications, segmentation, or product expansion) could the company develop that would help it make a profit while not breaking the marketing budget?

2. Familiarize yourself with the spreadsheet in table 2.1 provided as a sample model for quantifying different aspects of CLTV. Look at the spreadsheet to understand how all aspects of marketing—price (necessary spending and average dollars spent), distribution (conversion rate and retention rate), communication (cost per click), and product (gross margin)—become integrated into CLTV models. The shaded cells are inputs that you can manipulate to see how each of these variables affect key marketing metrics. The model has hypothetical inputs (not necessarily reflective of MotherNature.com's business), but you are strongly encouraged to challenge these assumptions.

   Looking at the customer lifetime value model, you can see how each input affects the cost per acquired customer, cost per retained customer, cost per click, and so on. Looking at all the variables (inputs) that affect the effectiveness of your marketing expenses, which of these variables (inputs) would you tackle first and why? Given your understanding of MotherNature.com, what could the company do to improve the ROMI? What would you propose to the board if you were Jeffrey Steinberg? Include a ROMI calculation for changes that involve marketing spending.

3. Imagine that you are a member of MotherNature.com's board of directors at the board meeting on April 7, 2000. You understand the challenges facing the company and must now evaluate the options. Your money and the fate of the company are on the line. What options will you support?

CHAPTER

3

Understand Customer Needs and Behavior

Introduction

Consumer understanding has two parts: (1) Understanding the customer's decision process helps marketing managers develop advertising, pricing, distribution, and service programs, and (2) understanding consumer needs helps companies design successful new products and services.

Customer Decision Process

We can begin to understand the customer by understanding a model of decision making—the process by which the customer reaches a purchase decision. To do this, we use an information processing model. Information processing in its simplest form comprises three activities: input, decision making, and output (see figure 3.1). Each of these steps includes many behavioral phenomena and related issues. At the first level of analysis, it is important for managers to ask: How do consumers obtain information? How do they interpret and consolidate this information to reach a decision? How do they learn from their experience and influence others?

Input

What makes the customer first think about buying? Marketing managers expose potential customers to a constant barrage of information (television, radio, print and Web advertising, billboards, sales calls, e-mail, telemarketing, and point-of-sale displays). But customers do not internalize all this information, given the limited information storage and processing capabilities of the human mind. The salience, vividness, and relevance of the information all affect whether the information is taken as input. It is not enough to expose potential customers to information—the message must attract the customer's attention if it is to be processed. An ad must have something special to stand out in today's advertising clutter.

FIGURE 3.1   Information Processing Model

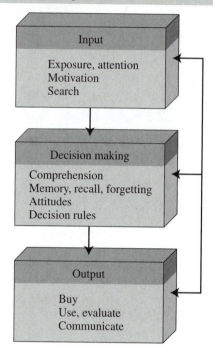

Source: Urban and Star (1991), p. 81.

Wireless technology offers a new information source. Customers can use their handhelds to access product information and prices before walking into the retail store.

When involvement with a product is low, it is usually more difficult to gain consumers' attention. On the other hand, when involvement is high, consumers not only pay attention but also actively seek information to fill their decision needs. This goal-oriented search may include Web site visits, shopping trips, talking with friends, and reading articles and reviews. The Internet amplifies the input search elements of the purchasing process, increasing the number of sources and the total volume of information accessible to purchasers. The Internet can also lower the motivation threshold. It is much easier to click to a competitor's Web site than it is to drive to a competitor's store.

Figure 3.2 depicts the customer decision process as it applies across channels. Alongside the flowchart are the questions you need to ask yourself at each step of the process.

Decision Making

After the customer has collected the requisite information, he or she must process that information in order to make an appropriate buying decision. Here, short-term and long-term memory play a role. Short-term memory is active memory and contains

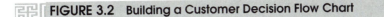

FIGURE 3.2 Building a Customer Decision Flow Chart

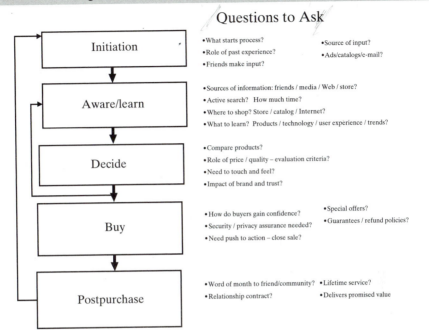

Questions to Ask

Initiation
- What starts process?
- Role of past experience?
- Friends make input?
- Source of input?
- Ads/catalogs/e-mail?

Aware/learn
- Sources of information: friends / media / Web / store?
- Active search? How much time?
- Where to shop? Store / catalog / Internet?
- What to learn? Products / technology / user experience / trends?

Decide
- Compare products?
- Role of price / quality – evaluation criteria?
- Need to touch and feel?
- Impact of brand and trust?

Buy
- How do buyers gain confidence?
- Security / privacy assurance needed?
- Need push to action – close sale?
- Special offers?
- Guarantees / refund policies?

Postpurchase
- Word of month to friend/community?
- Relationship contract?
- Lifetime service?
- Delivers promised value

information that is used to make current decisions. It usually includes a limited amount of relevant information that is forgotten rather quickly. Long-term memory is a much larger storehouse of information that can be drawn into short-term memory for the purpose of active decision making.

The Internet augments both short-term and long-term memory processes even as it gives customers much more to remember. On-line "shopping baskets" help customers remember which products they were considering. Customers can keep items in a shopping basket for days and refer back to them. E-mail alert systems keep customers apprised of developments on some interesting product or product line, reminding them of unmet needs or new purchase options. The most successful companies are using a blend of clicks and mortar. For example, Circuit City knows that in the decision process, customers need information, choice comparisons, and price details. But customers may also want to see the product and be able to immediately pick it up or have a repair location at the store. That is why Circuit City has a blend of technology and physical stores and blends it into the process of actual buying.

Information in memory decays over time, so marketers must renew their messages if they do not want them to be forgotten. If the interval between decisions is long, either new information must be made available for input and processing or information in long-term memory must be made accessible.

When faced with a plethora of information, customers use heuristics, or rules of thumb, to include or eliminate product options from consideration. For example, customers may have a price limit beyond which they will not go. Even if the product offers a vastly superior price–performance ratio (such as by having a much longer life or greater reliability), customers may reject the product if it exceeds this heuristic price limit. Or customers may decide that they do not need some feature that is common in products of the target class and will thus reject all alternatives that have that feature even if that feature is essentially cost free. By eliminating alternatives, customers evaluate only a small set of products when making choices. Such "consideration sets" are typically much smaller than the number of brands on the market.

Although it is the customer who ultimately decides what to buy, digital technology can aid in the decision process. The newfound ease of access to product reviews and purchasing guides means that the Internet has the power to create or influence heuristics (and companies can also use the Internet to uncover or document the heuristics being touted in this public medium). The recommendations or advice found on-line might cover product features ("make sure your new computer has at least 512 MB RAM") or even elements of the purchase process ("don't buy a computer monitor unless you have seen it in person in a store"). Whether these heuristics are strictly valid is irrelevant—that the customer will follow the heuristics is what counts.

The decision process explained here applies to both consumer and industrial buyers. The process with industrial buyers is more complex, however, because several people are involved in the purchase decision. These people form a decision-making unit (DMU). For example, a software purchase decision at a company would involve the end user as well as input from information technology and finance people. In formulating a marketing strategy, managers must identify the functions performed by each member of the DMU and how the people interact. The following is a list of the most important functions in multiperson industrial buying:

Functions in Multiperson Industrial Buying

Specifying: Defining the need and specifying the necessary attributes and performance requirements for the product or system

Gatekeeping: Determining whether a supplier will be recognized and qualified for consideration

Budgeting: Allocating funds for the purchase of a specific product

Generating Alternatives: Identifying solutions, products, and qualified bidders

Evaluating: Considering proposals and bids in order to select the one that best meets requirements

Selecting: Choosing the final supplier

Approving: Obtaining an OK from top management

Output

The decision process does not end with the purchase. After customers have made their decision and bought a product, several postpurchase phenomena take place. As consumers use a product, they gain information about how it performs, and they update memory with this new information. The postuse evaluation is critical for repeat-purchase products. If a product does not fulfill expectations, it is not likely to be purchased again.

Customers continue to evaluate their purchases, and this postpurchase evaluation impacts their subsequent decisions and actions. For example, customers may change the heuristic rules by which they make future purchases. Postpurchase processing can also affect loyalty decisions about choosing or avoiding particular companies, or it can cause them to return the purchased product and insist on redress for a faulty outcome. Even if the purchase is a one-time transaction with no potential for repeat business, customers often influence other potential customers through word-of-mouth communication. The Internet amplifies this aspect of customer behavior.

E-mail, chat, and on-line discussion forums represent new ways for person-to-person communication. These highly distributed communication forms give customers new power because their voices carry so much farther in these new communication media. Whether posting a book review on Amazon.com, giving a feedback rating of an eBay seller, or expressing opinions in an on-line discussion group, customers influence the purchase behavior of other customers.

By understanding the customer's decision process, you can make decisions about how to communicate, price, and distribute your product. In the following section, we look at customer needs. By understanding customer needs, you can design better products and extend the product line more effectively. In chapter 9, we explore the product design process in greater detail and look at additional digitally based market research techniques in addition to the on-line focus groups, virtual concept tests, and Web-based conjoint analysis described next.

图冠册 Market Research to Understand Customer Needs

The following five methods represent a hierarchy, from simplest to most advanced, of how to identify customer needs.

> Sixty to 80 percent of successful technologically based products have their idea source in the recognition of market needs and demands.

Talk to Your Customers

Often, companies can understand their customers by directly asking them about what they need, what they currently do, and what problems they encounter with how they currently do things. Examples of talking with customers can range from formal focus groups with customers to informal conversations with industrial buyers. This direct interrogation technique works well with industrial customers, who have a better understanding of their needs than individual consumers do. For example, Marketsoft (see chapter 10) interviewed sixty companies to identify the needs that drove Marketsoft's product development process.

Digital Technology Reduces Focus Group Costs

Consumer products giant Procter & Gamble is reducing market research and new product concept test costs by 50 to 70 percent by conducting focus groups on-line rather than in person. On-line focus groups cost one-tenth as much as in-person groups, deliver results in days rather than months, and provide richer, better information. For example, in a face-to-face group setting, one vociferous person may dominate the group. Or embarrassment or avoidance of conflict can suppress some points of view. But Procter & Gamble found that these dynamics do not happen in the on-line world.

Source: "Can the Internet Hot-Wire P&G?," Ziff Davis Smart Business for the New Economy, January 1, 2001.

Concept Tests

Individual consumers are often less able to explicitly define their needs than industrial customers, but they are able to react to need fulfillers when described. For example, the automotive industry would never have created the sport-utility vehicle (SUV) if they had waited for consumers to ask for "a big, square, trucklike vehicle." But if consumers were shown a concept of the SUV that was comfortable and safe and that had spacious hauling capacity and good performance, then they could respond more accurately. Concept tests gauge people's reactions to concrete and explicit ideas, asking about the likes, dislikes, price points, and overall interest in potential new products or services.

The Virtual Concept Test presents a small number of concrete design options (different models) at some set price level. The participant picks among these options while the price escalates. This tool elicits both preferences for particular models and price-sensitivity information.

Lead Users

The third level of analysis involves working with lead users. As Professor Eric von Hippel from the Massachusetts Institute of Technology showed, lead users are customers who not only know their needs but also have often developed their own solution to meet those needs because they were unable to find a solution on the market. Companies can capture input both about needs and about innovative solutions to meet those needs from lead users. For example, women's use of eggs along with their shampoos, to give more body to the hair, was the solution adopted in the protein shampoo market.

Search engines, on-line customer-contributed product reviews, and on-line discussion groups (either public or private) can help companies find and interact with lead users. People who contribute helpful tips to discussion forums are a valuable source of ideas about needs and solutions.

Idea Generation Techniques

The fourth level of needs analysis is to generate a large number of ideas and screen them by customer reaction. For this, managers and customers come together in a creativity-encouraging environment with a posed problem and an incentive to create the solution. Idea generation techniques yield insight into needs and solutions (see figure 3.3).

Formal Marketing Research

The fifth level of needs assessment uses formal marketing research techniques such as conjoint analysis and Listening In. Conjoint analysis uses very large numbers of comparison questions to statistically construct a model of a customer's desires and acceptable trade-offs. Customers often find the large number of questions frustrating, even though the underlying software does a good job of uncovering the customer's willingness to trade off features and prices. Thus, conjoint analysis and other formal market research techniques are the most advanced on the hierarchy of needs assessment. The Listening In technique involves Listening In on the clickstream at a company's Web site. You will learn more about Listening In in chapter 9.

Web-Based Conjoint Analysis presents the participant with a screen full of alternatives (different vehicles with different prices, engine sizes, and seating capacities). The software asks the consumer to pick products that he or she might buy. Through the clever presentation of various alternatives, the method of conjoint analysis can determine the consumer's preferences without asking too many questions, such as asking them to rate every possible product option.

Dell Case Introduction

The following case illustrates the complexity of the customer's purchasing process in an on-line environment. In particular, the case shows that customers do not follow a simplistic single-pass process of visiting a site, shopping on that site, and buying from that site all in a single sitting. The case also illustrates how, in digital technology, the key issue is increasing the conversion from products in a shopping cart to actual purchases. To increase this conversion, you need to understand the buying process. Note the process model in the Dell case and the loss of customers at each stage. Clickstream analysis allows an understanding of the shopping process and needs for information and PCs. The key question in the case is how to increase conversion rates by understanding the buying process and by thinking creatively about information needs and ways to fulfill them with site design.

FIGURE 3.3 Idea-Generating Flow

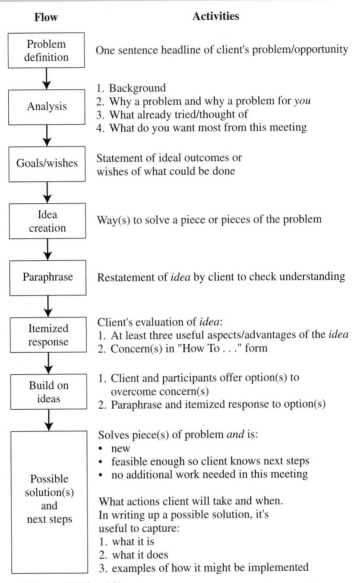

Flow	Activities
Problem definition	One sentence headline of client's problem/opportunity
Analysis	1. Background 2. Why a problem and why a problem for *you* 3. What already tried/thought of 4. What do you want most from this meeting
Goals/wishes	Statement of ideal outcomes or wishes of what could be done
Idea creation	Way(s) to solve a piece or pieces of the problem
Paraphrase	Restatement of *idea* by client to check understanding
Itemized response	Client's evaluation of *idea*: 1. At least three useful aspects/advantages of the *idea* 2. Concern(s) in "How To . . ." form
Build on ideas	1. Client and participants offer option(s) to overcome concern(s) 2. Paraphrase and itemized response to option(s)
Possible solution(s) and next steps	Solves piece(s) of problem *and* is: • new • feasible enough so client knows next steps • no additional work needed in this meeting What actions client will take and when. In writing up a possible solution, it's useful to capture: 1. what it is 2. what it does 3. examples of how it might be implemented

Source: Urban and Hauser (1993), p. 151.

REFERENCES

Bettman, James R. 1979. *An Information Processing Theory of Consumer Choice.* Reading, Mass.: Addison-Wesley.

Dahan, Ely, and John R. Hauser. 2002. "The Virtual Customer." *Journal of Product Innovation Management* 19, no. 5: 332–53.

Dahan, Ely, John R. Hauser, Duncan Simester, and Olivier Toubia. 2002. "Application and Test of Web-Based Adaptive Polyhedral Conjoint Analysis." MIT Sloan Working Paper.

Urban, Glen L., and John R. Hauser. 1993. *Design and Marketing of New Products.* Upper Saddle River, N. J.: Prentice Hall.

Urban, Glen L., and Steven H. Star. 1991. *Advanced Marketing Strategies.* Upper Saddle River, N. J.: Prentice Hall.

Von Hippel, Eric. 1988. *The Sources of Innovation.* New York: Oxford University Press.

———. 2001. "Perspective: User Toolkits for Innovation." *Journal of Product Innovation Management* 18, no.: 247–57.

4

Dell Online

Introduction

The Director of Dell Online's Home and Small Business Unit has just heard some contradictory statistics about online purchasing at Dell.com. On the one hand, Dell is enjoying 70 percent market share in the on-line PC market. Dell.com is selling $52 million per day on-line—more than half of Dell's total sales. On the other hand, less than 1 percent of Web visits to Dell.com resulted in an actual purchase. More than 99 percent of visitors to Dell.com drop out somewhere along the three-phase process that lies between the home page and the sale.

As the director of Dell Online's Home and Small Business Unit, you are concerned that you will not reach the goal of selling $60 million per day by the end of the fiscal year unless you can convert more of these opportunities (visitors) into sales (buyers). Even a small reduction in the attrition rate will lead to a large increase in on-line sales.

How would you improve the site to increase the conversion rate?

Dell Background

Dell is the largest seller of PCs in the world. The company sells build-to-order computer systems directly to a wide range of customers—from the largest enterprises and government agencies to individual home PC enthusiasts. Founded in 1984 by Michael Dell in his university dorm room, the company grew to $31.8 billion by fiscal year 2001. Commensurate with its meteoric rise, Dell has seen its stock soar by a factor of more than 400 times over the last decade. Dell's success is based on a direct-sales model of build-to-order PCs and the use of information technology (IT) to streamline all its processes from procurement to manufacturing to marketing.

Pioneer in Direct Sales of PCs

Dell pioneered the direct-sales approach, eschewing the then-dominant indirect model that interposes a network of distributors, value-added resellers, and retailers between

---

All data in this case are hypothetical and do not reflect actual Dell numbers.

the PC maker and the PC buyer. Selling direct lowered Dell's cost by 25 to 40 percent compared to competitors (by eliminating the markups of intermediaries). Dell passed these savings on to customers.

In Dell's early days, direct connections with customers were based on phone calls that Dell used to get customer feedback on its products. Michael Dell believed that by selling PC systems directly to customers, Dell Corporation could best understand customers' needs and provide the most effective computing solutions to meet those needs. Dell initially targeted technically minded customers who have a lower cost of service and tend to buy higher-end, high-performance PCs. Knowledgeable PC buyers are less likely to need sales assistance, are more comfortable with specifying the technical configuration of the PC that they want, and tend to buy more expensive, cutting-edge machines. Buyers who knew what they wanted bought from Dell.

Reducing Costs and Risks with Build-to-Order

Dell's direct-sales model, on the front end, is supported by a build-to-order manufacturing process on the back end. Rather than fulfill customer demand from an extensive inventory of prebuilt PCs, Dell builds each PC on demand. Customers can choose which components they want their computer to have when they order. Dell then assembles the requested hardware and software components and ships the order. This strategy not only improves customer satisfaction, as customers get what they want, but actually reduces costs and risks to Dell.

Customers place orders by phone or on the Web, and the orders are downloaded to Dell's factories. Dell has an electronic bill of materials that tells operators exactly what materials go into the ordered PC. Each PC is built from base components. Dell uses true build-to-order, not configure-to-order, manufacturing. (In configure-to-order, the manufacturer builds a machine, stores it while waiting for an order, and then opens it up and configures it for the customer after the customer has placed an order.)

Build-to-order offers important advantages for Dell. As Moore's law states, the PC industry contends with exponentially increasing price–performance ratios of most PC components. Many PC components lose value at a rate as high as 1 percent per week. Worse, obsolete components (e.g., last year's CPU chips and disk drives) have virtually no value because customers refuse to buy inadequately powered machines. PC companies that build inventories of PCs to meet inexact forecasts face a double penalty. First, the PC's components lose value while sitting in inventory. Second, the company faces the risk of having to write off obsolete machines. By contrast, Dell holds very little inventory. In 2001, Dell held an average of fewer than four days, worth of inventory, down from 11 days in 1998. By contrast, the industry average was six weeks of inventory.

Moreover, by holding an inventory of parts rather than of finished goods, Dell reduces business risk. Dell does not build computers in the hopes that they will sell—it builds computers after it receives the customer order. It is much less expensive to hold inventory of components and build the computer to customer specifications than it is to try to predict which computer systems customers will want and then hold much more expensive inventory. This practice also lets Dell be more responsive to changes in technology and component prices. When new hardware components are introduced, Dell can immediately offer them to its customers without having to worry about clearing or writing off obsolete machines.

Direct sales in conjunction with build-to-order is a powerful model for both Dell and its customers. Customers get to buy what they want rather than be forced to choose among a fixed set of options. Dell wins because by developing and building only those systems that customers want, Dell eliminates the excess cost of buying too many components, having high storage and inventory costs, and having to sell the surplus at a loss. Dell passes these savings on to the customer.

In addition to its own product innovations, Dell leverages its research and development (R&D) by spending collaboratively with industry partners to create relevant technologies for customers. This efficient approach helps Dell avoid costly and redundant R&D efforts on technologies that may never materialize in the market place.

SUMMARY OF ADVANTAGES OF DIRECT SALES OF BUILD-TO-ORDER PCS

- Reduced costs (sell at lower prices)
    - No markups for intermediaries.
    - Reduced inventory holding costs (build-to-order lets Dell hold low inventory).
    - Better prices on components (Dell purchases inventory later at the lower price).
    - Low cost of service for on-line sales.
- Reduced risk (by taking orders straight from customers, Dell builds its PCs to demand rather than to inexact forecasts)
    - Reduced risk of obsolescence of inventories.
    - Obsolescence risk limited to components (not expensive finished-goods inventory).
- Better relationship with customer
    - Customers select, customize, order and pay for systems on-line.
    - Customers can order exactly the PC configuration they want, not a standard model.
    - Dell owns the relationship with the customer.
    - Customer data and direct relationship enables more tailoring and value-added services.
- Faster cycle times
    - Faster payment: Converting an order to cash can take less than 24 hours for credit card and electronic payments, compared to the 16 days that Gateway waits to receive payment from intermediaries (or the 35 days that Compaq waits).
    - Reduces time to market for new products because Dell does not have to empty and fill distribution channels.

Customer Segmentation

Internally, Dell is organized by customer segment—being divided according to the size and nature of Dell's connection with the customer. Some 40 percent of Dell's customers are what Dell calls "relationship" customers. These are larger organizations (e.g., bigger businesses and government agencies) with whom Dell has a long-term negotiated relationship. Relationship buyers evaluate PC purchases on a broader set of factors, including vendor strength, standardization of their own technological infrastructure, and so on. Relationship buyers value Dell services such as DellPlus (in which Dell installs software on the PC).

Another segment of customers are "transaction" customers: individuals or smaller businesses who view each purchase individually, focusing on the lowest cost of each purchase. (The remaining segment of customers combine aspects of both relationship and transaction customers.) Transaction buyers must be won over each time they make a purchase decision, and they buy primarily on the basis of features and price. As the director of Dell Online's Home and Small Business Unit, all your customers are transaction customers—buying PCs one at time.

Dell is organized along customer segmentation lines rather than product lines for three reasons. First, the organizational scheme helps Dell understand its customer better. By grouping customers into increasingly granular levels, Dell can understand the needs of these customers and how they make purchase decisions and then devise specific sales and marketing processes for each group. Second, the segmentation has let the company see the growth rates, profitability, service-level performance, and market share in each segment and adapt its activities accordingly. Finally, segmentation lets the company measure the efficiency of each division in terms of its asset use. Dell can evaluate the return on invested capital to each segment and compare it with other segments. Each division is a complete business unit, with its own sales, service, finance, and IT technical support.

In an interview with *Harvard Business Review,* Michael Dell talked about his customer segmentation strategy:

> We look closely at financial measures like gross margins by customer segment— and we focus on segments we can serve profitably as we achieve scale. People are sometimes surprised to learn that 90% of our sales go to institutions—business and government—and 70% to very large customers that buy at least $1 million in PCs per year. . . . For years we didn't actively pursue the consumer market because we couldn't reach our profit objectives. So we let our competitors introduce machines with rock-bottom prices and zero margins. We figured they could be the ones to teach consumers about PCs while we focused our efforts on more profitable segments. And then, because we're direct and can see who is buying what, we noticed something interesting. The industry's average selling price to consumers was going down, but ours was going up. Consumers who were now buying their second or third machines and needed less handholding were coming to us. And without focusing on it in a significant way, we had a billion-dollar consumer business that was profitable. So we decided in 1997 that it was time to dedicate a group to serving that segment."[1]

〔己〕 Dell.com

In 1996, Dell launched on-line sales through its Web site, www.dell.com, being the first PC maker to do so. Dell's emphasis on tech-savvy PC buyers made on-line selling a natural. High-end PC buyers were obvious users of the Internet and early adopters of e-commerce. Moreover, because Dell sold direct, it did not need to worry about channel conflict (i.e., competing with an entrenched network of distributors and retailers).

---

[1] Joan Magretta, "The Power of Virtual Integration: An Interview with Dell Computer's Michael Dell," *Harvard Business Review,* March–April 1998, p. 77.

To succeed in selling on-line while giving customers the choice of components and features they want in their computer, Dell needed an on-line configurator. The configurator lets Dell customers choose among computer models and a variety of options, such as memory, size, hard drive capacity, and modem type. When a customer clicks on an option, the exact cost is immediately added. (Conversely, removing options subtracts costs.)

The configurator reduces costs for Dell (no salesperson or order entry clerk is needed), reduces errors, and increases speed—the order is processed immediately. The configurator also records buyer's preferences, giving Dell immediate access to buying patterns. This gives Dell real-time market knowledge.

By April 1997, Dell was selling $1 million of goods per day on-line. Internet efficiencies let Dell create that $1 million daily sales volume with only 30 people, compared to the 700 who would be needed to process a similar sales volume by phone. The following year, Dell was selling $3 million per day on its Web site. As early as 1998, one-third of Dell's consumer business was conducted on-line (and 50 percent of the Japan consumer business was done on-line). By 2000, on-line sales were running $50 million per day and made up more than half of all Dell product sales.

A Tale of Two Studies

Although Dell.com is undeniably successful, two studies of on-line PC buying gave Dell a confusing picture of the effectiveness of its on-line sales efforts. Internal data about visitors to Dell.com led to an alarming conclusion that only 1 out of every 100 visits to Dell.com results in a sale—99 percent of visitors leave before buying. Yet external data established that Dell enjoyed over 70 percent market share among on-line PC vendors. Dell needs to use careful analysis of these different data to understand PC buyer behavior and to focus on the best possible opportunities for on-line sales growth.

Napoleon's March: Slogging through the Web Site to Get to "Buy Now"

The first study revealed extremely high attrition rates among visitors to Dell's Web site. This study used internal Dell data on how visitors progress through Dell's site—how many of them leave and how many make it to the ultimate point of purchase. On-line PC buying involves three distinct phases: browsing, configuration, and checkout (see figure 4.1 in the appendix). At each phase, visitors can leave Dell.com. Only those visitors who work their way through all three phases become customers. The study showed that a discouraging 99 percent of visitors leave the site without buying a PC from Dell.

During the first phase, browsing, the visitor passes from the home page to various parts of the retail site to examine product information. Browsing includes a range of search and navigation activities in which the visitor learns about Dell's products and tries to find a suitable PC. Out of every 100 visitors to Dell.com, 50 leave during browsing. This implies that browsing has a 50 percent attrition rate.

The second phase, configuration, starts when the visitor has selected a particular Dell model and wants to configure the purchase. Because of Dell's build-to-order approach, most of its models are defined in terms of ranges, such as "as low as $1,899" or "as much as 1 GB RAM." Configuration includes selecting among these various model options, indicating the amount of RAM or CPU speed, and selecting associated peripherals (e.g., speakers and network interface cards). Configuration involves more than a dozen questions, the answers to which change the price by some amount. After the configuration process, the visitor learns the total price for their specific configuration. The prospective customer can then adjust the configuration and recalculate the price. For every 100 visitors to Dell.com, only 50 enter the configuration process. Of those 50, 48 leave. This implies that configuration has a 96 percent attrition rate.

The final phase is checkout. Once the visitor has selected and configured their PC, they must submit appropriate payment and shipping information, entering name, address, and credit card information. Checkout culminates in the final "Buy Now" button, which formally triggers the order. Of the original 100 visitors to Dell.com, only two reach the checkout phase. Of those two stalwart individuals, 50 percent drop out during this final phase. Thus, of 100 visitors to Dell.com, only one (1 percent) is converted to a paying customer.

This study paints a grim picture in which Dell's Web site is a gauntlet from which few customers emerge. As the director of Dell Online's Home and Small Business Unit, you know that converting even a few percent more visitors into customers could have a massive impact on sales.

Massive Market Share: Dell.com Is the Cream of the Crop

This grim analysis of attrition rates among visitors to Dell.com was counterbalanced by further studies of on-line PC buying habits (figure 4.2 in the appendix). Dell examined external Web data and competitor intelligence, drawing information from Nielsen Net Ratings, Jupiter Media Metrix, and ComScore. These external data sources helped Dell understand where its wayward visitors go when they leave and whether Dell is losing customers. These data sources elucidate patterns of visitation across multiple competitors and multiple sessions. Such data tell Dell how long people spend at different on-line PC sites, how many different sites they visit, and from whom they buy.

The foremost fact from these data is that Dell enjoys 70 percent market share among on-line PC vendors. Although Dell loses more than 99 percent of its visitors, these visitors are not just buying from Dell's competitors. Dell's high market share suggests that Dell is doing quite well on-line (customer satisfaction ratings bear this out). Moreover, working harder to steal customers from the on-line competition will generate only modest sales increases (even if Dell got 100 percent market share of current on-line buyers, its on-line sales would increase by only 25 percent, but if more people buy on-line the total on-line market sales would be higher). How can Dell reconcile a 1 percent conversion rate with a 70 percent market share?

Further examination of external Web data and competitor intelligence reveals that the visitor attrition rate figures are terribly skewed by an important element of buyer's behavior. PC buyers want to compare different products, so they shop around, visiting multiple sites multiple times before buying. Although 99 percent of visitors leave Dell.com before buying, many of them come back later. Indeed, the average buyer from Dell visits Dell.com six times before buying. This fact alone accounts for some, but not all, of the attrition rate.

Implication: Not As Bad As It Looks, Not As Good As It Could Be

Somewhere between the discouragingly high attrition rates and the encouragingly high market share is the real story of Dell.com. The key is to combine the internal and external data to infer the behavior of the visitors to Dell's Web site and of PC buyers in general.

The real lesson from these internal and external data is that a very large fraction of visitors to Dell.com do not buy from Dell or any other on-line PC provider. On the basis of attrition rates and visitation rates, we can infer that only about 4 out of every 100 visitors to Dell.com ultimately buy a PC from Dell. On the basis of Dell.com's 70 percent market share and assuming that customers of competing on-line PC makers also visit Dell.com numerous times, we can estimate that only 5.7 percent of Dell's visitors buy a PC from any on-line site. Thus, more than 90 percent of visits to Dell.com are by people who never buy a PC on-line. This analysis suggests that Dell has a substantive opportunity to increase sales by getting more people to buy PCs on-line—converting those visitors who normally would not buy a PC on-line.

Analysis

Your job is to formulate a plan (strategic goals with tactical initiatives) that will help Dell reach $60 million per day in on-line sales by the end of the fiscal year. Note that the question here is not one of customer acquisition. We assume that a steady enough flow of visitors is arriving at Dell's Web site. Instead, the objective of this case is to analyze ways in which the customer experience at Dell's Web site can be improved.

Task

Prepare a three- to four-page report presenting your top three recommendations for improvements to Dell.com that focus on customer conversion. To reference your recommendations, you are free to compare and use examples from any of Dell's competitors. As a hint, draw a behavioral decision process chart of customer buying and think about what elements are not met by the site experience. In addition, think of other types of clickstream or customer traffic data that could be helpful in the analysis.

Following is a list of questions that you might find helpful in leading you to your final recommendations:

1. To whom is this site targeted? It is tailored to experienced or inexperienced customers?
2. How can the site be improved? For example, are the pages built in the right way? Are customers directed properly? Are trust cues in place?
3. How does Dell's site differ from those of its competitors? Are there features within its site that you think are unique and that effectively increase conversion? Are aspects of competitors' sites unique?

Appendix

Clickstream Data

Clickstream data enable companies to calculate the conversion rate for a site and to calculate the retention at each stage of the process as visitors move through the site. Companies can obtain this raw data from "log files" that record each click a person makes while visiting the site. A company can easily capture log files on its site with available software from firms like WebCriteria or WebTrends.

Figure 4.1 shows a hypothetical clickstream analysis for Dell. With clickstream data, we can see how many people land on the home page and then click on product pages. If they leave the site after examining product information, we can calculate the fraction of the visitors lost after browsing. Likewise, we can see how many of the visitors who stay on the site click on "configure." From that, we can calculate the fraction of visitors lost between browsing and configu-

ration. Next, we can see how many visitors put a product in their shopping cart and click on "buy." This lets us calculate the retention from configuration to buy. Finally, we can see how many of those who click on "buy" actually provide credit card information and pay for the product. Such ratios provide the kind of data shown in figure 4.1. The total fraction of those who visit a site and then buy is called the site "conversion." In the figure, Dell's conversion is indicated as 1 percent.

Companies can also identify visitors who return to the site by attaching a cookie to the visitor's browser. This lets firms calculate the fraction of initial site visitors who eventually buy a product on their site. Figure 4.2A shows that Dell has a 4 percent unique conversion over three months. In other words, even though only 1 percent of visitors to the site buy on that visit, 4 percent of those who initially visit will ultimately

FIGURE 4.1   Dell Online: Hypothetical Site Flows

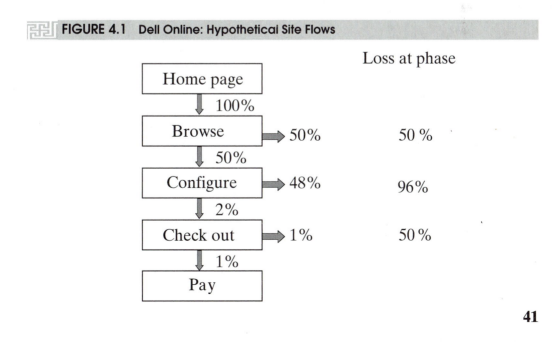

FIGURE 4.2

A. Conversion
- Dell visitors　　　1.0/session　　　4.0% unique[*]
- Gateway　　　　　.1%　　　　　　　.3%
- Compact　　　　　.2%　　　　　　　.6%
- HP　　　　　　　.4%　　　　　　　.8%
- IBM　　　　　　　.2%　　　　　　　.5%

[*]Unique buyers over multiple sessions in three-month period. All data are hypothetical.

B. Dell Buyers Minutes[*]
- Dell　　　　　20/session　　　　50 total
- Gateway　　　10　　　　　　　　30
- HP　　　　　10　　　　　　　　30
- IBM　　　　　8　　　　　　　　75
- Compaq　　　8　　　　　　　　25
- Apple　　　　5　　　　　　　　85

[*]All data are hypothetical

C. Market Share
- Share of on-line home computer sales[*]
  - Dell 70%
  - Gateway 12%
  - HP 6%
  - IBM 4%
  - Compaq 6%
  - Apple 2%

[*]All data are hypothetical.

D. Sites Dell Buyers Also Visit[*]
- Gateway　　　　35%
- HP　　　　　　25%
- IBM　　　　　13%
- Compaq　　　　22%
- Apple　　　　　20%

[*]All data are hypothetical.

buy over multiple visits in a three-month period. If we attach a timer to the site, we can calculate the initial time and ultimate time that visitors spend on the site. Figure 4.2B indicates that Dell visitors spend 20 minutes on their first visit and a total of 50 minutes over multiple visits in a three-month period.

A more expanded form of clickstream analysis allows capturing the clicks not only on the firm's site but on competitor sites as well. Such data are collected by third-party companies such as Jupiter Media Metrix, Nielsen Net Ratings, or Comscore. This data collection is done by installing software on a sample of Internet users (Nielsen and Jupiter Media Metrix) or establishing a virtual browser on their machine (Comscore). These panels typically have over one million users. With this monitoring, we can see which other sites customers visit and what they do there. For example, we can see how many of our one million panel members buy in a given period and the market share for each site. Figure 4.2C shows the market share for leading PC makers among those people who buy on-line. Although Dell's conversion is low, competitors' conversion is lower (see figure 4.2A), so Dell's market share is high. But this implies that many people visit sites but do not buy on-line at any of them. We can also see what sites people visit while they shop. For example, figure 4.2D shows that 35% of people who buy a Dell computer also visited Gateway, 25% HP, 13% IBM, and so on. This gives us a view of competitive visits and shopping behavior. Finally, we can see how many minutes visitors spend on these competitor sites (see figure 4.2B and D). With additional analysis, we could determine what they look at on these sites. For example, did they compare specific prices or just generally browse the other sites?

Clickstream analysis represents a wealth of information about how customers react to a site and how they shop. This analysis can be very useful for creating changes to a site to increase the conversion rates. Use the hypothetical data in figure 4.2 to formulate your suggestions for improving conversion in this case.

CHAPTER **5**

Formulate a Strategy to Fill Needs

Introduction

Having learned about customer needs, your next step as a marketing manager is to formulate a strategy to fill those needs. Formulating a strategy begins with assessing your company's strengths and weaknesses and balancing them against threats and opportunities. Your goal is to pursue opportunities that use your company's strengths while avoiding threats and overcoming weaknesses in target markets.

Strategy Formulation

Strengths and Weaknesses

The first step in formulating a strategy is to identify the key marketing strategic success factors for a given business and then rate your company on those factors relative to the competition. Figure 5.1 presents a list of common strategic success factors. Not all of these factors may be relevant in a given situation; others may be essential. For each factor, rate your company relative to the strongest competitor you face on a five-point scale of "much worse," "worse," "equal," "better," or "much better." The objective is to develop your company's strengths and overcome its weaknesses. If your company's strengths are greater than those of primary competitors, your company will have a strategic advantage.

After you have a comprehensive view of your firm's marketing strengths and weaknesses, you can match your company's profile to specific market opportunities and environmental threats in order to specify a platform for market selection, program evaluation, and resource allocation.

Threats and Opportunities

As a marketing manager, you should carefully examine trends in the environment to uncover the major changes that are likely to occur in existing markets. Using a formal

FIGURE 5.1   Strategic Success Factors

Sensitivity to changing market needs	Learning systematically from past strategies
Innovative response to customer needs	Understanding how and why customers buy
Ability to target and reach segments of market	Linkage of technology to market demand
Short time to market for new products	Linkage of marketing to production
Long-term view of market development and resources	Investment in growth markets
Knowing when to shift resources from old to new products	Product line coverage
Identify and exploit global market	Customer loyalty
Willingness to form interfirm coalitions	Strong brand image and awareness
Distribution coverage and delivery speed	Aggressive commitment when required
Advertising budget and copy effectiveness	Cooperative trade relations
Sales force size and productivity	Promotion magnitude and impact
High product quality	Customer service and feedback
Marketing research quality	Patent protection
Managerial ability and experience	Analytic support capability
	Quick decision and action capability
	Organizational effectiveness

rating procedure ensures that this diagnostic step is carried out comprehensively. Threats and opportunities can be listed as follows:

Threats

    Reactions from existing competition
    New competition likely to enter
    Competition by vertical integration
    Decreased entry costs for competitors
    Price/promotion war
    Customer power
    Change in consumer tastes and values
    Increasing segmentation
    Technological change
    Material scarcity and supplier price hikes
    Economic stagnation
    Inflation/deflation
    Regulatory changes
    Terrorism
    Foreign exchange fluctuation
    Political/social changes
    Environmental pollution
    Takeover/merger

Opportunities

Technological change
Customer power
Political, economic, and social trends
Size of market
Growth of market
High response to sales, ads, promotions
Unfulfilled customer needs
Market not segmented
Gaps in existing product positions
Merger
High margins
Stable price structure
Few or weak competitors
Low entry cost to new markets
Low exit barriers
Transfer cost experience
Low investment
Matches our strengths

The threats listed here reflect only some of the dangers likely to impact the success of a marketing strategy. Marketing managers must be careful not to be blindsided by unexpected developments. In markets characterized by rapid and/or discontinuous, environmental, and technological changes, it is essential to employ sensitive monitoring techniques and to have comprehensive contingency plans in place.

Note that some items appear in both lists. A threat in one situation can be an opportunity in another. For example, digital technology is a threat to the extent that it enables new competitors to enter your markets or that competitors might use technology to create new dimensions for competition, but is also an opportunity in terms of creating new channels and new means of interacting with customers.

Having assessed strengths, weaknesses, threats, and opportunities, you begin formulating strategy by mapping customer needs onto threats and opportunities. Some customer needs might represent opportunities, while changes in needs might reflect threats to existing marketing approaches. Because whole books have been written on the topic of strategy, this book concentrates on only two key strategic marketing issues: the trust versus push decision (this chapter) and the fundamental issues of segmentation and positioning (chapter 7).

The New Threat/Opportunity: Consumer Power

Consumer power in the Internet era is driven by three factors: more options, more information, and simpler transactions. The Internet provides a new channel for buying products and services, giving customers more options when buying a given product or service. The Internet also gives customers more information because it makes it easy for customers to learn about competing products and services, to compare offerings between companies, to use price-comparison engines, and to read third-party evaluations of product/service performance. Finally, the Internet makes executing transactions easier or

TABLE 5.1 Evidence of Growing Consumer Power

	Travel	*Automobile*	*Health Care*
Evidence of customer usage	Over 35% of leisure travelers use the Web for research, and over 15% of all airline tickets are sold via the Internet.	Over 60% of new car buyers use the web for research; 6% use Internet buying services.	Over 50% of adults on-line use the Internet to research health questions and inform themselves about health issues.
Change in industry structure and leadership	The role of the agent is diminished because consumers can research and purchase their travel without an agent.	Third-party information and selling services have become prominent, although the dealer network is still intact.	Comprehensive research sites on the Internet empower consumers to research their health needs.
Evidence of consumer power	Airlines discontinued commissions to agents. Over 2,000 brick-and-mortar travel agents have gone out of business in the last year	Consumers save an average of $450 per vehicle when using an Internet Buying Service rather than using the traditional buying process.	Consumers use the Internet to select health maintenance organizations and research illnesses. They now ask their doctors for specific products rather than passively being told which products they need.

more convenient. Consumers have more power when they can more easily find, select, and buy competing product or service offerings.

Evidence of Growing Consumer Power

Customer power has been increasing across many industries. For example, table 5.1 shows the evidence of consumer power growth in the travel, automotive, and health care industries. The table summarizes how customer use of the Internet in those industries has grown and how that usage has changed industry structure and power. The far right-hand column describes how companies have responded to this growth of consumer power.

Theory T Marketing

As described in chapter 1, customer power is a threat to the old way of doing things, forcing companies to adopt new theories about customers. In 1960, Douglas McGregor posed a new view of what motivates employees. The traditional view, Theory X, held that employees dislike work, avoid responsibility, and prefer to be told what to do. In contrast, McGregor proposed Theory Y, that employees are creative, willing to exercise self-direction, and willing to accept responsibility. Table 5.2 summarizes Theory X and Y for organizations.

Just as the concept of Theory Y provides a new view of empowered employees, so, too, Theory T provides a new view of marketing. Theory P marketing (push-based mar-

TABLE 5.2   McGregor's Theory X and Theory Y for Management

Theory X Management	*Theory Y Management*
Employees dislike work.	Employees will exercise self-direction.
Employees must be coerced before they will work.	Employees will become committed based on ego satisfaction.
Employees prefer to be directed.	Employees seek and accept responsibility.
Employees avoid responsibility.	Employees have imagination, ingenuity, and creativity.

TABLE 5.3   Theory T Marketing

Theory P Marketing	*Theory T Marketing*
Customers avoid decision-making responsibility.	Decision making is natural.
Customers are passive and must be coerced.	Customers are active and want to control the buying process.
Customers have difficulty learning and prefer to be influenced.	Customers prefer to learn and make an informed decision.
Customers have little imagination.	Customers have imagination, ingenuity, and creativity.

keting) led to push promotions and one-sided advertising. Theory T marketing, on the other hand, provides a view of empowered customers. The implications for Theory T marketing are trust-based marketing and companies being advocates for consumers (see table 5.3). Could this new view be a paradigm shift in marketing as Theory Y was in organizational theory in the 1960s?

Theory P thinking leads to a push-based view of marketing—that companies must "make" reluctant, apathetic customers buy products. In contrast, Theory T points to trust-based marketing and creating a mutually beneficial relationship with an empowered and responsible loyal customer following. Under Theory T, a company has the opportunity to partner with its customers and use the Internet as an enabler to provide information and offer customized advice.

Trust-Based Marketing

What Is Trust?

Trust is the end product of a four-level trust-building process. At level 1, the process starts as *belief:* customers thinking that a company's statements just might be true. At level 2, belief builds toward *confidence* as the customer becomes mentally convinced of a company's statements. Sufficient confidence leads to level 3, *reliance* as the customer comes to depend on the company. Level 4, *true trust,* is when the customer allows that company to make decisions and carry out actions on the customer's behalf without the foreknowledge and explicit permission of the customer.

The Four Levels of Trust

1. *Belief* that the company's statements might be true
2. *Confidence* in the statements of the company
3. *Reliance* on the company
4. *True trust:* customer delegates the right to make decisions and take action to the company

The Internet Enables Trust Building

Customers can feel overwhelmed by the myriad of purchase options and depth of information that is accessible on the Web. Thus, there is a tremendous opportunity for automated systems that help customers filter, sort, and select the best product for their needs. This leads to the notion of an on-line advisor or agent—a software construct that elicits information about the customer's needs, filters out irrelevant options, and recommends highly rated options.

GM's Auto Choice Advisor

GM created an on-line trust-based advisor that helps consumers find the car that is right for them, whether it is a GM car or not. GM's on-line advisor provides unbiased information not only on GM cars but on competitors' cars as well.

Auto Choice Advisor is designed for new car shoppers who are not sure which models might suit their needs. At the site, potential car buyers answer a few questions, such as how they plan to use the car, what features they want, and how much they are willing to spend. Based on their answers, GM shows them the top five choices matching their needs (from 150 makes and models available from all manufacturers). GM cars do not show up unless they meet the consumer's criteria. There is a button, however, that lets consumers see the closest matching GM car.

Strategic Choice: Push versus Trust

The weights-and-balance scale shown in figure 5.2 depicts three strategic choices: push marketing, full trust, and selective trust. The figure can act as a tool for marketing managers in determining which strategy to use. To use the tool, remove the blocks that do not apply and see which way the balance tilts. If it tilts to the right, use a trust-based strategy. If it tilts to the left, use a push-based strategy. If the balance is level, a selective trust strategy is best.

At the Theory P extreme is the pure push strategy, which involves virtually no trust on the part of customers. In a push-based strategy, a company tries to manipulate customers into buying products and services. The goal is to maximize sales, especially sales of high-margin items, without regard for customer satisfaction. Alluring, flashy ads

FIGURE 5.2   Push versus Trust

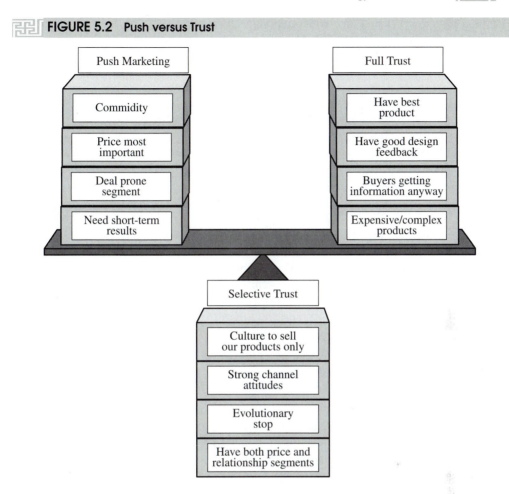

emphasize form over substance to create hype that drives sales. Fulfillment and after-sale support are minimal and very cost oriented. Under the push strategy, the goal is to get the next sale rather than the sale after that.

In the middle is a strategy based on selective trust. Here a company honestly tries to match customers to the products offered by that company. Such a company offers extensive and honest information about its own products, although it will not necessarily provide any useful comparisons to competing products. A selectively trust-based company has a value-based pricing strategy so that customers know that they are getting what they pay for. Companies in this middle category have adequate fulfillment and support services that deliver the promised value to the customer (e.g., good-quality products, adequate returns processes, and service guarantees). A selectively trust-based company is concerned about customer retention, but it may try to retain customers whose needs are no longer met by that company.

A fully trust-based Theory T strategy seeks to create customers who trust the company to act on their behalf at all times. Sales, marketing, fulfillment, and support all work together to underpromise and overdeliver. In seeking to unconditionally serve and satisfy customers, a fully trust-based business will actually occasionally act against its own short-term interests (e.g., by recommending a competitor's product or covering the cost of some extreme level of service). Because trust-based companies try to build customers for life, these companies strive to create reputations for impeccable honesty. Although a fully trust-based business can lose customers (whose needs or circumstances change), the quality of the experience means that even ex-customers recommend the company.

For example, a client may come to trust a private banker, letting that banker or investment adviser make financial decisions for that customer. Or a company might trust a supplier, letting that supplier take responsibility for inspecting the quality of the supplier's parts. True trust comes when one party delegates responsibility, with very little oversight, to another party. Trust implies that the customer knows that the company will act competently on that customer's best interests.

When to Use Which Strategy

Push marketing is suited to companies with commodity products and price-sensitive Theory P customers. Push marketing is also successful when customers are ill informed or the cost of gathering information is high. In the absence of specific information, customers are more likely to emphasize how much of a deal they believe they are being offered. Eventually, consumers will gain access to the information they need to make better judgments, and the seller's marketing efforts will be offset by consumer knowledge. Prerequisites for push-based strategies include the following:

- Your company must be the low-cost producer because the company will not be building a relationship with the customer.
- Your company must be in a market that does not value relationships.

The *fully trust-based strategy* is most successful for companies with the best products and an educated consumer base. Trust is important for products and services that are complex, that have hard-to-assess benefits or features, or that have a high impact on the customer. Examples include purchasing a car, picking the right bouquet of flowers, or working with a private banker. These factors also tend to be more stable in the long run, which is another advantage of being on this side of the scale. An educated Theory T consumer is able to better validate any corporate claims of product performance, and thus one would expect this customer to be more receptive to the notion of an advocacy relationship with the company. Prerequisites for trust-based strategies include the following:

- Your company must be a quality provider.
- Your company must be able to keep innovation to add value and differentiation to your products.
- Your company must be in a market that values relationships.

Digital technology is theory neutral. That is, digital technology can be applied to either push marketing or trust-based marketing. For example, marketing automation technology can be used to push advertising messages onto customers. Unsolicited push e-mail is called spam. But the same technology can be used in trust-based marketing for opt-in mail programs. With opt-in e-mail, customers sign up to receive information and promotions by e-mail.

Benefits of Trust-Based Strategies

Trust-based businesses can extract themselves from margin-killing price competition by proving to customers and to the marketplace that they deliver true value. More trust-oriented businesses have high customer retention and more stable revenue streams. Ultimately, trust-based businesses have higher sales volumes and lower marketing costs than push-based businesses.

Push-based businesses must acquire a continuous influx of new, uninformed customers to replace departing, dissatisfied customers. As the poor fulfillment and service levels of the company become widely known, a push-based business must spend increasingly large amounts of money on marketing to reach new customers and to convince them to buy. Although money spent on advertising and marketing can buy customers, the return on that investment is short lived if the customers are not ultimately satisfied with the delivered products and services.

By contrast, trust-based businesses accumulate customers with modest and decreasing marketing costs per customer. Satisfied customers, ratings agencies, and journalists all become very effective, free marketing resources for trusted companies with high reputations. When a customer trusts a company, the cost to serve drops because the customer and company spend less time negotiating sales, inspecting goods, and overseeing service. Admittedly, trust-based businesses must spend more on creating and delivering good products and services because a trust-based business cannot honestly recommend its own products if those products are not truly the best. But because these expenditures go directly to providing real value to the customer, they have a high and long-lasting return on investment.

In a study of 6,831 consumers, respondents were assigned one of 25 Web sites and asked to evaluate it using a questionnaire. The sites ranged from automobiles, finance, computers, sports, e-tailers, and portals. The purpose of the study was to identify characteristics of a Web site that engender trust. The results showed that characteristics like privacy, security, and no errors were important, but surprisingly characteristics such as easy navigation, brand, advice, and presentation proved to be just as important. The implication of this research for marketing managers is to design your Web site for trust by having (1) good navigational properties, (2) strong brand, (3) helpful advice, and (4) professional and friendly site design. These characteristics act as trust cues that convey the trustworthiness of your company.

Insite Case Introduction

As we have seen, there are many benefits to trust-based marketing. The following case of InSite Technology, however, presents a dilemma. The company offers a trust-based adviser, but they are not meeting with success. What is preventing their success, and what do you recommend InSite should do? This case presents a good opportunity for you to think about how trust-based marketing might work and how to formulate a trust-based strategy. This case also gives you a chance to apply the concepts of consumer buying behavior.

REFERENCES

McGregor, Douglas. 1960. *The Human Side of Enterprise.* New York: McGraw-Hill.

Morgan, Robert M., and Shelby D. Hunt. 1994. "The Commitment-Trust Theory of Relationship Marketing." *Journal of Marketing* 58: 20–39.

Novak, T. P., D. L. Hoffman, and Y. Yung. 2000. "Measuring the Customer Experience in Online Environments: A Structural Modeling Approach." *Management Science* 19: 22–42.

Urban, Glen L., Fareena Sultan, and William Qualls. 2000. "Placing Trust at the Center of Your Internet Strategy." *MIT Sloan Management Review,* fall, vol. 42 no. 1, 39–48.

CHAPTER

InSite Marketing Technology

Introduction

It is the summer of 1999, and the president and chief executive officer of InSite Marketing Technology, Stefania Nappi, is thinking long and hard about why the company's powerful product could be so promising and yet be selling so poorly. InSite sells trust-based on-line advisers—a software technology for helping customers select products on the Web and feel more comfortable with on-line buying. InSite's software is especially useful in buying situations in which customers choose from a complex array of product choices, such as pickup trucks and notebook computers.

InSite's software ameliorates the cold, impersonal nature of search-and-navigate Web sites by using a virtual salesperson and a dialogue-based user interface. The virtual salesperson is a "personality" that creates rapport with customers rather than a site that merely presents text-only questions. Behind the scenes, powerful software interprets customer interactions in terms of the likely needs, preferences, and expertise level. The software combines leading research from two areas: predictive statistical models and the psychocognitive basis of trust in business transactions.

Now, after nearly two and half years, InSite is running low on cash and is looking to raise a new round of investment. Nappi knows that the value proposition for the product is good and that e-commerce is booming. Although many companies are trying to figure out how to sell products over the Web, actual sales of the on-line adviser have lagged behind expectations. InSite needs to understand why sales lag, how to boost sales, and how to prove to potential investors that InSite has both a winning product and a winning plan for selling that product.

History

Three cofounders started InSite in February 1997 to commercialize new ideas about marketing and e-commerce that were arising at the Massachusetts Institute of Technology (MIT). Professors Glen Urban and John Little brought a wealth of new ideas on virtual buying environments, trust, discrete-choice modeling, customer segmentation, and product acceptance modeling. Jeffrey Stamen had been president of another company, Management Decisions Systems (MDS), which was cofounded by Professors Urban and Little. MDS, formed in the 1970s, was sold to IRI in 1980, and then Oracle bought a part of the combined company (essentially the part that was MDS) in 1995. With their long history of working together, these three cofounders formed the intellectual core of the company and recruited other key executives to the nascent firm. For example, they recruited Stefania Nappi, an MIT graduate with a 20-year history of building software organizations and former chief operating officer of IntraNet, to be the chief executive officer and president.

The three cofounders invested a total of $450,000 to self-fund the start-up, especially to fund the development of a prototype of a trust-based adviser. This money, along with some early revenues from General Motors and other clients, supported the company until the summer of 1998.

When Nappi joined the firm, her first two priorities were to hire a strong team and to develop a prototype to refine and showcase the ideas. "My philosophy was to hire a smaller team of higher-quality people," Nappi said. "We looked for both breadth and depth—a person who could do the work of three people, not because they worked three times as long but because they worked smart." For example, Nappi hired a software engineer comfortable with creating such a new product and a technical architect experienced in creating large-scale systems used by multiple users simultaneously. Besides hiring for solid experience and imagination, Nappi also looked for people who were committed to building a company. "That way, we'd be making technical decisions that were informed strategically," Nappi said.

The company started small and frugally, building its first prototype of what became the Trusted Advisor for only $100,000. Development was swift, and the first prototype was ready in May 1997. "Creating the prototype for not a lot of money was useful when we went looking for additional funding. Everyone was impressed with how much we had gotten done for so little money," Nappi said. In 1998, InSite raised $1.5 million from angel investors and increased its staff to 15 people.

Building the prototype began with the germ of an idea, informed by market knowledge, then tested extensively by prospective customers. "We wanted to make sure we designed a product that the market would want, so we used a very iterative design process," Nappi said. InSite's fourth employee was an expert in user-interface design who had designed CD-based games for *Toy Story* and the "Where in the World Is Carmen Sandiego" series. "We wanted a product that would be immediately accessible, just like a game, not something you'd need an instruction manual for," Nappi said.

InSite's initial target markets were any sales situation that involved a product with multiple decision options and a desire for individualized service. InSite had good receptivity from companies in electronics, financial services, and gift goods. It saw prospects in wholesale computing, petroleum, plastics, pharmaceutical, and medical industries as well (see figure 6.1 for InSite's customer prospects).

Understanding the need for a product like Trusted Advisor implies understanding the crucial differences between on-line retailing and traditional in-store retailing. InSite saw that companies would need to engender trust among customers and provide some form of personalized service if those companies were to fulfill their e-commerce dreams.

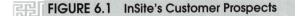

FIGURE 6.1   InSite's Customer Prospects

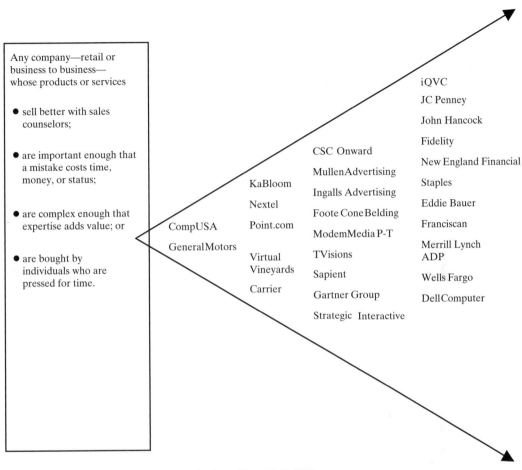

Any company—retail or business to business—whose products or services

- sell better with sales counselors;

- are important enough that a mistake costs time, money, or status;

- are complex enough that expertise adds value; or

- are bought by individuals who are pressed for time.

CompUSA
GeneralMotors

KaBloom
Nextel
Point.com
Virtual Vineyards
Carrier

CSC Onward
MullenAdvertising
Ingalls Advertising
Foote Cone Belding
ModemMedia P-T
TVisions
Sapient
Gartner Group
Strategic Interactive

iQVC
JC Penney
John Hancock
Fidelity
New England Financial
Staples
Eddie Bauer
Franciscan
Merrill Lynch
ADP
Wells Fargo
DellComputer

Source: InSite Marketing Technology, Inc., Business Plan, July 7, 1999.

Product Information and Selling on the Internet

As a new medium for sales, the Internet offers a powerful value proposition but hides a problematic reality. On the one hand, the Internet offers an unparalleled opportunity to get accurate, relevant information into the hands of consumers—aiding those consumers in their buying decisions. Web sites cheaply and efficiently store and disseminate vast volumes of product information. A Web site can "know" the minute details of millions of products in a way that no normal salesperson could ever know. A Web site can have the latest product information instantly, while a traditional sales organization is still drafting a memo to mail out to a far-flung sales force. The Web seems ideal for distributing product information and for increasing sales.

On the other hand, most Web sites put the onus on customers to serve themselves and force the customer to search and navigate through a confusing array of screens. They do not differentiate between knowledgeable and novice customers (e.g., customers who know the technical jargon of the product domain and customers who do not or customers who are already informed about currently available prices and features and customers who are not). On the Web, the information is all there, but the customer must work hard to find it. The problem is that while many companies like to think that they are "selling" on the Web, they are actually only barely allowing customers to "buy" on the Web (assuming that those customers are dedicated and determined enough).

To understand the impact of the Internet on selling information-intensive products, we must examine the sales process from the perspective of both the buying customer and the selling company and then highlight the differences between on-line and traditional sales. InSite's product attempts to reduce the gap between shopping on the Web and shopping in a store.

Buying Information-Intensive Products: Consumer's Perspective

For many products, consumers face an information-intensive buying process. Each of a range of product options carries a complex litany of features, strengths, weaknesses, and issues with an associated price tag. Obvious examples include cars, computers, and home entertainment equipment where a truly astronomical array of choices of faces threatens to overwhelm the consumer.

Buying a high-dollar durable good can be harrowing—consumers face substantive consequences from buying the wrong product. Worse, these types of products have very complex technical features—consumers face a burden of learning the jargon before they can even rationally compare the choices. Buying can be frustrating, and consumers may fear that salespeople will take advantage of them, pushing expensive, unnecessary bells and whistles with a convincing cloud of jargon. The point is that consumers would like to—and need to—trust the seller when those consumers gather information, solicit recommendations, submit sensitive personal information, and, ultimately, buy the product (table 6.1 shows how InSite's Trusted Advisor satisfies on-line customer needs).

Selling Information-Intensive Products: Sales Perspective

Information-intensive products present challenges not only to consumers but to the seller's sales and marketing organizations as well. The seller must translate the complex features of each new product into marketing pitches and sales talking points. Then the seller must distribute the information about the new product to the sales force, training them to sell the new product.

Training is a major cost for salespeople, as teaching each salesperson about each new product is time consuming. Training consumes the valuable time during which the sales force might otherwise have been making sales. In short, transferring product knowledge to salespeople so that they can use it is costly to companies on several levels (table 6.2 shows how InSite's Trusted Advisor satisfies on-line merchant needs).

On-Line Retail versus Traditional Retail of Information-Intensive Products

Traditional retailers rely on the personal knowledge and sales skills of the in-store staff. Salespeople help consumers find, select, and buy the right product.

TABLE 6-1	How Trusted Advisor Satisfies E-Customer Needs
E-Customer Need	*How the Trusted Advisor Fills the Need*
People want to buy from people.	The Advisor entails one or more **personas** as **virtual sales-people,** each of which is appropriately "cast" to deliver the optimal appearance, style, and expertise.
People want sales help, not self-service.	The Advisor's virtual salespeople **elicit** the visitors' **soft and hard issues, make** tailored **recommendations, reassure visitors** by educating them and addressing concerns, and **encourage sales** by saying why specific products are right for them.
People do not want to give up self-empowerment and control in order to receive sales help.	The Advisor is built on InSite's platform of **Trust-Based Marketing™,** an approach to marketing and selling that meets both the merchant's and the customer's goals while earning the customer's trust—and never taking control away from the customer. This is captured in InSite's **Trust Cues.**
People want warmth without surrendering their privacy.	The Advisor has at its core a proprietary **microsegmentation model** that allows the Advisor to make highly educated predictions of customer motivations and needs, without knowing a customer's name or even requiring that they do much work.
People do not want to be computer experts.	Customers using the Advisor are immersed in an intuitively supportive buying experience. InSite's designs reflect its **models of customer purchase behavior** and include **intuitive interfaces** with the immediacy of interactive games.

Source: InSite Marketing Technology, Inc., Business Plan, July 7, 1999.

Salespeople use a host of social cues and their innate intelligence to quickly identify the needs of each consumer and to guide that consumer to appropriate product offerings.

The key difference between traditional retail and on-line retail is that salespeople build a personal relationship with the customer. They ask questions, listen to responses, and observe the customer's behavior. Customers do the same thing: react to answers, observe the salesperson's behavior, and form opinions about the product, the salesperson, and the process, any or all of which can strongly influence their decision. By contrast, the plain world of Web pages lacks these important interactive social mechanisms. A clickstream is not a conversation.

Worse, because the Web is a new medium filled with young companies, consumers may not be ready to trust the Web for their purchasing. In traditional retail, consumers can immediately judge the resources of the seller by judging the environment of the retail outlet. A clean, well-lit store with amply stocked shelves and professional-looking sales staff inspires confidence in consumers. Consumers can also examine the goods to personally judge the features, quality, and styling of the product. By contrast, on the Web, it is hard to determine whether the Web site is backed by a billion-dollar corporation or a student in a dorm room. Judging products on the Web

TABLE 6.2   How Trusted Advisor Satisfies E-Merchant Needs

E-Merchant Need	*How the Trusted Advisor Fills the Need*
Companies need differentiators.	The satisfaction e-customers receive from the Advisor during the buying process is an extremely powerful differentiator. Further, the Advisor's **Template Library** (configurable templates that incorporate InSite's state-of-the-art interface designs and harness the power of InSite's Trust Cues) makes it possible to create a unique look and feel for each merchant.
Companies need greater Internet return on investment.	The Advisor's ability to **completely satisfy e-customers** during the buying process directly improves a merchant's Web results
Companies need effective alliances between marketing and technology.	The Advisor, built by a team of proven technology-savvy marketing scientists and marketing-savvy software staff, **bridges the gap** so companies do not have to.
Companies are overwhelmed by the effort needed for e-commerce.	The Advisor **integrates transparently** into Web sites, so existing investments are leveraged, not discarded, and development efforts can continue without disruption.
Companies want solid solutions, not hype.	The Advisor is an industrial-strength scalable **turnkey solution** that continually gathers **built-in measurements** of its results. Further, as it operates, it observes uncontaminated customer behaviors. As part of its **Intelligence Service,** InSite's market analysts synthesize these into **actionable insights for e-merchants** and increased effectiveness for the Advisor.

Source: InSite Marketing Technology, Inc., Business Plan, July 7, 1999.

is also harder, as one lacks the ability to "kick the tires." On the Web, consumers wonder whether the seller will deliver as promised, will keep credit card numbers safe, and will be there if something goes wrong with the product. Trust is both more important and harder to convey on the Web than it is at traditional bricks-and-mortar retail outlets.

Information-Intensive Products: InSite's Solution

InSite saw an opportunity to create a trust-based advisor that would reduce the gulf between browsing a Web site and talking with a salesperson. The technology would combine research on trust cues, purchasing behavior, virtual buying environments, and software capabilities.

The goal was to blend the low cost of information service with the personal attention of a salesperson. InSite's Trusted Advisor system would help customers research and buy products in much the same way they would if they had the help of an effective and trustworthy human sales counselor. The system provides unbiased product information (presenting both the good and the bad, avoiding brand favoritism) and uses a core engine to translate customer preferences into justifiable product recommendations. The Trusted Advisor works by translating each customer's needs and preferences into technical product features and narrowing the field of likely candidates.

The following is a summary of the types of products that are information intense and that need Advisor-like technology:

1. Information breadth
   - Multidimensional feature sets
   - Wide array of alternatives
2. Information depth
   - Customer needs trustworthy knowledge
   - Price-performance trade-offs
   - Complex product configuration process
3. Risky purchases
   - High-dollar, durable goods
   - High-impact goods
   - Volatile or dynamic markets (rapid changes in price/performance)
   - Infrequent purchases of time-varying products
   - High-visibility, status-related goods

Technological Core

The basis of InSite's Trusted Advisor technology is sophisticated database and decision analysis tools that segment consumers on the basis of the attitudes and preferences they reveal as they shop on-line. Visitors are presented with dynamically generated Web pages that provide an experience customized to the visitor's needs and goals. The Advisor engine takes known information about the visitor and uses rule-based predictions to create a customized experience. The engine uses the visitor's behavior as well as market segment predictions to infer information about the visitor without asking a lot of information. Through a combination of techniques (microsegmentation, utility/preference theory, and expert product knowledge), the Advisor brings products to shoppers rather than requiring shoppers to find and distinguish between the products on their own.

In addition to the Advisor, InSite's technology has sophisticated measurement ability to tally the revenue and cost savings delivered by the Advisor. Moreover, it measures the impact of individual components of a purchasing experience to evaluate whether a specific approach is effective.

InSite offers two performance levels for the Trusted Advisor. Implementing a full-featured Trusted Advisor requires about three months of elapsed time with one staff-year of effort. A streamlined, simplified Advisor can be implemented in less than one month of elapsed time and three staff-months of effort. These implementation times reflect the substantive amount of work required to translate knowledge about customers and product specifications into an automated system. Nonetheless, these implementation times are not large compared to the costs of creating sales force literature, distributing sales force materials, and training a large sales force. The software was available in application service provider (ASP) mode or ready to install in house.

Buyers of Trusted Advisor, such as CompUSA, participate in the implementation process by providing expertise about the customer base and product domain. InSite personnel use this to customize the solution correctly. For example, the buyer must provide lists of product attributes and valid combinations of components/features and identify customer segments. InSite translates this knowledge into the rules and Web screens of the Trusted Advisor Web site. Finally, buyers test the Advisor, approving the questions/answers and the recommendations to each exemplar. After implementation, the buyer is responsible for maintaining the product data in the Advisor database.

Pricing of the Advisor was based on the software business model. An initial license was priced at $100,000 plus a monthly maintenance fee (including updates) of $5,000 per month plus consulting services. A typical engagement would cost $200,000 to $300,000 for the first year and $100,000 per year thereafter. Early customers were offered discounts, and the philosophy was to do what was necessary to get initial customers on board.

Alternatives to InSite

InSite's trust-based advisor technology is not the only approach to improving sales on the Internet. The massive opportunity associated with e-commerce is driving many companies—both retailers and technology vendors—to create processes and technologies that improve the on-line buying experience. These alternatives address various facets of the on-line buying conundrum, such as helping consumers choose appropriate products, creating a social connection in an otherwise asocial medium, creating trustworthy information, and creating trust in the on-line retailer.

Augmenting Self-Service with Personal Service

A number of on-line companies augment Web-based self-service with some form of personal service. Retailer Lands' End, for example, pioneered Lands' End Live on its Web site in 1999. The service lets shoppers speak to customer-service reps live over the Web via chat or voice. If a customer cannot find an item, the rep can take the shopper's browser to it. Similarly, a customer with a question about an item can guide a rep's browser to the relevant page. Other on-line retailers use a "Call Me" button in which the customer enters their phone number and the retailer calls the customer to discuss the customer's needs. At the low end of the spectrum is e-mail-based personal service (which can be partially automated). These tactics do add personal service, although they also burden on-line sales with significant labor costs.

Product Selection via Clever Questioning

Other companies also have software technologies to aid product selection. These technologies pose a series of questions to the buyer and deduce buyer preferences from the answers. Various schemes rely on various styles of questions, such as pairwise comparisons, ranking the importance of features, or weighing dimensions on a scale of 1 to 10. A host of theoretical frameworks underpin these tools, including statistical decision theory, fuzzy logic, utility theory, and optimization theory. Each tool strives to derive the best product recommendation from the fewest questions.

Collaborative Filtering: Customers Helping Customers

To date, collaborative filtering systems have been most often used to recommend taste-based products, such as books or music, to customers. Collaborative filtering uses the past purchase behavior of one customer to recommend items to another customer who is in some way similar to that customer. For example, if two customers buy the same book and the first customer also buys a second, related book, then Amazon.com's recommendation engine suggests that the second customer might also like the second book. Thus, Amazon.com can tell a customer who is considering buying book XYZ that "people who bought book XYZ also bought book ABC and PDQ." Collaborative filtering relies on large numbers of purchases to identify coherent similarities. Collaborative filtering can also segment by workplace (e.g., Amazon also knows the "most popular" books at various businesses around the country) or by geography (the most popular books in Boulder, Colorado).

Third-Party Rating Services: A Seal of Approval

Another approach to the trust issue involves third-party rating services. Third-party agencies, such as TRUSTe, provide independent verification that a company is acting responsibly. TRUSTe is a nonprofit privacy initiative that has developed a third-party oversight "seal" program. The seal alleviates users' concerns about on-line privacy and establishes Web site credibility through a complex assurance process. TRUSTe does not directly recommend products. Rather, it evaluates the overall privacy of a site so that users are more comfortable when making on-line purchases. Other companies, such as BizRate, ask customers to rate a Web site after they have made a purchase. Customers rate the Web site experience and their satisfaction with delivery. BizRate aggregates this information, presenting customer satisfaction ratings for participating retailers.

Examples: Trusted Advisor in Action

CompUSA

InSite's first major customer, CompUSA, signed on in March 1998. CompUSA wanted an on-line advisor that would help customers buy notebook computers at cozone.com, an on-line arm of the giant retailer.

InSite designed an advisor that embedded the best salesperson skills and knowledge into an application with 24/7 availability. The advisor, named "Jill," helps customers select the notebook computer that best meets their needs by posing nonintrusive, easy questions. The customer can answer the questions or ask for recommendations immediately (see figure 6.2).

"We went live on CompUSA's Web site selling laptops," Nappi said. "Customers were extremely receptive—they loved it. The advisor was warm, friendly, and useful. CompUSA felt it differentiated the company because it looked good and was different from anything the competitors had." Even better, the software worked. "I've been in the software business 25 years, and it's amazing how often a product just doesn't work. Ours worked right from the start, and CompUSA was impressed. They said, 'It differentiates us, it tests well, it's a piece of cake for us to use, and it works—there's nothing we don't like about it.'"

In early testing, Jill was used by 25,000 visitors in three months. CompUSA saw a 6 percent increase in sales, 65 percent longer site visits (which increase mind/market share), and increased customer satisfaction.

Research Prototype: TruckTown

InSite cofounder Professor Glen Urban had been working on an advisor prototype as part of his research at MIT. He published the results in the open literature, and InSite used this public work and extended it to a proprietary version based on improved algorithms.

FIGURE 6.2   CompUSA's Trusted Advisor, "Jill"

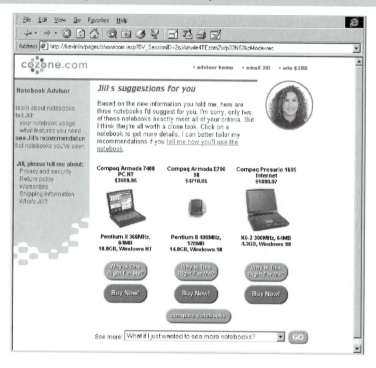

The research prototype was called TruckTown. TruckTown is a demonstration project that illustrates the use of a series of simulated personalities to guide customers to a purchase decision on a new pickup truck. The prospective customer gets information from and answers posed by one of several "personalities" (e.g., one of the personalities is "Craig Lynch, owner of Hillside Garage"). An algorithm based on Bayesian statistics continuously narrows the list of candidate trucks by asking relevant questions. Check boxes and trade-off sliders let each customer describe how he or she will be using his or her truck and what features are most important. Ultimately, the advisor provides a recommended truck model. During the research project, the vast majority of test subjects who have used the advisor ascribed a high level of trust to it and even indicated that they would be willing to pay about $100 for such an advisory service.

Promising Sales Leads Lead Nowhere

InSite does not lack for sales leads and customer interest. Prospective customer companies grasp the value of creating a more personal on-line selling process. But agreeing with InSite's value proposition is not the same as agreeing to buy InSite's technology. To date, InSite's sales have not met projections.

A team of four MIT-Sloan MBA students revealed some of the reasons why companies were not buying the Trusted Advisor. The team interviewed e-merchants to understand their perceptions and the adoption behavior of the Trusted Advisor. The team identified the following points as contributing to the low adoption of the Advisor on the market (see figure 6.3 for points and diagram).

"Our product seems to fall in the 'nice-to-have' category, not the must-have," Nappi said, explaining the slow sales. Many companies are just in the process of putting up their sites and are concentrating on the basics. "Some companies put up a recommendation engine that asks one or two questions, like 'How much do you want to spend?' and steers the customer to one half of their product set or the other half. Apart from that, they don't feel like it is worth it to create a better sales experience. By analogy, it's like going to a store that has aisles full of merchandise, but you can't find a salesperson because the store doesn't want to invest heavily in a salesforce." On-line retailers are focusing on putting up shopping carts and being able to ship products. Creating good proactive sales capability seems to be on the back burner.

The Trusted Advisor optimizes for customer satisfaction. It is more complex, warmer, and gives more targeted advice, and customer satisfaction always rises whenever the Advisor is used. But installing a two-question engine that leads customers some acceptable products is faster to implement. It appears that the e-commerce companies do not yet realize that customer satisfaction during on-line buying is important. By the end of the summer of 1999, InSite was reaching the end of its resources. The cofounders are using their own money to meet payroll while the company searches for a way to move forward. Venture Capitalists liked the idea, but they were unwilling to invest without a growing list of happy customers and a healthy pipeline of potential buyers. A good idea will die unless the company can convince investors (and customers) that the product is worth the price.

FIGURE 6.3

A team of four MIT-Sloans MBA students interviewed various e-merchants and identified the following points as reasons for the low adoption of the Advisor on the market:

1. **Customers are satisfied with status quo of the Web for their products**
   - The Web provides objective information.
   - Product attributes are difficult to verbalize/categorize.
   - Current status quo avoids channel conflict with sales representative.
   - Companies can serve customers through "FAQ" and "Search" functions.
2. **Customers adopt other concepts**
   - Push-oriented marketing gives more control on the output.
   - End users perceive collaborative filtering to be more fair (users trust other buyers more than the merchant itself).
   - There are other forms of personalizing Web sites (e.g., Broadvision platform).
   - Advisors are homemade.
3. **Customers do not perceive the benefits**
   - The Trusted Advisor technology is complex and difficult to understand.
   - The time needed for the Advisor to have an impact on results is too long for Internet.
   - Data to support the benefits of Advisor is hard to obtain and measure.
4. **Customers perceive high costs**
   - Implementation time is extremely long.
   - Price is high, and there is no reason for such high prices.
   - Customers are afraid of hidden costs (upgrades and maintenance).

QUESTIONS

1. How can InSite convince Venture Capitalists that Trusted Advisor has good sales prospects? How would you convince Venture Capitalists of the salability of InSite's product?
2. Given low sales of Trusted Advisor, why do companies not seem to be buying Trusted Advisor? What would you do about the problem?
3. If you were the marketing director at a firm that wants to sell on-line, would you consider purchasing Trusted Advisor?

FIGURE 6.3 Continued

THE TEAM ALSO INVESTIGATED THE BUYING DECISION
OF E-MERCHANTS ON ADVISORS:

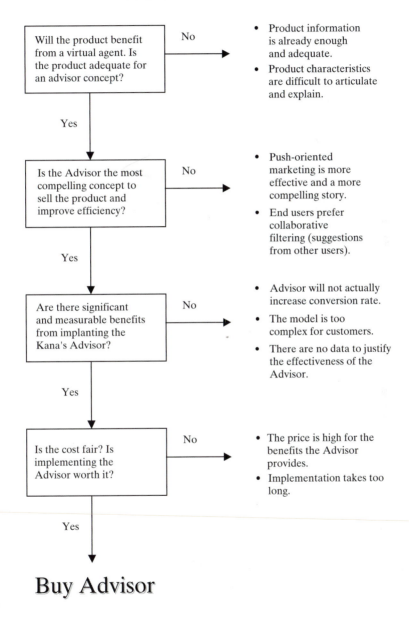

| Will the product benefit from a virtual agent. Is the product adequate for an advisor concept? | No → | • Product information is already enough and adequate.
• Product characteristics are difficult to articulate and explain. |

Yes

| Is the Advisor the most compelling concept to sell the product and improve efficiency? | No → | • Push-oriented marketing is more effective and a more compelling story.
• End users prefer collaborative filtering (suggestions from other users). |

Yes

| Are there significant and measurable benefits from implanting the Kana's Advisor? | No → | • Advisor will not actually increase conversion rate.
• The model is too complex for customers.
• There are no data to justify the effectiveness of the Advisor. |

Yes

| Is the cost fair? Is implementing the Advisor worth it? | No → | • The price is high for the benefits the Advisor provides.
• Implementation takes too long. |

Yes

Buy Advisor

Segmentation and Positioning

Segmentation and Positioning

Introduction

Having determined the strategic approach (push-based versus trust-based marketing), the next step is to determine which customers to target and how to position your product/service relative to the competition.

Why Segment?

Segmentation involves dividing the market into parts and devising alternative strategies for some or all of these parts. Differences in consumer preferences and needs are the primary reason for segmentation. Consumers are willing to pay more for a product tailored to their specific needs than for one designed to fit the average preference.

Although heterogeneity in preferences is the major driving force in segmentation, segmentation offers other benefits as well. For example, it may reduce competitive pressure when competitors do not have a product tailored to a particular segment's needs. A competitor with one product that fits average preferences will lose share to a firm with multiple products fitted to particular segment needs, assuming similar prices. Within the segment, the tailored product is relatively insulated from the effects of price wars and can generally maintain a price premium.

Given the advantages of segmentation, why not treat each consumer individually? The drawback of extremely fine-grained segmentation is cost. The trade-off between the increased costs of narrower segments and the potential gains to be made from offering products targeted at specific segments is a fundamental managerial concern. Two key questions that must be addressed are (1) how many segments should we deliver, and (2) how should customers be grouped in these segments to best define a market?

Digital technologies lower the cost of reaching customers. In the past, ads could be delivered only via mass media such as television, newspaper, radio, and billboard. Reaching a narrow segment of the population was difficult and expensive.

Assurances that the right segment saw the ad and reacted to the ad were limited. Now, technologies such as e-mail, the Internet, wireless technologies, video on demand, and rich media ads make it possible and inexpensive for marketing managers to reach their targeted audience. There are three reasons for this. First, ad server companies can compile and assemble much narrower demographic segments than can magazines, cable channels, or other mass media. Second, the cost to deliver an ad is small and may even be done on a commission basis. Third, user log-ins and cookies let marketers know the specific individuals who are seeing an ad and what they do after seeing an ad impression (click through, shop now, buy later, abandon shopping cart, and so on).

Segmentation Strategies

If the preference difference between consumers are large, then offering products for each segment can be profitable. This is especially true if some of the product and marketing costs can be shared by one or more products (i.e., brand marketing or marketing a product family). If costs cannot be shared because of the uniqueness of each segment, it may be more effective to target only one or a few segments. For example, a company may offer premium-quality homes and not participate at all in the low-cost, low-quality subdivision segment of the housing market.

The goal is to segment the market for the purpose of maximizing profits. This is a challenging task because of the many ways to segment markets: It is often difficult to access segments selectively, there is frequent overlap between segments, and segments can change markedly over time. We need to define the criteria for grouping customers, specify the number of groups, and decide how to vary our product offering across segments. Let us now look at a number of common bases for segmentation and the analytic tools available to support segmentation strategy.

Customer Relationship Management

A major part of Customer Relationship Management (CRM) is CRM software, which aids in tracking and managing a company's front-office interactions (sales calls, sales leads, purchases, and so on) with each of its customers. CRM software is most useful for companies that maintain direct channels to the customer (e.g., financial services, industrial suppliers, telecommunications, and on-line/mail-order retailers). Although CRM promises the potential of one-to-one segmentation, other factors (product design, advertising, and distribution) limit the company to macrostrategic segmentation. Thus, CRM is a texturing method for individualizing the positioning within a segment—helping to pitch the right products and services to each customer. Some companies also use CRM and associated data to derive crucial customer-related variables, such as the profitability of individual customers or the probability that the customer is about to defect. CRM software is just one example of the new enterprise software technologies that improve the efficiency and sophistication of a company's operations.

Bases of Segmentation

One of the most important decisions in segmentation is the designation of the dimensions on which customers will be grouped in an effort to find internally homogeneous segments. By "internally homogeneous," we mean that the members within each segment would share a common set of needs, preferences, and predilections to purchase the company's products and services. For example, in automobiles, the segments could be based on age, attitudes toward car ownership, product feature importances (fuel economy, stereo quality, safety, capacity, and power), or something else (number of children or how the car is used). There is no one correct segmentation. A best grouping can often be found through the use of statistical criteria to define similarity between customers. Next we discuss the most common bases for segmentation.

Demographics

The most obvious and clearly measured differences between customers are often demographic. Sex, age, marital status, family size, age of children, income, occupation, geographic location, mobility, home ownership, education, race, religion, and nationality are all candidate variables for the definition of segments. Demographic segmentation aids in identifying market changes that represent a future threat or opportunity. For example, in the next 30 years, the fastest-growing segment in the United States will be the over-55 age-group. In industrial markets, commonly used demographic variables are size of company (scales volume or number of employees), SIC code business designation, or geographic location.

Attitudes

Although demographic data are generally easy to collect, attitudes may be a better basis for identifying differences in response. Attitudes can be measured with market research questions (see Churchill, 1998). Attitudes may relate to overall social issues (religion, politics, or work), personal interests (family, home, job, or health), or specific product attitudes ("the highest-quality product is usually the best long-run buy" or "Mercedes-Benz is for rich people").

Importances

The most direct measure of differences in preferences between customers consists of the importances they attach to product benefits and characteristics. For example, some consumers may select toothpaste on the basis of its whitening properties, while others may select it on the basis of its protection against gingivitis. Price is another importance category. For industrial customers, importance categories might include price, product quality, and service level in making deliveries.

Usage

Importances are not always easy to estimate—verbal statements of importances may not correlate well with purchasing behavior. Sometimes observed behavior is a more practical correlate to preference differences. Heavy users of a product may represent a meaningful segment because they account for such a large proportion of cases. In many markets, the top 20 percent of customers in usage account for 80 percent of sales volume.

When a product has a number of possible uses, segmentation as a function of use may be appropriate. For example, it might make sense to market differently to customers for preengineered steel buildings used for schools, auto dealerships, and barns.

> Segmenting the market is like looking at a three-dimensional object from different perspectives. The real object is the same, but it looks different from various angles (see figure 7.1 for several orthogonal views of a solid object). In marketing, the object (i.e., the market) is more complex than the object represented in figure 7.1 because there are many more than three dimensions, the hierarchies may have multiple levels, and some segments may overlap. Fortunately, a number of analytical support tools offer help in segmenting complex markets, as the next section illustrates.

FIGURE 7.1 Two-Dimensional Views and Solid Object

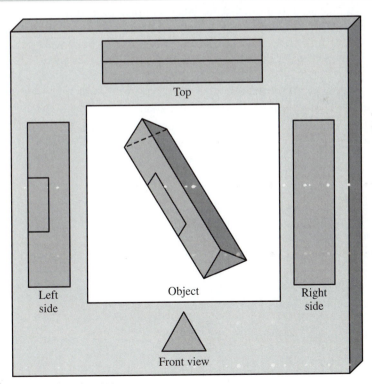

Source: Urban and Star (1991), p. 124.

Analytical Support

The aggregation of customers into internally homogeneous groups can be formalized by a simple statistical technique called *cluster analysis*. Clusters of consumers are formed by aggregating consumers on the basis of similarities.

Demographics

Clustering methods have been used by commercial research and consulting firms to analyze demographic data. One system, called PRIZM,[1] uses ZIP code areas rather than individuals as microdata inputs. PRIZM classifies U.S. households into one of 62 unique "clusters." Each cluster has its own name and set of attributes. For example, the "Blue Bloods" cluster is much higher in the professional/managerial career attributes than the general population (51.2 percent in the cluster compared to 22.7 percent in the U.S. population). The cluster profile reflects higher incomes, education, home ownership, likelihood of being middle age, and average household size. Although the cluster represents only 0.7 percent of the U.S. population, it would be vitally important to companies selling luxury goods.

Attitudes

Clustering methodology can also be applied to attitudinal responses. This kind of segmentation is called *psychographic segmentation.* Commercial services have clustered attitude measures obtained from large samples to determine segments. One of the best known of such services is called VALS.[2] It is based on attitudes toward issues such as the importance of work, strength of religious belief, and personality ("I like to be outrageous" or "I prefer a quiet evening at home to a party") (see figure 7.2).

Data mining is a powerful digital technology for analytically processing a company's data to learn more about customers, among other things. As computers have become more powerful, companies have created data warehouses to store voluminous amounts of data on business operations and customer transactions. Analyzing such data helps the company spot trends, identify segments, and detect problems. For example, Capital One created a 12-terabyte data warehouse to learn which of 14,000 credit card pitches worked and which did not. Retailers use POS (point-of-sale) data to do market basket analyses—to understand and segment consumers by the sets of products that they buy. Companies now have the data storage capacity and computer processing power to perform cluster analysis on low-level transaction data.

Sources: "Loyalty Programs," *American Banker,* September 15, 1998, and Stan Davis and Christopher Meyer, *Blur: The Speed of Change in the Connected Economy* (Reading, Mass.: Addison-Wesley, 1998).

---

[1] PRIZM is a registered trademark of Claritas, Inc.
[2] VALS is a registered trademark of SRI Consulting Business Intelligence.

FIGURE 7.2 Psychographic Segmentation of Stomach Remedy Market

The Severe Sufferers

The Severe Sufferers are the extreme group on the potency side of the market. They tend to be young, have children, and be well educated. They are irritable and anxious people, and believe that they suffer more severely than others. They take the ailment seriously, fuss about it, pamper themselves, and keep trying new and different products in search of greater potency. A most advanced product with new ingredients best satisfies their need for potency and fast relief, and ties in with their psychosomatic beliefs.

The Active Medicators

The Active Medicators are on the same side of the motivational spectrum. They are typically modern suburbanites with average income and education. They are emotionally well adjusted to the demands of their active lives. They have learned to cope by adopting the contemporary beliefs of seeking help for every ill, and use remedies to relieve even minor signs of ailments and every ache and pain. In a modern product they seek restoration of their condition and energy, mental recovery, and a lift for the active lives. They are influenced by a brand's reputation and by how well it is advertised. They tend to develop strong brand loyalties.

The Hypochondriacs

The Hypochondriacs are on the opposite side of the motivational spectrum. They tend to be older, not as well educated, and women. They have conservative attitudes toward medication and a deep concern over health. They see possible dangers in frequent use of remedies, are concerned over side effects, and afraid of remedies with new ingredients and extra potency. To cope with these concerns, they are strongly oriented toward medical authority, seeking guidance in treatment and what products they should use. They hold rigid beliefs about the ailment, and are disciplined in the products they use and how frequently they use them. They want a simple, single-purpose remedy that is safe and free from side effects and backed by doctors or a reputable company.

The Practicalists

The Practicalists are in the extreme position on this side of the motivational spectrum. They tend to be older, well educated, emotionally the most stable, and least concerned over their ailment or the dangers of remedies. They accept the ailment and its discomforts as part of life, without fuss and pampering. They use a remedy as a last resort, and just to relieve the particular symptom. They seek simple products whose efficacy is well proved, and are skeptical of complicated modern remedies with new ingredients and multiple functions.

From W. D. Wells, "Psychographics: A Critical Review." *Journal of Marketing Science,* Vol. 12 (May 1975), p. 203.

Product Positioning

Segmentation analysis provides a definition of the market and allows us to target one or more market opportunities (note that different segmentation analyses will provide different market definitions). Product positioning takes place within a target market segment and tells us how we can compete most effectively within that market segment. If we are to make good positioning decisions, we need to know (1) what dimensions in-segment consumers use to evaluate competitive marketing programs, (2) how important each of these dimensions is in the decision process, (3) how we and the competition differ perceptually on these dimensions, and (4) how consumers make choices on the basis of this information. In this section, we examine perceptual mapping as a method for understanding positioning issues.

Perceptual Maps

Perceptual maps represent the positions of products on a set of primary customer needs. While tables can be used to represent product positionings on several dimensions, a graph or "map" is more effective in portraying the options. Perceptual maps help managers understand a product category and recognize opportunities by providing a succinct representation of how customers view and evaluate products in a category. They can also be used to identify gaps that may represent opportunities for new products (see figure 7.3).

FIGURE 7.3 Perceptual Map of a New Pain Reliever after Home Use

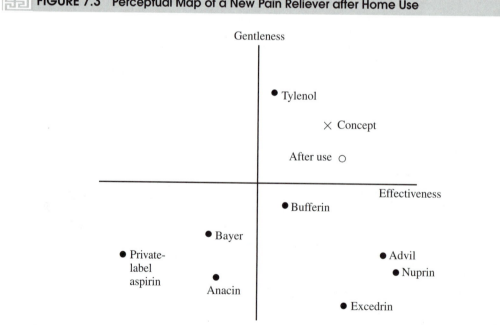

Source: Urban and Hauser (1993), p. 220.

FIGURE 7.4 Conjoint Analysis Can Link Features to Perceptions and Preference

Source: Urban and Hauser (1993), p. 273.

Conjoint Analysis

Recall conjoint analysis from chapter 5. Conjoint analysis provides a way to link product features directly to customer preferences, to link features to perceptual dimensions, or to link features to customer needs (see figure 7.4). For example, a target position of a new deodorant might be that it "goes on dry, keeps you dry." To achieve this position, the new product team must determine the features (e.g., chemical ingredients; scent; form; such as powder, stick, spray, or roll-on; package size; and package color) that best achieve the target position. One method to identify the best features might be to try every combination of features, determine which is the best, and select that combination. That is basically what conjoint analysis does except that only a fraction of all combinations need to be tried and a formal model is used to help the team measure and quantify the effect of each feature.

Terra Lycos Case Introduction

The Terra Lycos case raises issues about global segmentation, branding, and positioning. Two companies, Terra and Lycos, have segmented along different lines (one geographically by country, the other by computer demographics and psychographics). Then the two companies merged. What recommendations can you suggest for how the merged company can expand its business and its profitability?

REFERENCES

Churchill, G. A. 1998. *Marketing Research: Methodological Foundations.* Hinsdale, Ill.: Dryden Press.

Green, Paul E. "Conjoint Analysis in Marketing: New Developments and Directions." *Journal of Marketing* 54, no. 4: 3–19.

Leavitt, Theodore. 1981 "Marketing Intangible Products and Product Intangibles." *Harvard Business Review,* January/February, 83–91.

Urban, Glen L., and John R. Hauser. 1993. *Design and Marketing of New Products.* Englewood Cliffs, N.J.: Prentice Hall.

Urban, Glen L., and Steven H. Star. 1991. *Advanced Marketing Strategies.* Upper Saddle River, N.J.: Prentice Hall.

C H A P T E R

Terra Lycos

Introduction

Terra Lycos faces a trio of business issues as it begins life with the combined assets of two global Internet companies, Terra Networks and Lycos, Inc. Executives of the combined company must make decisions about branding, business model choice, and technical strategy. Many of the decisions relate to the issue of localization versus globalization and the strategies by Lycos and Terra that were pursued prior to the merger, particularly in Latin America.

Lycos: Scrappy Dot-Com Start-Up

Lycos, Inc., was a poster child for dot-com start-ups. The company's core search engine technology was spawned in the labs of Carnegie Mellon University by Michael Mauldin in 1994. CMGI, the Internet investment conglomerate, nurtured the upstart financially with funding through CMGI@Ventures in 1995. The company then settled in the tech-heavy Route 128 corridor of Massachusetts. A mere 10 months after hiring its first employee, the company went public in April 1996. Lycos rode the on-line wave of search engines, portals, and Netscape.

As worldwide Internet penetration rose, Lycos expanded beyond the United States. For the most part, Lycos leveraged the experience of local partners as it expanded globally. In June 1997, Lycos and media giant Bertelsmann AG cocreated Lycos Europe, a localized version of the Lycos site throughout Europe. Lycos expanded further in Europe by snapping up other portals, including Scandinavia's Spray and France's MultiMania. Then, Lycos teamed up with Sumitomo to expand into Japan in 1998. The following year, Lycos advanced into Korea and beefed up its Asia presence with the formation of Lycos Asia with Singapore Telecom. In 2000, Lycos launched Sympatico-Lycos, a Canadian business-to-consumer Internet portal, in partnership with Bell Canada.

As Lycos was expanding globally through partnerships and acquisitions, it also expanded laterally into a diverse range of content arenas. In 1998, the company acquired Tripod (home page building—www.tripod.com), wisewire (directory building), and WhoWhere (directory services—www.whowhere.com). Then in 1999, it acquired Sonique (Internet music distribution—www.sonique.com), Quote.com (financial information Web site—www.quote.com), and Gamesville.com (interactive entertainment company—www.gamesville.com). Lycos also announced a joint venture with Quack.com to develop a voice-accessed portal and launched a cobranded automotive Web site with Autoweb.com (Lycos took a 10 percent stake in Autoweb). Finally, Lycos began offering free Internet access and created LycosLabs to finance other Internet start-ups.

In late 1999, Lycos turned its attention to Latin America. Until the time of the merger, Lycos Latin America had 20 employees. Although Lycos Latin America had been up for only a few months, Lycos had already closed significant cobranding deals in Latin America countries. By 2000, Lycos had established a presence in Argentina, Brazil, Colombia, Chile, Mexico, Peru, and Venezuela. As with its other global expansion activities, Lycos closed significant cobranding deals in Latin America countries in order to gain access to needed content to meet local needs and interests.

At the time of the merger, the company's Lycos Network was visited by nearly 31 million people each month and featured services such as Web searching, chat rooms, e-mail, on-line shopping, news, auctions, streaming video programming, home pages, and even free (ad-supported) Internet access. Lycos had a wide-ranging global presence that included more than 30 countries scattered across North America, South America, Europe, and Asia. Overall, Lycos had about 900 employees in the United States and had been profitable since 1997. Revenues for the fiscal year ending August 2000 were some $300 million. Lycos derives the vast majority (70 percent) of revenues from advertising, with the remainder coming from e-commerce activities and a variety of licensing deals.

Terra: Big Phone Company Spin-Off

Terra came of age far from the realm of U.S. Internet technologists and venture capitalists. It arose within Telefónica, which was the dominant, newly privatized traditional telephone company of Latin America and Spain. Initially, Telefónica played the role of ISP (Internet Service Provider) by offering dial-up modem access to consumers and small businesses. Telefónica grew its Internet business by purchasing and integrating existing portals and ISPs in Spanish- and Portuguese-speaking countries.

In late 1998, Telefónica spun off these Internet activities to create Telefónica Interactiva. The spin-off took control of the various Internet companies in which Telefónica had stakes as well as the wholly owned Spanish and Latin American Internet subsidiaries of Telefónica. Assets included the Spanish portal Ole; Internet companies ZAZ (Brazil), Infovia (Guatemala), and Infosel (Mexico); and several companies belonging to Telefónica subsidiaries in Chile and Peru. In 1999, the spin-off changed its name to Terra Networks, and its parent (Telefónica) floated a 30 percent stake in an IPO.

Over time, Terra expanded both geographically and into other Internet arenas. Terra acquired portal Chevere in Venezuela and La Ciudad in Colombia in 2000. As it expanded to create a presence in most Spanish- and Portuguese-speaking countries, Terra expanded its range of offerings. Terra bought a 30 percent stake in DeRemate.com, a provider of on-line auctions in Latin America. Terra partnered with the wireless arm of Telefónica (Telefónica Moviles) to create Terra Mobile, a wireless portal for the European and Latin America region. These wireless Internet activities focused on WAP—an early standard for providing Web-like browsing on the small screens of cell phones. Terra also teamed with Lotus to develop Instanterra (instant messaging solution).

At the time of the merger, Terra Networks was the world's leading provider both of ISP services to residential and small office clients and of content for the Spanish- and Portuguese-speaking markets. The company operated in 16 countries: Spain, Brazil, Mexico, Chile, Peru, Uruguay, Guatemala, Argentina, Costa Rica, Venezuela, Colombia, El Salvador, Honduras, Nicaragua, Panama, and the United States. Overall, Terra employed around 2,000 employees; around 60 percent of Terra's workforce was located in Latin America. For the six months ending in June 2000, revenues totaled 82.5 million Euros. Net loss totaled 267.3 million Euros. Terra's revenues derived from ISP subscriptions (40 percent), advertising (29 percent), and e-commerce ventures (50 percent).

閼 The Merger

On May 16, 2000, Terra reached an agreement to buy Lycos and merge with it. The complex deal consisted of stock swap and a massive cash infusion. Lycos shareholders would receive somewhat less than half the shares in the new company, Terra Lycos. Telefónica (still 67 percent owner of Terra) agreed to underwrite a secondary offering to add $2 billion in cash to the new company. At the time of the offer, the stock-based acquisition was valued at $12.5 billion, but the value of Terra Networks' American-listed shares plunged during 2000, cutting nearly $7 billion off the buyout price. Despite the deteriorating stock market, the deal would guarantee the new company a cash horde of $3 billion, making it one of the world's best-capitalized Internet companies.

The merger had benefits for both Terra and Lycos. For Terra, the merger would propel the company out of Spain and Latin America and into a broader global arena. The combination would also help Terra move toward profitability (Lycos had been profitable since 1997, but Terra was still in its money-burning growth phase).

For Lycos, the merger would help it move from being a second-tier Internet portal to being a larger global company. Lycos knew it had to take action to keep up with competitors. While Lycos had only 3 percent year-on-year growth in March 2000, its competitor Yahoo! had 50 percent growth. Worse, Lycos' first attempt to diversify had failed—shareholders stymied its 1999 attempt to merge with Barry Diller's USA Networks. Fortunately, at a special meeting for Lycos' stockholders held in October 2000, 99.4 percent voted in favor of merging with Terra. Since the board at Terra had already voted unanimously to make the offer, Lycos shareholder approval cleared the way for the creation of Terra Lycos.

The combined company will be a major player in the global Internet, operating in 41 countries in 20 languages and reaching 91 million unique monthly visitors worldwide. The company's self-described mission is to be the most visited on-line destination in the world. Terra Lycos aggregates services and local and international content from leading providers from around the world and provides on-line advertising and marketing, e-commerce, and other Web services.

Terra Lycos is headquartered in Barcelona, Spain, but its operations headquarters are in Waltham, Massachusetts. Terra Lycos' chief executive officer is Bob Davis (former Lycos chief executive officer), and Terra Lycos is expected to have pro forma calendar year 2000 revenues of approximately $500 million.

Terra Lycos will hold the leading position in four of its eight primary markets: Canada, Korea, Latin America, and the U.S. Hispanic market. Terra Lycos will be number two in Asia (including Japan), number three in Europe, and number four in the United States. Moreover, Terra Lycos provides Internet access to more than five million customers throughout the world.

The merger was a sound decision for both Terra's and Lycos' board. Both companies complemented each other well, and joining forces would create a global Internet player that could improve both companies' market positions. The company would also leverage its important partners. It would use Bertelsmann (the third largest media company in the world) and Telefónica (a leading telecommunications company) to provide content, commerce, and connectivity assets, giving the company a distinct market differentiation. See figure 8.1

Contrasting Internet Strategy

Although both Lycos and Terra are global Internet portal providers that link Internet users to on-line content and e-commerce, the two companies have markedly different approaches to the Internet. The differences are most striking in the areas of content creation and technical infrastructure. The differences in these two areas arise from the different histories of the two companies.

Terra's historic role as an ISP defined its Internet strategy. Creating modem pools and points of presence meant that Terra had sizable local infrastructure investments. And because Terra created its network by acquiring local Internet companies, Terra chose to leverage the acquired local assets at the expense of creating a unified global architecture. By contrast, Lycos was more the idealized Internet company—offering service anywhere in the world from anywhere in the world by connecting its servers to the Internet backbone.

Content: Cobrand versus Buy and Make

Lycos and Terra used markedly different strategies for aggregating the content that attracts browsers and advertisers to their respective sites. Lycos used a cobranding strategy, leveraging the offerings of local third-party content providers. Lycos worked with local content providers so that externally created content was in a Lycos-usable format. The content resides on the developer's network but appears at Lycos' portal. Lycos' Web site then routes traffic to partner content providers and shares the associated advertising revenues. Lycos developed 57 of these cobranding partnerships. The advantages of Lycos' cobranding approach are the following:

- It leverages local expertise without acquisition costs.
- It chooses the best content providers from the marketplace of all players.

FIGURE 8.1 The Terra Lycos Network of Companies

Terra.com (www.terra.com)

Terra's portals offer users across the whole Spanish- and Portuguese-speaking world the widest variety of local and global content and services. Terra's success lies in its ability to satisfy the needs of both dial-up and broadband users, excelling at developing a state-of-the-art live entertainment and multiplatform content.

Lycos.com (www.lycos.com)

Lycos.com, a leading portal, offers Internet users a fast, easy, and efficient way to make sense of the Internet and manage its vast resources. It combines leading Web search and navigation resources, deep content in vertical areas, communications and personalization tools, and a complete shopping center.

AnimationExpress.com (www.animationexpress.com)

Animation Express is an entertainment destination featuring some of the best animations on the Web. The site features a range of animation styles produced by amateur and professional artists from all over the world.

Angelfire.com (www.angelire.com)

Angelfire makes building home pages simple, giving users a centralized file manager and their choice of a one-step HTML wizard or an advanced editor for direct control. Angelfire focuses on the home-page-building experience rather than communities and content and provides users with a variety of tools and utilities to publish great pages.

A Tu Hora (www.atuhora.com)

Atuhora.com is an e-commerce site launched in conjunction with Telepizza. The site offers delivery of convenience products, such as books, discs, drinks, food, and beverages within one hour to consumer homes.

Gamesville.com (www.gamesville.com)

Gamesville.com produces the Web's leading interactive entertainment community where members compete for prizes by playing massive multiplayer real-time games and is consistently named by Media Metrix as one of the "stickiest" sites on the Internet. Gamesville's unique approach to interactive entertainment enables thousands of registered contestants to simultaneously vie for prizes in unique, proprietary live games, such as poker and other card games, sports, trivia, and bingo.

HotBot.com (www.hotbot.com)

HotBot.com is an award-winning smart, sophisticated search engine with more than 40 tools to help users better articulate their searches and get relevant search results quickly and easily.

htmlGEAR.com (www.htmlgear.com)

htmlGEAR offers Web publishers at every skill level a fast and easy way to add compelling and interactive content to their sites. The professional Web add-ons, or Gears, can be used out of the box to easily add an instant upgrade to a home page or be customized or more tightly integrated into a commercial or professional Web site.

FIGURE 8.1 *(continued)*

Invertia.com (www.invertia.com)

Invertia.com is a financial portal offering global solutions for personal finance with real-time information and tools. It has presence in Argentina, Chile, Mexico, the United States, and Venezuela.

Lycos Zone

Lycos Zone is a free, engaging, and safe on-line haven for children featuring educational content, fun and games, and homework resources. Lycos Zone offers children, teachers, and parents the resources they need to explore the world from their PC.

Matchmaker.com (www.matchmaker.com)

Matchmaker is the leading on-line community enabling secure connections between people with similar interests and needs. Looking for a lifetime lover, a weekend workout partner, or a local wine connoisseur, *Matchmaker.com* is the place to meet all types of people across the world. *Matchmaker.com* has created a global constellation of city-centric and lifestyle-specific communities.

Quote.com (www.quote.com)

Quote.com brings Wall Street–quality information, tools, and trading capabilities to independent investors. Quote.com is one of the Internet's leading providers of streaming quotes and one of the top financial information sites on the Web.

Rumbo.com (www.rumbo.com)

Rumbo is a travel portal that provides the ability to research and purchase flights, hotels, rental cars, and vacation packages in real time. This Web site provides users with news articles and in-depth profiles and other information about travel destinations.

Sonique (sonique.lycos.com)

Sonique is one of the most popular audio players, supporting many audio formats, including MP3, and is consistently in the top five of the most popular downloads on *www.downloads.com*. The free audio player technology decodes music files and formats them to be played from the desktop.

Tripod.com (www.tripod.com)

Tripod offers premier, easy-to-use personal publishing tools and services, making it fast, fun, and easy for members to build professional-looking home pages, whether they are beginners or experienced users.

Web monkey.com (hotwired.lycos.com/webmonkey)

One of the first sites written by Web developers for Web developers, Webmonkey is the comprehensive source of information for professional and amateur Web enthusiasts, offering daily articles and technical updates as well as an archive of more than 200 features and tutorials.

Whowhere.com (www.whowhere.lycos.com)

WhoWhere.com provides a variety of comprehensive directory services that make it easy to find people on the Internet. The directories include E-mail Address Lookup, Phone and Address Lookup, Personal Home Page Lookup and People in U.S. Government.

(continued)

FIGURE 8.1 The Terra Lycos Network of Companies *(continued)*

Wired News *(Wired.com)*

Launched in November 1996, Wired News quickly rose to become an essential source for daily news and analysis of the technologies, companies, and people driving the information age.

Lycos Ventures

The Lycos Ventures investment strategy is simple: fund early-stage companies with the foresight and the product to make the Internet more interesting, more useful, faster, and better. In addition to capital, Lycos Ventures can contribute distribution and cobranding via the Terra Lycos network of Web properties, which receives 91 million unique visitors each month. This helps portfolio companies build value, visibility, and branding power more rapidly.

LycosLab

LycosLabs is Boston's unique full-service business incubator that offers entrepreneurs early-stage funding, resources, and guidance based on real-world Internet experience. Located in the western suburbs of Boston, LycosLabs offers New England and mid-Atlantic entrepreneurs the opportunity to be one of a very select group of companies that will reside on the campus, with a team that has thousands of man-years of highly relevant Internet experience.

From strategy, marketing, and corporate development to operations and international deployment, LycosLabs harnesses the experts who have built Lycos into one of the world's largest and most profitable networks of Web destinations. E-commerce, infrastructure, technology, and viral applications are a few of the areas that LycosLabs will consider for investing and active business acceleration.

- It does not incur development costs.
- It uses an efficient "format once, use many times" approach.

Terra, by contrast, tended to develop content itself after acquiring local companies to acquire local expertise. This strategy followed from Telefónica's original strategy of creating an Internet presence in different Latin American countries by purchasing local ISPs or content companies. In some cases, Terra also used exclusive contracts to outsource content development, but it never cobranded content. In general, Terra sought control and ownership. The advantages of Terra's approach are the following:

- Acquisition brings local expertise in house.
- It can create content to meet unsatisfied needs (for which no third-party provider exists).
- It has a greater degree of control over the content portfolio.
- Terra owns everything and can extract maximum value from it.

On balance, each strategy worked for its respective company.

Technical Infrastructure: Global Standards versus Local Assets

Because Terra kept the disparate technical architectures of its acquired ISPs, it had a more fragmented infrastructure. Terra's portal in Argentina looked very different from Terra's portal in Mexico, and content could not be easily shared between these two systems. In contrast, Lycos tried to create a common technical infrastructure that supports reuse of content in multiple countries. In theory, any piece of content could be put into a Lycos-friendly format and distributed around the world. Of course, Lycos faced some exceptions to this ideal of global leveraged standards. For example, Lycos is interested in acquiring firms in Asia that have built the specialized double-byte-enabled tools (chat or messaging software) that lets users type and read Asian-language characters. Whereas Lycos created a global platform, Terra conglomerated different technical platforms as it bought different country-specific Internet companies.

卐 Contrasting Latin American Strategy

Latin America is the only place of substantive overlap that Lycos and Terra had prior to the merger. Looking at the potential market, the population in the region is 508 million people with 53 percent of the population concentrated in two countries: Brazil and Mexico. The number of Internet users in Latin America is currently small—only 2.4 percent of the population uses the Internet today (12.4 million Internet users). But the number of Internet users is expected to grow nearly 30 percent per year.

Potential revenues from the Internet in Latin American markets differ from the United States. First, the per capita gross domestic product (GDP) in Latin America is very low (U.S.$3,946, which is one-eighth of the per capita GDP in the United States). Second, also unlike in the United States, access revenues account for a significant amount of revenues today (69 percent) and will continue to play a major role in Latin America for the next few years. Finally, the growth potential of revenues is high: Internet revenues are expected to grow 54 percent annually (from the $5.6 billion figure in 2000). Growth will come mostly from e-commerce revenues (82 percent growth). Advertising revenues are expected to grow the fastest (91 percent overall), but they will continue to account for less than 5 percent of the total Internet revenues.

The most obvious contrast between Lycos and Terra in Latin America is that Lycos is a new entrant into Latin America, whereas Latin America is virtually the home turf of Terra. Lycos is a very global company, with operations in Europe, Korea, and Japan, but it was late in coming to Latin America. Lycos' Latin America division accounts for a mere 2 percent of the company's staff. Moreover, Lycos' Latin America headquarters is not even located in Latin America—it is in Miami, Florida. By contrast, 60 percent of Terra's staff resides in Latin America (world headquarters are in Barcelona, where Telefónica resides). Terra's staff has a strong presence in its various country-specific outposts, the former purchases made by Telefónica and then by Terra.

But the contrasting Latin American strategies of Lycos and Terra are only partially explained by the new-entrant-versus-home-turf difference. The bigger difference is that of strategic choice. Terra chose a local strategy, whereas Lycos pursued a unified strategy. The result is that Terra's sites are different in each country, whereas Lycos' sites have the same global look and feel across all countries. See figure 8.2 to 8.4 for Internet pages.

FIGURE 8.2 The Terra Lycos Management Team

Joaquim Agut, Executive Chairman

Joaquim Agut serves as executive chairman of Terra Lycos and is responsible for the strategic direction of Terra Lycos. Prior to the combination of Terra and Lycos in October 2000, Agut was chairman of Terra Networks.

Prior to joining Terra, Agut was leader of the European Corporate Executive Council, (CEC) of General Electric (GE) and was the first executive of GE in Europe. At GE, Agut previously held the roles of vice president and general manager of marketing and sales, president and chief executive officer of GE Power Controls, and GE national executive for Spain and Portugal and chairman of the Pan European GE Quality Council.

Agut has also been active in the local and national business community, responsible for Spain's industrial electronic sector integration in the European Economic Community. In 1984, he was awarded the Young Businessman of the Year Award from a leading Spanish economic magazine.

Agut earned a bachelor of science degree in electrical engineering from the University Politécnica de Catalunya in Barcelona, Spain, and an MBA from IESE at Universidad de Navarra.

Robert J. Davis, Chief Executive Officer

Robert J. Davis serves as chief executive officer of Terra Lycos and is responsible for the day-to-day operations of Terra Lycos. Prior to the combination of Terra and Lycos in October 2000, Davis was president and chief executive officer of Lycos, Inc., and was Lycos' first employee in June 1995.

Davis transformed Lycos from an Internet search engine to one of the most powerful Internet hubs and media companies worldwide. In just five years, Davis led Lycos from a company with $2 million in venture capital to a multi-billion-dollar business. Under his leadership, Lycos jumped from the fastest IPO in Nasdaq history, a mere nine months from inception to offering, to an esteemed member of the Nasdaq 100. Through a string of strategic partnerships and investments along with eight major acquisitions, Davis led Lycos in developing the Lycos Network, a pioneering Web media model that delivers mass reach and diversity of audience and programming.

Davis holds a bachelor of science degree, summa cum laude, from Northeastern University and an MBA, with high distinction, from Babson College. He also received an honorary Doctor of Commercial Sciences from Bentley College in May 1999 and an honorary doctorate from Northeastern University in June 2000. In addition to the Terra Lycos board, he serves on the board of directors of several other public and private sector entities. Davis is also cochairman of Massachusetts E-Government Task Force, formed to improve and expand the state's e-government capabilities.

Abel Linares, Chief Operating Officer

Abel Linares serves as chief operating officer of Terra Lycos. Prior to the merger of Terra and Lycos in October 2000, Linares served as chief executive officer of Terra Networks.

Linares was appointed chief executive officer of Terra Networks, S.A., in February 2000. At Terra, he helped the company achieve 448 percent growth in subscribers,

FIGURE 8.2   *(continued)*

---

550 percent growth in advertising, and 500 percent growth in e-commerce revenues, respectively, from June 1999 to June 2000. During this period, Terra launched operations in Venezuela, Colombia, El Salvador, Guatemala, Costa Rica, Nicaragua, Honduras, and the U.S. Hispanic and the Caribbean region. Linares played a key role in the transactions involving De Remate, Uno-e, Tu Ciudad, IDT, Ifigenia, the JV Terra Mobile, A Tu Hora, Motor Press and Meta 4, positioning the company as the undisputed leader in the region.

In January 1999, he was appointed board member of TPI-Páginas Amarillas and was responsible for its IPO. TPI experienced a 350 percent revalorization in the first six months of trading, reaching a market capitalization of U.S.$6.3 billion. In 1998, Linares was appointed board member of Telefónica Centro America as well as president of Telefónica El Salvador. Under Linares, as general subdirector of Telefónica International, Telefónica entered the market as a start-up and within six months held the world's highest market share in mobile phones and international long-distance benefits. In 1994, Linares joined TPI as general manager, responsible for 600 salespersons. Following this period, he was appointed general subdirector of sales and customer services of Telefónica España, directly responsible for U.S.$6.4 billion in sales, 12 million clients, and 11,000 employees. He has played a key role in the liberalization of the telecommunications market in Spain.

Between 1984 and 1994, Linares held the position of director of sales and marketing in Prime Computer and Computervisión, American multinationals, leaders in the information technology sector, CAD-CAM/CAE/GIS, and consulting aimed to reengineering processes and reduction of time to market. Linares holds an aeronautic engineering degree.

Terra grew by acquiring major portals and ISPs in each country (such as Ole in Spain, Gauchonet in Argentina, and Infoset in Mexico). It kept the specialized technology and content of each country. (Visit the links www.terra.com.mx, www.terra.com.br, and www.terra.com to see the differences among Terra sites.)

In contrast, Lycos implemented a standard Web site for each country, giving each site a similar look and feel even though the content is specialized for each country.

Contrasting Business Cultures

Finally, the two companies have contrasting business cultures. These cultural differences arise both from the business histories and from the national origins of the two companies. Whereas Lycos is a product of the Internet start-up craze, Terra represents the seasoned business activities of a traditional phone company. Although Telefónica's investments in the Internet and its spin-off Terra show that the company is forward thinking, Telefónica (and Terra) retain some of the bureaucratic mind-set of a regulated monopoly.

A. Lycos Mexico

B. Lycos Brazil

A. Terra Mexico

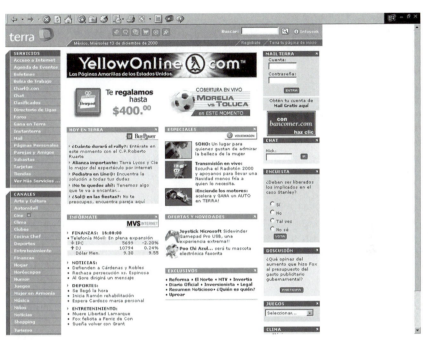

B. Terra Brazil

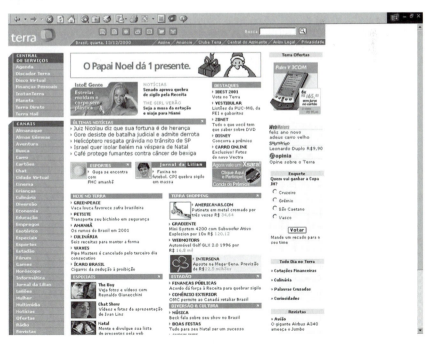

National cultures also create some differences between the companies. Whereas American entrepreneurial culture is about breaking old rules, Spanish and Latin culture is more respectful of those rules. Whereas Americans want to get down to business and "just do it," Spanish and Latin culture feels less time pressure and enjoys more emphasis on creating strong, long-term personal relationships. Reflecting the gulf between the cultures of corporate governance and of technical wizardry, the new company chose Barcelona for its corporate headquarters, and Waltham for its operations headquarters.

[logo] Terra Lycos' Latin American Challenges

As the integration of the two companies takes place, Lycos and Terra management face difficult issues in Latin America. Management needs to make a decision on two important issues. Management must decide the brand strategy for the region and the best model to apply in the region.

Latin America is a major part of Terra Lycos' global reach, leveraging Terra's strength in the region. Latin America is very important to Terra Lycos because the merged company intends to pursue a global growth strategy. But Terra Lycos must define a strategy for the region. Is it sustainable to have a strategy for Latin America that is different from the global one? Should Terra Lycos pursue a global brand strategy or tailor the brand to each region? Terra Lycos' challenges clearly are strategic.

Prior to the merger, Lycos and Terra each had different geographic coverage, with Latin America being the only geographic overlap. At the time of the merger, Terra had a strong, established presence in the region and a location-specific model. Lycos, on the other hand, had a regional strategy and was creating the Latin America division. After the merger, Terra Lycos must define its strategy for Latin America. As the integration period begins, Terra Lycos has two Web sites and two brand names for Latin America: the strong local Terra brand name and the international Lycos brand name.

QUESTIONS

Prepare to discuss answers to the following questions:

1. Compare and contrast Terra's global strategy with Lycos' global strategy. What should the global strategy for the combined company be? How can Terra Lycos achieve and accelerate global profitability?
2. What should Terra Lycos' model be for the Latin America region? Is it possible to have a model for the region that is different from the model for other places in the world?
3. What should Terra Lycos do with the brand in Latin America? What implications would Latin America brand strategy have in the global strategy? What should Terra Lycos do with the Web sites in Latin America?

C H A P T E R

New Products

Introduction

To stay competitive, firms must maintain a steady stream of profitable new products. Yet 41 percent of products fail in the marketplace after introduction. Many more fail before they are even introduced. Through the cycle of idea generation, design, testing, and launch, 74 percent of ideas are weeded out before they get to market (Griffin, 1997). Taken together, this implies that 85 percent of ideas are not successful on the market. The probability of a new idea reaching successful launch is low. Nonetheless, new products are vital to company success. Research (Griffin, 1997) shows that 49.2 percent of sales at best-practice firms come from products commercialized over the past five years, about twice the rate of the rest of the firms.

In this chapter, we discuss why new products fail and how to avoid those failures. We look at the structured process for product development and the use of new methodologies, such as Information Acceleration and Listening In, to improve premarket forecasting of products. Finally, we discuss the life cycle of products and what marketing managers need to do at each stage of the life cycle.

Digital Failures

During the Internet's early days, 90 percent of Internet companies that were launched failed. Although that failure rate may look higher than the failure rate for nondigital products, in fact the total rate is similar. The reason is that traditional companies weeded out poor ideas before putting them on the market. At the start of the Internet era, however, people forgot to do the structured product development process. In their rush to market, dot-coms forgot to screen, test, and do the design work necessary for successful product development. Internet companies got capital simply on the basis of an idea and launched it. As a result, companies themselves became very expensive concept tests. It is not surprising that so many companies failed.

Preventing New Product Failures

Success depends on many factors—the extent to which the product satisfies customers' perceived needs, the relative advantages in terms of the competition, the size and growth rate of the target market, the creativity of the marketing plan, and so on. One useful approach to preventing new product failure is to understand the reasons for failure and then use a systematic process from the inception of the idea through the life cycle of the product.

Understand the Reasons for Failure

Research has identified specific reasons for new product failure. The major reasons are the following:

1. **Too Small a Market:**   Although a segment with differentiated needs has been identified, demand is inadequate to make the product profitable.
2. Poor Positioning: The product is poorly positioned because management misunderstood customers' perceptions, relative importance weights, and price trade-offs.
3. Little Benefit Relative to the Competition: The product does not provide significant advantages over alternatives already available to customers.
4. Not New/Not Different: Although the product is technically or physically different, it is not new from the customer's point of view.
5. Forecasting Error: Sales potential and/or rate of diffusion were overestimated.
6. Poor Timing: The product entered the market too late or too early. If too late, the cycle time was too long and missed the window of technology or marketing opportunity. If too early, customers were not yet conditioned to adopt the product or necessary supporting technologies, products, or services were not in place.
7. Shift in Technology: The company was blindsided by a radical change in technology, stayed with an old technology too long, or chose a new technology that was not adopted in the marketplace.
8. Change in Customer Tastes: There was a shift in preferences that the company did not detect.

Use a Structured Process

Companies can avoid new product failure by following a systematic new product development process. Following a systematic development process helps avoid these pitfalls by providing disciplined checkpoints at each stage of development (see figure 9.1). Using a sequential Go/No Go decision process, "poor" projects are eliminated early, and "good" projects are given priority. For example, the market definition stage of Opportunity Identification checks the market for sales volume potential and thus avoids the "market too small" reason for failure or pitfall. Pitfalls 2 to 5 are avoided through careful design and market testing, and pitfalls 6 to 8 are avoided by continual monitoring of the market, competitive environments, and product launch strategy.

FIGURE 9.1 New Product and Service Development Process

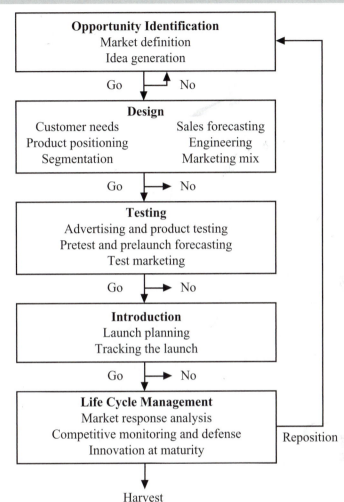

Source: Urban and Hauser (1993), p. 38.

In research conducted by Mercer Management Consulting and *R&D Management* magazine, companies in the top one-third in product development cycle time, innovativeness, success rate, and revenue contribution used a customer-centered, disciplined product development approach.

FIGURE 9.2 Decision Process

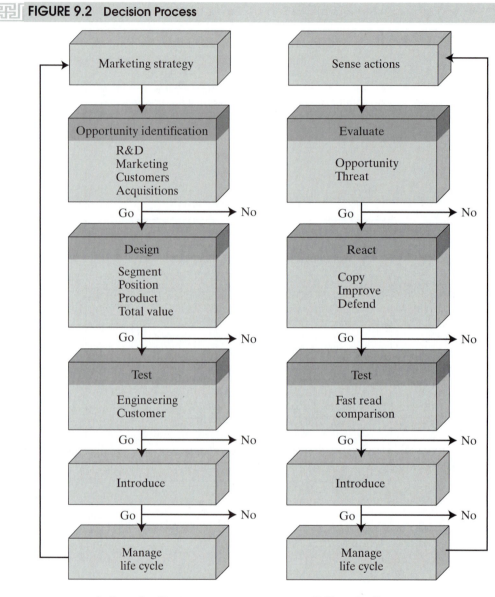

A. Proactive Strategy   B. Reactive Strategy

Source: Urban and Star, p. 289.

Figure 9.2 shows two simplified sets of decision sequences intended to minimize the risks of falling victim to one of the failure pitfalls. Figure 9.2A delineates a series of steps to be followed by a firm engaged in a proactive new products strategy, while the sequence shown in figure 9.2B would be more appropriate for a company employing a reactive strategy. Let us consider each of these approaches in turn.

〔〕 Proactive Product Development

Proactive new product development is driven by marketing strategy. *Opportunity identification* should be based on a systematic search of the target domain. New technological capabilities, when assessed in terms of customer needs, may be a major source of potential advantages. Similarly, an in-depth understanding of customer requirements and buying behavior provides insights useful for identifying appropriate new technologies.

The traditional process of generating a very large number of ideas and then screening them is rapidly being replaced by one of identifying a few high-potential ideas in strategic areas where the firm has a competitive advantage and then evaluating them in depth. If a good opportunity is found, the company makes a Go decision and begins design efforts. If no adequately attractive opportunity is found, the search process recommences, generally with a modified set of targeting criteria.

> Rather than letting 1,000 ideas bloom to find the one winner, it is better to do more strategic work up front. By first understanding the structure of markets and customer needs, companies can design the one or two products most likely to succeed.

Converting attractive opportunities into product *designs* involves several steps. The first step is to define the target market segment and specify the core benefit proposition (features, perceptual dimensions, importances, and ratings versus the competition). The next step is to begin the actual design process with concept specification and testing. The product features must fulfill the previously specified (and, it is hoped, tested) core benefit proposition and achieve the desired "positioning" in terms of the target market segments. Other elements in the "bundle" (e.g., price, advertising, promotion, selling, distribution, and service) complete the design of the product. Finally, this total bundle of utility is presented to potential customers for their judgment. Depending on their response, the project may be aborted, or there may be a Go decision for full-scale testing. A typical development process involves a series of such milestone Go/No Go decisions, after each of which the product is iteratively improved and further evaluated.

After the product design has been completed, it is essential to conduct a comprehensive *test* of customer reactions. This study should assess, from the customer's perspective, whether the newly designed product meets its target specification and then provide inputs to the development of a sales forecast for the new product. Often, customer evaluation at this point in the process leads to the discovery of new needs or criteria. The outcome of this research may be a decision to Go to introduction, to refine the product further, or to terminate the project (a No decision).

Customer testing at this stage is critical, as is engineering evaluation to ensure that the product is of high quality and will meet customer requirements easily. Effective linkage among marketing, engineering, and manufacturing is increasingly important, as customers have become more sophisticated and markets more competitive.

Introduction can now occur on the assumption that the new product does indeed satisfy real needs and that adequate levels of profits and return on investment can be earned with a minimum of risk. At a later point the product may be restaged (note arrow back to Marketing Strategy in figure 9.2A) or dropped from the product line.

Cross-Functional Integration in New Product Strategy

Over 84 percent of innovative new product development projects use multifunction teams (Griffin, 1997). New product development cannot focus solely on technology or solely on customer needs—both are essential to success. Consider the example of designing cell phones. A company needs to know how customers will use their phones as well as the technical standards to use for transmission. A successful product resides at the intersection of technical standards, manufacturing capabilities, and customer needs. Multifunctional teams help find or create this intersection.

Marketing input is important at the beginning of the development and during the launch phase. In the beginning phase, marketing is responsible for representing the customer in the design process. Research and development (R&D) is most important in the early phases of development and decreases in activity as launch nears. Marketing must give R&D correct input on customer needs or bring in lead users, and R&D must design a product to fit those customers' needs. But R&D must also design a product that can be manufactured at high-quality levels and low cost. This "design for manufacturing" is increasingly important.

In addition to the critical marketing-R&D interface, the skills and resources of production and finance are also needed to ensure that the product can be built at a cost level (and therefore a price level) and quality level that customers demand. If not enough is spent on R&D, the firm's core technologies cannot be maintained. If not enough is invested in production process technology, products will not meet quality standards. If not enough is spent on marketing, customer needs may be misread, forecasting may be deficient, and the launch intensity may be insufficient to capture a dominant position in the target markets. Given that funds are often in short supply, however, financial decisions must be integrated with the R&D, production, and marketing strategies so that the resources can be allocated to maximize the long-run return on the funds invested in new product development.

Reactive Product Development

Although most firms seek to develop new products proactively, it may be more appropriate to adopt a reactive new product strategy when doing so promises to reduce both costs and risks significantly. If such a strategy is to be effective, it is essential to put in place processes to *sense actions and changes* in the market rapidly and accurately. Figure 9.2B delineates a series of steps that are more appropriate for a company employing a reactive strategy. Competitive moves must be recognized quickly. New competitive products, for example, should be discovered while they are still in test market (or even earlier by watching markets, talking to customers, and interviewing suppliers).

After a competitive product or activity has been identified, the next step is to *evaluate* it as a potential threat or opportunity. If it has the potential to reduce company margins or profits, marketing managers should formulate a reactive strategy to defend the product line. Even if no direct threat seems present, it may be a wise to emulate a competitive entry because of the opportunity it represents.

A company's *reaction* may be to either copy the competitive entry as exactly as possible or to improve on the competitor's concept or execution. Responses might be to reposition an existing product, add a new product to counter the threat, or vary the price, promotion, advertising, or selling tactics.

Introduction and *managing the life cycle* are much the same as under a proactive strategy, except that these steps should be implemented more rapidly and less expensively. When employing a reactive strategy, it is especially necessary to modify the marketing program as soon as new competitive actions are diagnosed.

Which Strategy to Use?

Which strategy you select will depend on the characteristics of the market concerned and on your firm's competitive advantages.

Prerequisites to the Proactive Strategy

If your firm has strong R&D skills and marketing power, a proactive strategy will generally be most effective, especially if the market responds to premium benefit products and rewards the pioneer in a product category with incremental sales. If your company is pursuing a Theory T marketing strategy, then you will need to use the proactive product development approach because Theory T requires that a company be innovative and continually differentiate its products.

Prerequisites to the Reactive Strategy

If, on the other hand, your firm is flexible and agile and the market is one where price is important and products are not perceived as widely differentiated, then a reactive strategy may be appropriate. If the experience curve is not too steep, you may be able to charge lower prices as a reactor because your development and introductory advertising costs will be lower. Finally, if your company is pursuing Theory P marketing, then you will need to use the reactive approach to product develop in order to keep your costs low and be the low-cost provider.

State-of-the-Art Market Research to Support Proactive Strategy

As we saw in chapter 3, digital strategies reduce market research costs, make it easier to do market research, and provide richer stimuli compared to traditional market research techniques. Next we describe two state-of-the-art market research techniques that can be done entirely on-line.

Listening In

Listening In is another good example of how digital technology changes the practice of marketing—lowering the cost of gathering information about customer needs while accelerating this process. Listening In is a practical methodology in which a virtual engineer "listens in" to a customer's Internet dialogue with a trusted virtual advisor. The fraction of people using the Internet for information and advice is large (62 percent in autos, 70 percent in travel, and 56 percent in health), and advisors are becoming more common. Listening In provides a means to capture the information in these dialogues. By monitoring and analyzing the clickstream dialogues, Listening In identifies the potential for unmet needs. Once unmet needs are identified, automated interventions both gather more detail on the unmet needs and enable the customer to express his or her own solutions. Listening In represents a natural source of new information that is there for the taking (since the dialogues occur as the customer searches for product information on the Web). Moreover, the information is much easier to gather and use than traditional focus groups. Automaker General Motors used the Listening In process to identify unmet needs in full-size trucks. The Listening In methodology identified the need for better maneuverability of full-size pickup trucks, leading the company to introduce four-wheel drive in order to improve the maneuverability of its top-of-the-line pickup truck (the latest model of GMC Denali). The new truck is selling well. In short, the Listening In methodology extends the use of virtual advisors, using them to identify unmet customer needs.

Information Acceleration

Information Acceleration (IA) is a market research and modeling methodology used in the premarket forecasting of high-tech products. The methodology is particularly effective for forecasting how customers will respond to cutting-edge products because it provides customers with a multimedia virtual buying environment. This environment simulates both technological and environmental conditions and provides all the information they will have when making the decision in the future. For example, IA was used to forecast the sales of new electric cars. Respondents viewed multimedia presentations, read on-line articles about the new product, talked with users of the vehicle, visited a showroom, and were able to virtually get into the vehicle and talk with salespeople. The IA system measured their preferences, perceptions, and choice during the information gathering process. Measurements were taken on probability of purchase and perceptions at various points in the customer information process. Finally, IA used the customer decision flow model to forecast sales and simulate changes in product design.

In the electric vehicle example, IA was used to determine the following:

- Whether the electric vehicle would be a viable business venture at its target launch date
- Whether the firm should plan for improvements in technology that would reduce the price and/or increase benefits enough so that the venture would be profitable
- Whether the firm should stop development

The Toyota Prius

After using IA, Toyota launched a new vehicle, the Prius. The Prius is the world's first mass-produced hybrid vehicle, combining a gasoline engine and an electric motor. The Prius' onboard system recharges the batteries while the vehicle is being driven, eliminating the need to plug the car into an electrical source. IA simulated the market and provided consumers with the ability to do research on-line, visit a virtual showroom, test the car, and talk with users and salespeople. IA recommended that a hybrid vehicle would sell the best, and Toyota's results have proved that forecast correct. The Prius has sold 50,000 units. Using IA greatly reduced the costs of market research while providing a much richer simulation of the new product than traditionally possible.

Managing the Life Cycle

Products and industries pass through life cycles just as plants and animals do, progressing sequentially through phases of introduction, growth, maturity, and decline. Marketing managers take different actions at each phase of the life cycle.

Diffusion of Innovation

According to the diffusion theory, innovators adopt first and then communicate the product's benefits through word of mouth. (Recall from chapter 3 that interpersonal communication often plays a major role in consumer decision making.) Diffusion is characterized by a slow start but a subsequent rapid increase in sales as the innovation is accepted by the majority of the market. If the market has a limit, there comes a point when most of those who intended to buy the product have already purchased it. Saturation sets in, leading to a decline in annual sales. A decline in sales also occurs when the product is substituted for one that has a newer technology. Companies that take a pioneering, proactive strategy must be most concerned with the rate of diffusion (Will adoption be sufficient?). Companies that take a follower/reactive strategy may be most concerned with the rate of saturation (Will any potential sales be left?).

Introduction Phase

In this first phase, marketing managers emphasize expanding the market. Heavy expenditures of advertising, selling, sampling, promotion, and distribution are made to facilitate initial purchases and to stimulate diffusion of innovation. Efforts are undertaken to achieve awareness and positive purchase attitudes in the target market. Companies will focus on pleasing early adopters—maximizing positive feedback from early adopters in order to increase the rate of diffusion. Product performance must be good at introduction, and it must be constantly improved so that the innovating company can continue to preempt competitors who might be considering entering.

Profitability will be affected by the introductory marketing budget. *Pricing* is a key strategic decision that will affect life cycle return on investment. Should price be set high to "skim" the market demand, with resultant slow sales growth but high profit levels, or should price be set low to "penetrate" the potential market, encourage diffusion, build market share, and achieve greater profits later in the life cycle? In today's market, the skimming strategy is often ineffective because it allows competitors to enter under the price umbrella and built market position. They can copy the innovation and not suffer the time penalties usually experienced by a late entrant. Only if the originator is protected from competition (e.g., by a strong patent) or if the strategy is to take profit and then move to other markets would skimming be recommended. Penetration is an aggressive strategy; pricing below initial cost is especially risky because, if costs do not decline with volume, profits may never be earned.

Growth Phase

Once critical market acceptance has been achieved, the firm's focus shifts to holding and building market share as competitors enter. Product improvement continues, more product variants are introduced, the market is segmented into basic components, competitors differentiate their products, and channels of distribution widen. Emphasis switches from stimulating diffusion to capturing a dominant share of consumer preference and choices.

Maturity Phase

In the mature phase, competition intensifies, and price erosion is likely. Price promotion is common. The cost to acquire a new customer climbs, so companies focus on maintaining loyalty. More segmentation occurs in an attempt to find higher-margin sales opportunities, and efforts are made to differentiate within each segment.

> **Pricing**
> During the life cycle, prices often fall and competition increases unless you can innovate and differentiate your products and services with value-added features.

Decline Phase

As sales decline, a firm has two basic strategic choices: It can milk the product to obtain whatever potential residual profit remains, or it can rejuvenate it to begin the growth phase of a new life cycle.

Milking the product entails reducing marketing expenditures—passively reaping the profits from residual sales instead of actively recruiting new customers at increasing expense. Product sales depend on consumer loyalty to maintain high margins. The harvesting strategy allows the product to die gracefully and profitably.

Rejuvenation entails finding new needs or uses for the product and fitting the product to them to produce a new spurt of sales. Marketing managers can delay decline by creating new uses or new customer markets for a product. Nylon, for example, produced by DuPont for parachutes and women's hosiery in the 1940s, would probably have followed the traditional life cycle, reaching maturity and decline, if DuPont had not developed new uses for nylon, such as broad-woven fabrics, tire cord, and sweaters. With these new applications, nylon was kept in the growth phase for over 25 years.

Introduction to MarketSoft Corporation Case

In the MarketSoft case, company managers used customer needs to develop and launch a very successful product. The company is now facing a challenge: how to expand its product line and position it against the competition.

REFERENCES

Griffin, Abbie. 1997. "PDMA Research on New Product Development Practices: Updating Trends and Benchmarking Best Practices." *Journal of Product Innovation Management* vol. 14, no. 6: 429–58.

Urban, Glen L., and John R. Hauser. 1993. *Design and Marketing New Products.* Englewood Cliffs, N.J.: Prentice Hall.

Urban, Glen L., and John R. Hauser. 2002. "Listening In to Find Unmet Customer Needs and Solutions." Working paper, MIT Sloan School of Management.

Urban, Glen L., and Steven H. Star. 1991. *Advanced Marketing Strategies.* Upper Saddle River, N.J.: Prentice Hall.

Urban, Glen L., Bruce Weinberg, and John R. Hauser. 1996. "Premarket Forecasting of Really-New Products." *Journal of Marketing* 60, no. 1: 47–60.

CHAPTER 10

MarketSoft Corporation

We want to own every dollar that VPs of marketing spend on software!
—GREG ERMAN, FOUNDER, PRESIDENT, AND CHIEF EXECUTIVE OFFICER,
MarketSoft Corporation

Introduction

The chapter-opening statement summarizes Greg Erman's ambitious goal for MarketSoft. Erman has raised $45 million from a recent round of venture funding with which he can grow the company and reach profitability. So far, the company has a strong customer-focused product development strategy, a successful sales strategy, and an initial set of three well-received products and is growing rapidly. But Erman wonders about the optimal strategy for capturing more sales. He is choosing among many directions in which to grow his company and prepare for an eventual IPO.

MarketSoft has grown from under $100,000 in sales in fiscal year (FY) 1999 (June 30, 1998, to June 30, 1999), to $1.7 million in FY 2000, and to $6.7 million in FY 2001. Revenue goals are $20 million in FY 2002 and over $40 million by FY 2003. The company is losing money, but with its recent capital infusion of $45 million (January 2001), the company plans to reach profitability by FY 2004 without additional financing.

Company Founding

Erman founded MarketSoft in May 1998. Previously, he founded Waypoint Software Corp., a firm that developed software to put business-to-business marketing catalogs on the Internet. Erman founded Waypoint, recruited the management team, raised venture capital, and sold the firm in four months, giving institutional investors a 426 percent return on their investment.

Buoyed by the success of Waypoint and aware that he did not want to work at the large firm that had acquired Waypoint, Erman was eager to start another firm. He felt it was imperative, however, that the firm respond to a clear market need, so he investigated potential business ideas.

By the time he resigned from Waypoint in December 1997, Erman had narrowed down his next business idea to one of two choices: Web-based training or lead management software (software that helps sales and marketing professionals manage leads to prospective customers). Although a venture capital firm was ready to fund the Web-based training idea, Erman rejected the offer. His rationale, based on interviews with corporate training managers, was that training managers had limited purchasing authority. In contrast, Erman reasoned, vice presidents of sales had greater authority to say yes and had a greater sense of urgency than training managers.

Erman's first step after settling on the lead management idea was to build a management team. His first contact, Nancy Benovich-Gilby, was recommended to him by venture capitalists. Benovich-Gilby had worked in a series of start-ups, most recently Firefly Networks, where she was vice president of engineering. Her solid experience in engineering, product development, and raising capital made her an ideal choice, and she signed on as MarketSoft's first employee. Erman's desire to create a customer-driven product rather than a "cool technology" product persuaded Benovich-Gilby to join. Having worked for companies developing "cool solutions" and then trying to sell customers on the need for the solution, Benovich-Gilby welcomed working for a company whose mission was to develop a product that met existing customer needs.

After hiring Benovich-Gilby, Erman tapped Benovich-Gilby's network of other capable engineers with whom she had worked over the course of her career at five start-ups. Together they hired John Mandel as director of engineering, Charlie Everett as lead architect, and David Tiu as principal engineer. All three had previously worked with Benovich-Gilby. Filling out the roster was Bob Hiss, an industry veteran recommended by a venture capital partner and known as the "best implementation manager in the business." Hiss became MarketSoft's vice president of client services.

Needs-Focused Product Development Process

MarketSoft's product development process for its first product was very methodical and strongly focused on uncovering the real needs of sales and marketing professionals. MarketSoft spent three months on the market research for its first product, eLeads. Specifically, a six-member team (Erman and his first five hires) interviewed 60 companies for 1.5 hours each over a two-month period. The interviews were conducted on-site at companies in the Boston area (20 companies) and by phone for the 40 companies outside Boston. Interviewees were primarily marketing vice presidents and marketing reps from blue-chip companies in the high-tech industry. The companies had to have over $300 million in annual revenues and a sales force equipped with laptops and Internet access. Marketsoft added the laptop stipulation for two reasons. First, tech-savvy marketing departments would provide the greatest insight into how such companies might want to use computers to support marketing processes. Second, such companies would be an easy sell for marketing software.

The interviews followed a detailed protocol designed to elicit the customer's needs articulated in the customer's own words (in contrast to asking leading questions that might bias the interview toward validating preexisting assumptions or building a product based on engineering language). MarketSoft wanted to start with a blank page and create product specs based on actual customer needs. All the interviews were recorded, transcribed, and put into HTML (Hypertext Markup Language). Following each interview, the interview team conducted a half-hour internal debrief discussion in which they identified 5 to 10 quotes that best captured the major points of the interview.

After completing all the interviews, the team compiled the previously selected 5 to 10 quotes per interview into one big list of about 400 quotes. Then they discussed each quote one by one. After the discussions, each team member voted on which two quotes were most significant in each category.

This rigorous market research process created a clear vision for the product, one that the entire team understood because they had been involved in the process. In particular, the team identified three "pain points" that customers experienced with their existing lead management procedures:

- **Poor Lead Assignment:** Leads were not getting to the right salespeople.
- **Poor Lead Qualification:** Salespeople were not satisfied with the leads they were getting.
- **Poor Effectiveness Tracking:** There was no method for tracking the effectiveness of leads that had been pursued.

Moreover, other industry data supported these three pain points:

- **Lead assignment:** Less than 40 percent of all marketing leads get to a sales rep.
- **Lead Qualification:** Less than 10 percent of sales reps are satisfied with the quality of leads they receive.
- **Lead Tracking:** Less than 5 percent of channel leads are tracked.

Solving these three customer pain points became the mission of MarketSoft's product development effort. Armed with this customer and industry data, MarketSoft began the seven-month process of developing the eLeads product.

Sales Strategy: Accelerating the Sales Process for Software

Specialty software applications, such as MarketSoft's applications for marketing, can face a complex, time-consuming customer decision process. Both the department that will use the application (marketing and sales in the case of MarketSoft products) and the information technology (IT) department have a say in the purchase decision. Moreover, software purchase is a capital expenditure, which typically requires approvals from the finance department. MarketSoft found that it is harder for marketing vice presidents to directly purchase software because buying and implementing the software requires the skills of the purchaser's IT department. The involvement of the IT and finance departments slows the purchase approval process and reduces the chance of making a sale.

Therefore, MarketSoft positioned itself as an application services provider (ASP) in addition to a software solution provider. (Most of Marketsoft's competitors have also implemented an ASP model.) In contrast to buying the products, marketing vice presidents can more easily "rent" MarketSoft products on a hosted basis because that model involves less IT effort on the purchaser's side. Accordingly, MarketSoft's pricing model moved to a hybrid model based on perpetual licensing or Web-hosted subscription services. MarketSoft is now experiencing dramatically reduced sales cycles because buyers no longer have to make the huge up-front capital/licensing investments that the prior model mandated. They can commit to the hosted model much more quickly. MarketSoft makes its products easy to use so that marketing departments can run the software themselves. For example, The eOffers product features an easy-to-use rules engine that lets marketers define which customers should get which offers.

MarketSoft's current eLeads product allows decisions to be distributed across the firm and to channel partners. Agents can implement the programs and rules locally, and the end user need not depend on IT personnel to implement the system. (Many competitors, including Siebel, have complex centralized systems that often require system programmer intervention to implement rules and generate reports.) Using this feature, MarketSoft can direct the sales pitch toward marketing buyers, IT professionals, or both. Other competitive dimensions could include pricing, level of service, ease of use, customization capability, analytic power, data provision, vertical markets, integration with current systems, multichannel communication support, product development, scalability, channel relationships, brand equity, and continued innovation.

Progress: Fame, Fortune, and Products in the Field

By March 1999, MarketSoft had grown dramatically and received numerous accolades. The company had expanded to 100 employees and filled all the key positions. In the last quarter of 2000, MarketSoft successfully closed a third round of financing, which was noteworthy because the financing took place after the rupture of the dot-com bubble. MarketSoft raised $45 million, and the terms of the financing round were extremely favorable to MarketSoft, considering the tough market conditions. According to MarketSoft's business plan, this cash infusion is sufficient to take the company to profitability.

MarketSoft has also enjoyed tremendous client traction. Among its clients are industry leaders such as IBM, Cisco, American Express, and Fidelity. The company also boasts a litany of industry awards, including Top Private Company and Top Ten Overall in Upside's "Top 150 eBusiness Solution Providers," Demo 2000's "Company to Watch," Peppers and Rogers' "Accelerating 1-to-1 Innovator," and Computerworld's "Top Company in 2001."

MarketSoft's Product Suite

MarketSoft entered the e-marketing category through products for lead management and offer delivery. The e-marketing product arena is moving quickly as both start-up and established firms jockey for competitive position. MarketSoft chose lead management as its initial area of focus with its eLeads product. Next, MarketSoft developed two other products (eOffers and eLocator), applying the same customer-focused product development process as it applied to eLeads; that is, MarketSoft talked extensively with customers to get a deep understanding of customers' "pain." With the knowledge of customer needs, the MarketSoft team developed technology to eliminate that pain. MarketSoft frequently approaches customers for their input. A fourth product, eCampaign, is offered through an alliance with PrimeResponse.

eLeads

eLeads manages leads across the extended enterprise and increases revenue from marketing's leads. Some of the benefits of eLeads include the following:

- Coordinates leads across all channels

- Delivers leads to the right person at the right time
- Improves lead quality
- Ensures that leads get acted on (through rewards and accountability)

eOffers

eOffers is MarketSoft's product in the Internet direct-marketing category. The package itself is a commercial application that allows marketers to target specific customer groups in an automated fashion with their on-line marketing strategies. eOffers consumes the "data dump" coming from clickstream analytical tools (e.g., Net Perceptions) and customer call center dialogue. The program analyzes these customer data and is then able to develop/link optimized offers to the right customer at the right time in real time (based on individual profiles). Some of eOffers' benefits include the following:

- Coordinates messages across all channels to speak with one voice
- Enables cooperative marketing with business partners
- Triggers those offers that are more relevant
- Builds customer relationships via next-generation permission marketing

eOffers, introduced in March 2000, applies analytics and artificial intelligence to the management of marketing campaigns. It analyzes proposed marketing messages and marketing campaigns using rules that are set by each company's marketing managers. eOffers filters multiple messages that may be directed at the same customer and selects the most appropriate one. It detects redundant messages and controls the frequency of messages to the same customer.

eLocator

eLocator is a Web-based solution that connects prospects to the optimal partner. eLocator makes it easy for a company's customers, partners, call center staff, and sales force to quickly find appropriate, trusted business partners. eLocator does so while providing them with a resource to identify and locate the right organization from which to buy their products and services. By fulfilling demand in real time, businesses increase customer acquisition and retention rates and shorten sales cycles. eLocator's benefits include the following:

- Finds optimal partners by searching for proximity, business attributes, and customer feedback
- Creates new revenue opportunities by triggering relevant partner offers
- Ensures immediate follow-up by generating qualified leads
- Eliminates dependency on external vendors

eCampaign

eCampaign provides users the functionality for operational planning and campaign execution. Unlike the other three products, which MarketSoft developed in house, eCampaign is offered through an alliance with PrimeResponse. MarketSoft wanted to add this key piece of functionality, and an alliance was seen as more cost effective than from-scratch product development. eCampaign enables comprehensive automated scheduling, rescheduling, execution, and monitoring of all tasks associated with marketing campaigns. Users can define campaign targets, parameters, and campaign components (such as Internet or e-mail) more efficiently than with traditional software solutions by using eCampaign's embedded tools and prompts. Users can build winning campaigns by matching relevant offers with the right channels and customer segments. The intuitive graphical user interface lets users quickly assemble a full range of campaigns, from one-time offers to fully integrated, event-driven marketing campaigns that span months.

Broader Market Forces: The Rise of e-Marketing

Although MarketSoft began its product line by focusing on lead management, lead management is only one of many possible products that a marketing vice president might buy. MarketSoft's customers are seeing a broader need for e-marketing—a more comprehensive approach to electronically enabled marketing efforts. This comprehensive approach ties together the various elements of marketing processes (of which lead management is part) into a holistic, efficient end-to-end system. These broader market forces drove MarketSoft to create its other products and will play a role in MarketSoft's future growth strategy.

Four Trends Driving the Rise of e-Marketing

Four trends underpin the rise of e-marketing. The first two reflect shifts in the overall business environment and business culture. The latter two reflect the negative and positive impact of the Internet on marketing. The confluence of these trends is driving the creation and adoption of rigorous e-marketing tools, such as the products of MarketSoft and of its competitors.

Increased Need for Differentiation

Many of MarketSoft's customers face a marketplace that is more fast paced and fiercely competitive than before. Global competition, new technologies, and rapid changes in the economic environment make the world a more competitive arena. This competition brings an increased need for differentiation. Marketing helps companies achieve this differentiation.

Rising Demand for Marketing the Measurement of Return on Investment

New information technologies for the back office (e.g., enterprise resource planning) have created a business culture based on objective measurement—expenditures and investments are now judged for expected tangible results. As all other parts of the firm have implemented systems to enhance productivity and measure return on investment, marketing vice presidents are realizing they need measurement of return on investment in their realm as well.

Internet-Created Rising Volumes of Leads

Previously, many companies found that ad hoc lead management was fairly manageable albeit disjointed. But the Internet makes lead generation much easier. The proliferation of the Internet has exponentially increased the number of leads that a given firm receives (Web/e-mail inquiries). For example, Toyota generates 1.5 million leads per month from its Web site alone. Homegrown systems cannot scale to coordinate this type of volume growth.

Increased Adoption of Internet Technologies to Solve Problems

Lead management is especially suited to the Web because of the fundamentally distributed nature of leads generation and leads usage. Internet architectures support many-to-many mapping from multiple channels of lead generation (e-mail, customer databases, and Web) to multiple users of leads (sales, marketing, and forecasting). In contrast, the traditional client/server architecture is not built with this wide dispersion in mind.

Three Components of e-Marketing

MarketSoft views e-marketing as consisting of three components that are rooted in the core process of marketing. Figure 10.1 illustrates this cyclic marketing process with its three main phases. First, the "Create Demand" phase kicks off marketing efforts that dessiminate marketing messages, product information, and offers to prospective customers. In this phase, e-marketing software would help create and manage marketing campaigns. Second, the "Fulfill Demand" phase supports the conversion of leads into

FIGURE 10.1 E-marketing Suite Proposal and Competitors

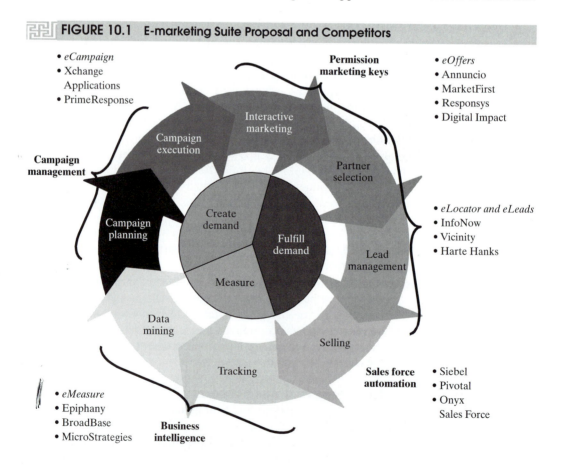

- *eCampaign*
- Xchange Applications
- PrimeResponse

Campaign management

- Campaign execution
- Campaign planning

Permission marketing keys

- Interactive marketing
- Partner selection

- *eOffers*
- Annuncio
- MarketFirst
- Responsys
- Digital Impact

Create demand

Fulfill demand

- *eLocator and eLeads*
- InfoNow
- Vicinity
- Harte Hanks

- Lead management
- Measure
- Data mining
- Selling

- Tracking

Sales force automation

- Siebel
- Pivotal
- Onyx Sales Force

- *eMeasure*
- Epiphany
- BroadBase
- MicroStrategies

Business intelligence

customers. E-marketing software would help manage leads, connect prospects to partners, and support the sales force. Third, the "Measure" phase closes the cycle by assessing the effectiveness of marketing and sales efforts with the intent of designing and executing better marketing campaigns in the future. E-marketing software plays an obvious role in collecting, collating, and analyzing the reams of data generated by the prior two phases.

Competitive Positioning for the Future: Depth versus Breadth

As seen in figure 10.1, MarketSoft's current products cover substantive parts of the cycle, but they do not close the loop. (MarketSoft's products in each area are indicated in italics and competitors products in standard type.) MarketSoft has established depth in terms of expertise in one process category (lead management), built expertise in two other process categories (eLocator and eOffers), and co-opted expertise using an alliance for a fourth category (eCampaign). MarketSoft's self-appointed quest for "every dollar spent on software" suggests that one potential avenue for growth is to expand its range of products to fill in the cycle. Using this growth strategy, MarketSoft would lay claim to every element of the e-marketing cycle using a combination of product development and alliances. The result combines depth and breadth in a full suite of e-marketing products. Figure 10.2 depicts the positioning strategy which MarketSoft is pursuing.

An expanded, integrated broad product range will allow MarketSoft to cross-sell products and provide a complete marketing solution to customers. However, numerous other competitors are also aiming to produce a suite. The competitive arena for e-marketing software contains a myriad of niche vendors, and MarketSoft faces different competition in each segment. Figure 10.1 lists some of these competitors in the respective parts of the marketing cycle.

Siebel is the greatest threat to MarketSoft's plan to dominate this space (see this chapter's appendix for more information on Siebel). A giant market leader in sales force automation (SFA), Siebel has been expanding its offerings beyond its corner of

FIGURE 10.2   Product Mix and Corporate Positioning

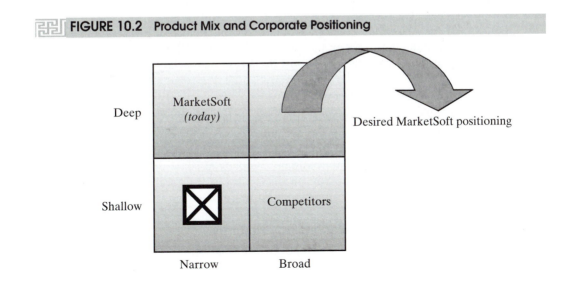

the marketing cycle. Other smaller players are also potential suite competitors. Finally, leaders in back-office software (such as SAP and Oracle) would like to move their enterprise software systems to encompass the front-office applications, such as customer relationship management (CRM) and SFA.

MarketSoft needs a defensible competitive strategy that assures leadership in the newly integrated e-marketing arena. Fortunately, MarketSoft develops each product using a similar architecture to facilitate the integration between its products. This common architecture facilitates this growth strategy. The challenge is to build a product suite that will develop a dominant position against current and potential competitors.

Growth through Lateral Penetration in Customer Companies

MarketSoft could target both business-to-business and business-to-consumer segments, but the company has focused primarily on the former, helping businesses manage their marketing efforts toward other businesses. MarketSoft is building strong relationships with big corporations. One of its future challenges is to use those relationships to increase its product range and penetration within a given corporation. Bill Price, MarketSoft's chief financial officer, gave a clear example: "One of our most important customers is Fidelity Investments. We implemented eLeads in the Fidelity retail organization. The performance and return on investment helps us to extend the product to the institutional and retirement organization. Now we must sell them other products." Other customers that use MarketSoft for business-to-business marketing activities include Cisco and Dun & Bradstreet. Once a large corporation uses MarketSoft in one part of the organization, MarketSoft would like to expand its presence to other divisions of that organization.

Growth through Indirect Channels

Some companies grow revenues by selling products through multiple channels, leveraging the expertise, market penetration, value-added services, or sales forces of partner firms. Thus far, MarketSoft has adopted a direct-sales model in order to focus resources on product development and positioning. When additional products are ready, MarketSoft may pursue an indirect-sales channel, allowing Original Equipment Manufacturers (OEMs) and integrators to sell MarketSoft's products. As Price expressed it, "We have not developed an indirect channel nor OEM relationships yet. We focus on building the right and scalable products. We will build the indirect channel later." Building new channels could boost MarketSoft's reach and awareness.

Growth through Global Expansion

Another avenue for growth is geographic expansion. MarketSoft wants to become a global company. Although being global is not a prerequisitite for the company's eventual IPO, a plan of geographic expansion would be very helpful for the IPO filing. MarketSoft must become an international company at some point. To achieve a successful global expansion, MarketSoft products must be truly scalable, multilingual, and multicurrency, and the value proposition must be complete and sound.

Growth through Alternative Technology Platforms

MarketSoft could also increase the range of the IT platforms on which its products run. Some potential customers would like the product to work in other platforms (e.g., Unix or Db2) that MarketSoft does not support. Having a scalable product is crucial to increase the sales and reach of the products. MarketSoft is currently working on and assigning considerable resources to adapt its products to new platforms.

The Goal of Growth: Preparing for an IPO

MarketSoft is preparing the strategic move of an IPO, raising more cash and a higher profile by selling shares in the company. Although early 2001 finds the IPO window closed, MarketSoft wants to be ready with a "Go" profile when the market again accepts IPOs. If the firm can broaden its product line, develop a preeminent competitive positioning, and create marketing awareness, the company could be poised for a public offering. MarketSoft would like to have an IPO-friendly profile by the end of 2001. For the IPO, MarketSoft must achieve $4 to $5 million in sales for the trailing quarter (last quarter before IPO date) and profitability close to the IPO.

Thus, MarketSoft must create strong revenue growth in a slowing economy and build a strong case for profitability. MarketSoft faces difficult challenges to hit the numbers. As Price explained, "To hit the $4 to $5 million per quarter, we must execute our sales. We have to build the pipeline and generate leads for the sales force to work on. Our sales force efficiency is increasing. Our sales pitch is clear, but we must provide leads to the sale reps. We also need to create brand awareness and presence in the market. MarketSoft is an unknown name to a lot of corporations."

The IPO target brings the urgency for MarketSoft to decide and work on other issues as well. First, which channel strategy should MarketSoft pursue until IPO? When is the right time to build the indirect channel? Second, should MarketSoft plan the global expansion before IPO? Third, should MarketSoft broaden the technology reach of the suite to work on different technologies? Finally, should MarketSoft complete the development of its suite and offer a broad e-marketing solution?

QUESTIONS

Develop a "Change the World Marketing Plan" for MarketSoft to achieve profitability before the end of the year. Many aspects are involved in such a plan, but we will concentrate on two elements of the plan: product suite (product strategy) and competitive strategy.

1. Evaluate the strengths and weaknesses of MarketSoft's product development process. What suggestions would you make to improve or extend it?
2. Evaluate MarketSoft's current plans for a product suite. What are the strengths and weaknesses of the proposal in figure 10.1? What new products would you target for next development priority? Would you build an SFA product, or would you broaden the products in areas where you have strength? How would you build in the analytic skills of measurement? Is the alliance with PrimeResponse the only product suite capability you need in campaign management?
3. What competitors are you most concerned about? What competitive positioning would you recommend? On which positioning dimensions would you excel?
4. What priorities would you set for changes in the product suite versus other growth opportunities (e.g., indirect channels, global expansion, platform compatibility)?

A p p e n d i x

Siebel Systems Products

This appendix describes a MarketSoft competitor, Siebel Systems, and its products.

Siebel Systems (www.siebel.com)

Siebel Systems (SEBL) is a publicly traded software company that provides customer relationship management (CRM) software. Tom Siebel, formerly the top salesperson at Oracle, founded Siebel Systems in 1993 and has achieved impressive growth rates since that time, with a mantra of 100 percent customer satisfaction. Originally starting with sales force automation (SFA) software, Siebel has expanded its product suite to include applications that link service, call centers, and marketing efforts into the integrated software suite. Siebel has been very effective at using its business partners in strategic roles to promote and propagate its products. At the current time, Siebel is by far the dominant player in the software-based CRM market, with a market share greater than 50 percent and was ranked second in *Fortune* magazine's 2001 ranking of the "100 Fastest Growing Companies."

Financials

Market Cap: $8.134 billion
Stock Price: $17.67 (October 19, 2001)
Cash: $1.5 billion (as of September 30, 2001)
Revenues: $1.795 billion (FY 2000)

Looking for greater depth and leveraging its industry-leading CRM position, Siebel has expanded far beyond its original SFA software and has developed a wide range of products to better serve more needs of today's corporations. All of Siebel's applications are Web enabled, so that the costs of deployment are significantly decreased (access is available through any standard browser). The Web-based architecture also enables companies to share information easily with their partners, clients, prospects, and other interested parties. Siebel has just released Siebel 7, which integrates CRM with employee relationship management (ERM) and partner relationship management (PRM). Siebel product suites include the following:

• **Siebel Sales** is the market-leading SFA software that helps firms manage their selling efforts throughout the cycle. Included in the applications of this suite is the core Sales application, which incorporates contact management, pipeline management, and effective tracking and identification of opportunities while allowing data to be shared throughout the organization. Additional applications include Incentive Compensation, eLearning, and Mobile Sales, the last of which is designed for the increasingly important wireless data world. In a recent CRM comparison by the research firm AMR, amidst close competition, Siebel's contact center application won "Best in Class" honors (*CRMDaily.com*, October 25, 2001).

• The **Siebel Marketing suite, including Siebel Analytics,** helps organizations plan, enhance, and evaluate their promotional activities. This set of applications promises more efficient, highly targeted marketing campaigns as well as cross-channel tracking and offer delivery. Siebel recently acquired nQuire to enchance the functionality of the Analytics offering.

- The purpose of the **Siebel Service** product family is to make sure that the customer is taken care of, no matter what channel they use to contact the company, whether through its Call Center, through its Web site, or out in the field. This suite of applications includes the following:
  - Call Center
  - Web Service
    - eMail Response
    - eService
    - eCollaboration
  - Field Service/Mobile Service
  - Siebel Professional Services Automation

- Siebel's **Interactive Selling Suite** helps organizations manage and give direction to their sales efforts, whether through the Web, telesales, partners, or direct or indirect sales channels. This is done through a variety of different applications that include the following:
  - Siebel eAdvisor
  - Siebel eSales
  - Siebel eConfigurator
  - Siebel ePricer
  - Siebel eAuction

- Siebel's **Industry Applications** are designed to offer turnkey eBusiness functionality tailored to a variety of different industries. Current industry offerings are Financial Institutions, Healthcare, Insurance, Communications, Energy, Consumer Sector, Life Sciences, Public Sector, Automotive, and Travel & Transportation.

- Siebel's **Partnership Relationship Management** program allows companies to increase the efficiencies of working with partners by automating many of the typical business processes and interactions.

- Siebel's **Employee Relationship Management** (ERM) assists in the human resources function, including employee recruiting, development, and management.

- Siebel's **Siebel 7 MidMarket** suite allows medium-size and smaller firms to experience a robust group of sales, marketing, and customer management applications. The traditional set of Siebel applications was often prohibitively expensive for smaller firms.

- In addition, attacking another of the growing segments in the marketplace, Siebel offers a self-service, Web-based service that AMR rated as the best in a recent study, with PeopleSoft following closely behind (CRMDaily.com, October 26, 2001).

Siebel's Strategy

Siebel seems very aware about the growing skepticism and concerns about the business value of CRM systems. With this in mind, they have designed a preemptive strategy of securing the support of executives, especially those of high-visibility accounts, and communicating these words of confidence to their smaller or potential clients. Their message seems to be, "If these large companies, whose operations are in an order of magnitude that is 10-fold yours, can have confidence in our system, and if they are able to quantify value from our systems, then so can you."

Siebel is telling potential clients that in this tough economy, an investment in Siebel systems is wise because it

1. yields a positive return on investment, despite the system's total cost of ownership;
2. provides an integrated set of e-business applications for marketing to, servicing, and meeting the needs of customers; and
3. can be integrated into a company's customer and business strategies and can be implemented in multiple channels, such as the Web, call centers, field sales

support, reseller channels, and retail and dealer networks.

Siebel will begin to customize its products for small to midsize companies and begin marketing to them. These are the markets in which the best-of-breed companies, not comprehensive suite players like Siebel, have competed. If Siebel succeeds with this goal, the industry will face intense competition as other large firms (e.g., Oracle, IBM, and Microsoft) recognize that this is a viable, attractive market in which to compete.

CHAPTER

Communication and Selling

Introduction

After you have targeted your market and uniquely positioned your product, you need to communicate the benefits of your product to your target customers. This communication traditionally takes the form of advertising and personal selling. In this chapter, you will consider how to evaluate advertising options and how much to spend. You will study how to access the effectiveness of advertising and use decision support models. Two approaches to selling (push-based and trust-based selling) are described. The chapter concludes with a look at multichannel communication and the use of the Internet to improve the buying process.

Advertising

Advertising agencies help companies create, place, and assess advertisements. By using an ad agency, a company can outsource part or all of the multistep advertising process. First, advertising agencies help advertisers generate specific advertisements. In on-line media, new types of advertising agencies emerge that not only generate the ads but also help firms optimize the mix of traditional and on-line advertising to create effective ad campaigns. Second, agencies help advertisers choose specific media (e.g., alternative Web publishers) and configure when and where the on-line ad will appear. On-line ad agencies also help clients create methods to record relevant data (e.g., page views, click-throughs, qualified sales leads, and resultant sales) in order to measure the effectiveness of a particular campaign.

How to Evaluate Media Copy

Advertising must be more than simply creative if it is to be effective. Evaluating proposed advertising requires careful consideration of numerous factors. Figure 11.1 is a rating sheet that you can use to evaluate ads. The rating sheet enumerates 10 factors in addition to creativity that are important to assess when choosing which ad to run. You will need to balance clever, attention-getting copy against your communication objectives and action needs. Use the sheet provided in figure 11.1 to rate each ad on the important

FIGURE 11.1   Ad Evaluation Form

Your weight of each dimension		Your rating of an ad: (1 = extremely bad, 7 = extremely good)						
		1	2	3	4	5	6	7
10	High attention						X	●
7	Positive brand association					●	X	
8	Brand recall			●	X			
8	Positive perception		●		X			
7	Information		●	X				
9	Core service proposition			●	X			
5	High emotion		X			●		
10	Action—visit site/buy		●			X		
8	Creativity				X		●	
10	Target group effectiveness				●		X	

Total score = sum of weight × rating

X = 375, ● = 319

dimensions. Then assign a weight to the importance of each dimension and sum up the weights times the rating. For example, in figure 11.1, circles are the ratings for one ad (Ad ●) and Xs are the ratings for the other (Ad X). The total score for the circles is 319, and the total score for Xs is 375. Overall, therefore, Ad X best meets your communication objectives. Ad X is less creative but has more action results. Using this simple ad evaluation tool can help you understand the trade-offs in finding the best ad for your product.

The Role of On-Line Advertising

Companies place their ads on-line in order to boost brand awareness and sell their products. For advertisers, the Web holds a tantalizing promise: getting the advertiser's message directly to the eyes of a targeted, receptive audience and providing a mechanism for instant action. Traditional advertising (e.g., print, television, and radio) suffers from the gulf between creating the perception of need and satisfying that need. In contrast, on-line advertising lets the audience click through to buy the product, subscribe to the service, gather more detailed information, or immediately contact the company that placed the ad.

The Advent of Rich Media

Internet advertising started as banner ads placed alongside text. The ads were static graphic files (using the Graphics Interchange Format) sitting atop a Web page. But as the Internet evolved, the techniques of advertisers evolved as well. In particular, there is a movement toward rich media, which are dynamic, multisensory, interactive ads that engage the viewer's attention (see figure 11.2). Rich media add sound, moving pictures, and interactivity to create a new form of advertising.

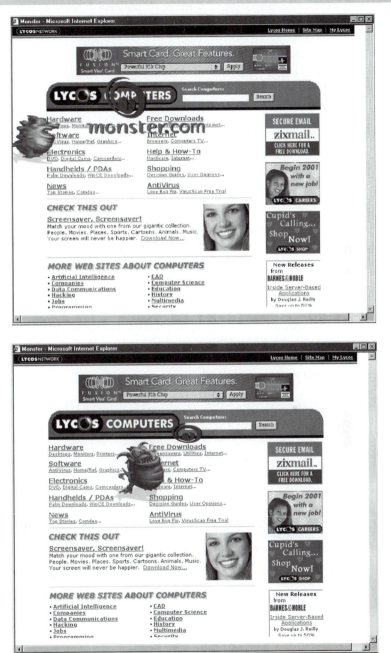

Early rich media ads replaced static, print-inspired picture ads with animated visuals (spinning logos, slideshows, scrolling images, cartoonlike animations, and sound). Newer rich media advertising is moving toward the techniques of television advertising by using full-motion imagery and sound. But rich media transcend television advertising by adding interactivity. Where television advertising presents a single linear mass-market viewer experience, rich media present a nonlinear, interactive, individualized viewer experience.

For example, interactivity can take the form of simple pop-up information that brings up additional layers of information as the user's mouse moves over the ad. This interactivity adds depth to the ad without committing viewers to click on the ad and leave the page they are currently viewing. Other ads have moving features that track the movement of the user's mouse, creating eye-catching motion. Some advertisers even create minigames within rich media banner ads ("See if you can click on the speeding monkey to find out if you have won!!!"). Interactivity creates engagement and adds depth to the advertiser's message. A *ClickZ* article estimated that rich media are twice as effective as standard ads (in click-throughs) while costing only 8 percent more.

Rich media are more complex than any other form of advertising. The interactive aspect of rich media implies that no two individuals experience the ad in the same way because different individuals might interact with the ad differently. Creating an interactive ad becomes more like developing software than laying out or scripting a print, radio, or television ad. Interactivity brings nonlinearity to the ad, meaning that ad creators must consider all the different interactions or paths through the material. For example, the ad copy must make sense even if the viewer skips to the bottom of the ad before going to the top. Although effective, the downside of rich media is the possibility of customers seeing the ad as intrusive, and this could have a negative effect on their buying the product.

New Media

The Internet helps deliver ads that position a company against the competition. New, more interactive rich media create more compelling, informative, and eye-catching on-line ads. Demographic data collected during registration at a Web site help that site segment its user base and help advertisers make the right pitch. Moreover, the Internet encourages experimentation and rapid feedback processes. A company can easily try a number of different ads or ad sequences pitched to different unique visitors. The company can then gauge response and use the most successful ads (based on click-through and conversions) more widely. Cookies (small data records left on the customer's computer and retrieved by the Web site during later browsing) help companies know which ads and promotions a customer has seen. Cookies also help companies keep track of what the customer is trying to do over multiple visits.

How Much to Spend Where

Deciding how to best spend your advertising dollars is becoming more complex (see the "Increasing Complexity" sidebar). This complexity brings the need for decision support tools that help you assess the payback that you are getting for your advertising budget. The types of questions marketing managers typically want answered are the following:

How much in incremental sales and profits did a promotion generate?

Would it be worthwhile to enlarge our advertising budget to increase consumer trial of our new product and obtain leverage from a heavy investment in point-of-purchase displays?

What would happen if we shifted some of our personal selling resources to other channels?

Marketing decision support systems (MDSS) help you model the effects of deploying alternative resources, thereby improving your decisions on advertising levels, sales efforts, promotions, and repositionings. With the right data and the right analysis, you can select the levels of these variables that lead to the best long-term profit. MDSS use both internal company data as well as data from external databases and let you run "what if" simulations to determine the most profitable level for each marketing variable before you spend a penny. MDSS use statistics to forecast and understand data and generate exception reports to help you identify problems, perform analysis, and run models to find solutions. For example, you can identify problems (e.g., loss of share or margin) and identify why the problems seem to have occurred (e.g., ineffective promotion, competitive actions, or category trends).

Increasing Complexity

On-line advertising is significantly more complex than traditional advertising for several reasons. First, on-line ads are often placed or delivered to individuals rather than to mass markets. As a result, firms must place and track massive numbers of ad impressions rather than place a single ad that will be seen by thousands or even millions of audience members. Second, on-line advertising yields far more data that can be used to evaluate the effectiveness of the ads. Data may range from straightforward information, such as the number of impressions or click-through rates, to complex information about individual audience members and their behavior relative to a particular ad or campaign. Third, advertisers are increasingly turning to rich media advertisements for on-line campaigns. The additional technical complexity of these types of ads calls for more coordination between the advertiser and the media seller. Fourth, whereas traditional media have relatively simple payment schemes (i.e., pay for placement with some postpublication adjustment for ratings), on-line media have varied and dynamic payment schemes (e.g., pay-per-page-view, pay-per-click-through, and commission-sales payments). Rather than making one payment for bulk placement of a traditional ad, on-line advertisers may pay varying amounts for each day that an ad appears, and the rates vary further, depending on the results of that ad. Finally, the Internet is a disaggregated medium. Ads televised on major networks will likely reach an audience of millions. To reach a similar Internet audience, advertisers place ads on several Internet publishers, creating additional planning, tracking, and evaluation needs

(continued)

for both buyers and sellers of on-line advertising. The increased complexity of on-line advertising implies greater need for automated work flow software. Companies such as Solbright, Inc., develop and sell work flow automation software for firms involved in the buying, selling, and managing of on-line advertisements. The software aids in planning, executing, and overseeing on-line advertising.

At the same time that overseeing advertising is becoming more complex, the amount and quality of data to help you with the decisions is also improving. For example, data from firms such as Jupiter MediaMetrix and Comscore help media buyers determine how many unique audience members visit a particular Web site, how long they stay, how often they return, and whether they buy on-line. Although measuring click-through rates is fairly common, such measurements do not necessarily reflect the total effectiveness of a particular on-line campaign. It is more informative to work with the clickstream data arising from on-line advertising to understand where customers came from, what they saw on the site, how long they stayed, whether they returned, and how much they ultimately bought.

When to Use Which Type of Advertising

The purpose of traditional print and television advertising today is to build product awareness rather than to generate immediate sales. One-sided 60-second ads that push a consumer to buy a product do not work as well as in the past. First, given the sheer volume of ads, it is difficult for any ad to rise above the clutter. Second, people are watching less television. Third, the amount of information that a company needs to convey about a product is also increasing, and 30- to 60-second commercials are too short to convey all that information. Therefore, it is more prudent to use advertising to build awareness and sustain a brand but then direct consumers to a Web site for more information.

Another useful tool is the opt-in mailing list, in which consumers sign up to receive information from the company. Opt-in mailing lists build more personalization, enabling companies to target those customers who would be most interested in the product being offered. Advertising is increasingly seen as part of a multichannel communication system.

Selling

Two Approaches to Selling: Push-Based Selling and Trust-Based Selling

The steps of the push-based selling process are to find a large list of prospects, screen the list for qualified buyers, present the "sales pitch," and go for the close. If the potential buyer is not interested, the salesperson moves on to the next prospect. This produces the traditional funnel of selling: amass lots of prospects in the top, and some will drip out from the bottom.

Trust-based selling involves targeting a few high-potential prospects, researching their problem, and building a relationship with them. Salespeople help potential customers solve their problems, becoming a trusted advisor for them. Trust-based selling often involves working with all members of the decision-making unit. In selling to an industrial decision-making unit (see chapter 3), the salesperson will orchestrate the sales process but not necessarily do it alone. In the approach, many leads are considered to set priorities, but the focus is on a small number of clients and a high flow of these prospects to the sales commitment.

In contrast to push-based selling, trust-based selling involves directing intensive effort on a few key prospects. The growth of customer power, as we saw in chapter 5, suggests that companies will need to do more trust-based selling over time as customers become more knowledgeable and demand more from their product and service providers.

The key to choosing your selling approach is to match it to your strategic marketing approach. Is your strategy push based or trust based? If you are pursuing a push-based marketing strategy, then using a push-based selling program is the way to go. In contrast, if you are using a trust-based marketing approach, then a trust-based sales approach is called for. In both cases, the selling approach will be coordinated with your company's overall strategy and advertising.

Trust-based selling involves sharing the pluses and minuses of your product with your customer. That is, instead of painting the product as perfect, you portray how it can solve the customer's problems. The selling process involves much more of a listening process.

Multichannel Communication

In the past, the selling function was conducted all in person, in a face-to-face meeting between a salesperson and the prospective customer. Now, other media are being used to substitute for some of the high-expenditure personal selling. Figure 11.3 shows that in the past, selling was used to generate awareness, build the perception of the product, convince customers of its value, and lead them through the purchase. Figure 11.4 shows how other methods are now substituting for the personal selling function of moving customers from awareness to purchase at a minimum cost.

FIGURE 11.3   Functional Substitution

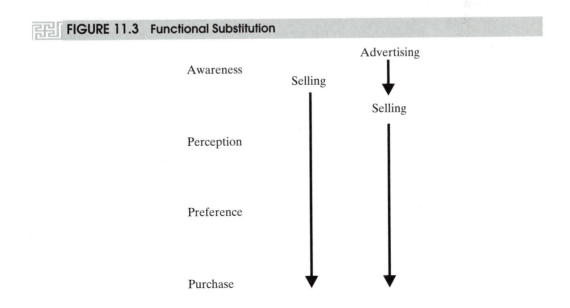

FIGURE 11.4 New Methods

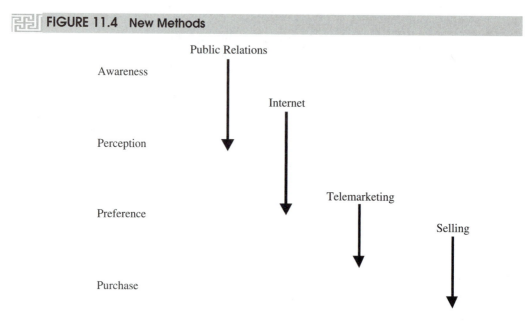

Figure 11.5 shows a more detailed view of the adoption process of traditional channels in comparison to the role of the Internet, advertising, retail outlets, and service. To be effective, all elements must be coordinated. The Internet allows each phase to be more effective. The challenge is to optimize the progression down the behavioral process with traditional and new technologies.

Word of Mouth on the Internet

Pharmaceutical firm Aventis is using the Internet and the dynamics of word of mouth to sell its arthritis drugs. Rather than pushing the product on patients, Aventis created a patient-focused (i.e., customer-focused) on-line community called RAwatch.com for people with rheumatoid arthritis. The Web site provides a powerful array of features: on-line information sources, chat rooms, opinion polls, threaded discussion databases, and an instant messaging–style tool for talking to others who are at RAwatch.com. The on-line patient community helps patients deal with the various medical, psychological, and life-impacting issues of their condition. The true trust-based aspect of the site is that Aventis allows frank discussion among patients about its drugs and other competitor drugs. For example, on-line discussions at RAwatch actually included unfavorable stories about Aventis' arthritis drug (Arava) and favorable mentions of competitors' treatments. Aventis did not suppress this unfavorable commentary because it did not want to lose the trust of patients and destroy the community. Reading the honest opinions of other customers may lead some patients to choose a competitor's drug. But Aventis' goal is not necessarily to sell to all possible patients but to sell to those for whom the drug would be most effective.

FIGURE 11.5

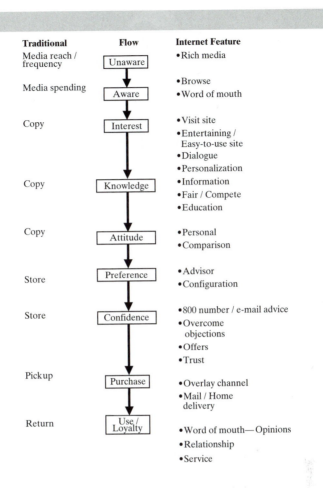

Traditional	Flow	Internet Feature
Media reach / frequency	Unaware	•Rich media
Media spending	Aware	•Browse •Word of mouth
Copy	Interest	•Visit site •Entertaining / Easy-to-use site •Dialogue •Personalization
Copy	Knowledge	•Information •Fair / Compete •Education
Copy	Attitude	•Personal •Comparison
Store	Preference	•Advisor •Configuration
Store	Confidence	•800 number / e-mail advice •Overcome objections •Offers •Trust
Pickup	Purchase	•Overlay channel •Mail / Home delivery
Return	Use / Loyalty	•Word of mouth—Opinions •Relationship •Service

Introduction to OSRAM Case

OSRAM Sylvania Inc. (OSI) successfully launched a sell-side Web platform, mySylvania.com, to its target group of small customers ("small" in this case is in contrast to the large industrial accounts and master distributors). Following the big initial success of the site in communicating to customers and encouraging more effective interaction, OSRAM Sylvania executives wonder how to proceed with their customer relationship management strategy.

REFERENCES

Davenport, Thomas H., Jeanne G. Harris, and Ajay K. Kohli. 2001. "How Do They Know Their Customers So Well?" *Sloan Management Review* 42, no. 2: 63–73.

Little, John D. C. 1975. "BRANDAID: A Marketing Mix Model, Structure, Implementation, Calibration and Case Study." *Operations Research* 23, no. 4: 628–73.

Maqister, David, C. H. Green, and R. M. Galford. 2000. *The Trusted Advisor*. New York: Free Press.

Shapiro, Benson P. 1985. "Rejuvenating the Marketing Mix." *Harvard Business Review* 63, no. 5: 28–34.

CHAPTER 12

OSRAM Sylvania

Introduction

In late fall 2001, Greg Schmidt, vice president of e-business for OSRAM Sylvania Inc., is sitting at his desk reviewing the company's e-business sell-side strategy. Schmidt and his group worked hard and reaped the benefits during the prior year. The team got OSRAM Sylvania's sell-side Web platform mySYLVANIA.com up and running and enjoyed the resulting improvements in sales processes and reductions in costs. As Schmidt reflects on the accomplishments to date, he sees that the group is just beginning to develop a full customer relationship management (CRM) system for the company. Thinking about the next steps, Schmidt wonders how he can leverage the mySYLVANIA.com portal to lock in customers with the company. He also ponders what to do with the "ocean" of customer behavior and transaction data that flows from the Web site.

At the same time and on another floor, Denise Champagne, marketing manager for the Industrial and Commercial Lighting channel, was creating her marketing plan for the coming year. She is thinking about the impact of mySYLVANIA.com on her sales reps. The Internet has reduced the amount of labor consumed by low-value administrative tasks, letting her reps focus more efforts on selling. She is eager to roll out new marketing campaigns that target specific channels and is wondering how the Web might support her plans.

The Lighting Market

The general lighting market, including light sources, ballasts, and fixtures, is a highly concentrated global market that generates an estimated $12 billion to $15 billion in revenues annually. The global light source market is dominated by three major players: Philips Lighting, General Electric Lighting, and OSRAM Sylvania. General lighting includes all types of lightbulbs or "lamps" used in common lighting, such as the ubiquitous incandescent bulbs and fluorescent bulbs, as well as the newer high-intensity discharge lamps and compact fluorescents.

Although the standard household 75-watt incandescent bulb is a commodity in the marketplace, the three major competitors are continuously introducing more higher-end, value-added products that increase the life of the bulb, improve the quality of the light, and lower energy costs of the user. This last point is important because lighting consumes between 15 and 20 percent of the world's energy, and general lighting is responsible for up to 60 percent of the energy demand in office and commercial buildings.

OSRAM Sylvania Background

Headquartered in Danvers, Massachusetts, OSRAM Sylvania is the North American subsidiary of OSRAM GmbH, together with its parent company, it is the second largest lighting and materials enterprise in the world, serving customers in more than 140 countries. OSRAM Sylvania manufactures and markets a wide range of lighting products including automotive, electronic and magnetic ballasts, and precision materials and components for industrial and commercial users, original equipment manufacturers and customers, sold primarily under the Sylvania name, but also under the OSRAM brand. The company has seven principal organizational units: General Lighting, Precision Materials & Components, Automotive Lighting, Electronic Control Systems, OSRAM SYLVANIA LTD./LTÉE, OSRAM Mexico, and Photo-Optics (see figure 12.1 for details).

OSRAM Sylvania Products

OSRAM Sylvania's general lighting product line consists of incandescent, fluorescent, and high-intensity discharge lightbulbs as well as ballasts. (For a complete product overview, see www.SYLVANIA.com). Customers include consumers who purchase lightbulbs for their homes, contractors who purchase ballasts and lamps for new or renovated private and commercial buildings, and large accounts, such as hotel chains or retail stores, that purchase ballasts and lamps in bulk.

FIGURE 12.1   OSRAM Sylvania's Organization (Partial)

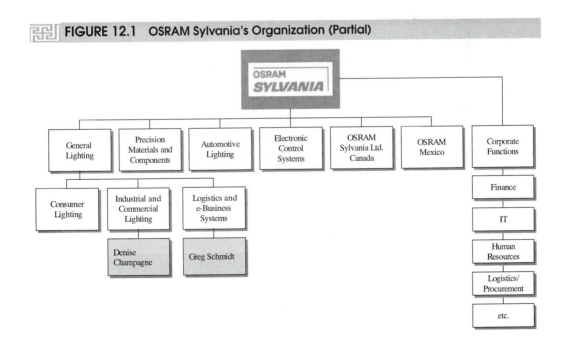

The company distributes its products via several different channels. For consumer lighting products, OSRAM Sylvania uses retail channels like hardware stores, supermarkets, and do-it-yourself super centers. In the business-to-business arena, handled by the Industrial and Commercial Lighting channel OSRAM Sylvania utilizes a two-pronged approach, selling through distributors and directly to large customers. The channel is divided into three groups: Field Sales, National Accounts, and Corporate Accounts. The Field Sales group is split into 10 regions around the United States and serves smaller-scale customers and end users. The National Accounts sales force is responsible for large national distribution chains, and its salespeople act as key account managers. Finally, the Corporate Accounts sales force targets large end-user groups, such as banking chains, hoteliers, and national retailers.

Sales force efforts are split mainly between business end users and channel partners, but there are many other players in the business-to-business lighting market space. In the new construction market, architects, engineers, and designers all influence buying decisions and are important foci for OSRAM Sylvania's marketing. In the existing buildings market, property managers are often product specifiers for the types of products that OSRAM Sylvania offers (see figure 12.2 for schematic of channel structure).

Creating OSRAM Sylvania's Web Presence

The company established a confidential e-team in 1998 to begin discussing how best to utilize the Web to forward the company's business objectives. The team began as an undercover unit to analyze the opportunities the Web offered before a major initiative was announced in the conservative company. The team included individuals from the information technology (IT) department who were eager to exploit the promises of the Internet as well as representatives of the lighting business. At this early stage, IT was leading the organization toward the Web.

Goal: Business-to-Business Sales Process Improvement

The first focus area of the initiative was on the business-to-business sell side. Given its extensive distribution network, the company had no interest in a business-to-consumer initiative that would sell individual lightbulbs to end consumers via the Internet. Rather, the sell-side strategy was to improve the internal selling process. Greg Schmidt, vice president in charge of e-business, emphasizes that the company has 20,000 price quotes active at any one time with customers and receives hundreds of requests for quotes every week. With this much data floating around in an off-line world, productivity gains were sure to be had.

The IT group worked with the marketing and sales departments to ensure that the system's functionality met all the necessary business requirements. Based on knowledge from the sales side, the decision was made to use the Web to offer personalization at the channel level and build a customer-only Web site called mySYLVANIA.com, which allows users to self-select their channels and then view information customized to those channels. There are approximately 14 lighting communities set up on mySYLVANIA.com for its different channels. The site also uses

FIGURE 12.2 Schematic of OSRAM Sylvania's Channel Structure

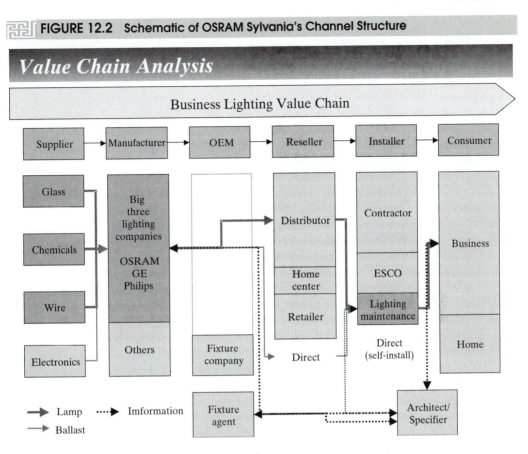

Value Chain Analysis

Business Lighting Value Chain

a user-name and password log-on to offer secure one-to-one communication between the company and the customer (see figure 12.3 for a screenshot progression of the mySYLVANIA.com Web site).

Using SAP for the Front Office

OSRAM Sylvania built the site using SAP as the backbone. It had already implemented SAP R/3 as an enterprise resource planning system for the company's back-office operations. Using software from this same vendor for OSRAM Sylvania's front-office Web initiative made sense for the following reasons:

- It decreased complexity from the IT side.
- It simplified upgrades to software.
- It provided the lowest total cost option.
- It provided the least amount of pain.

OSRAM Sylvania's chief information officer, Mehrdad Laghaeian, explains, "We never bought into the whole idea of front-office versus back-office applications. We've looked for a way to build systems that are seamless and can economically share information. The front-office and back-office distinctions don't matter much to end-users. They are simply seeking information."

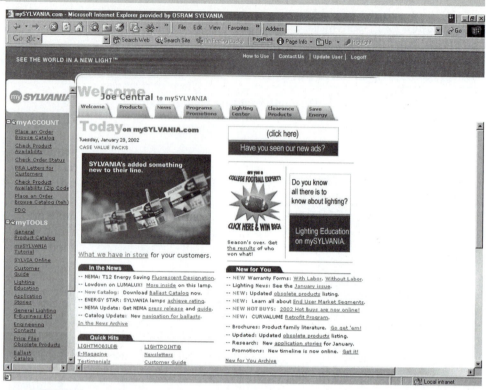

FIGURE 12.3   www.mySYLVANIA.com Web Site (continued)

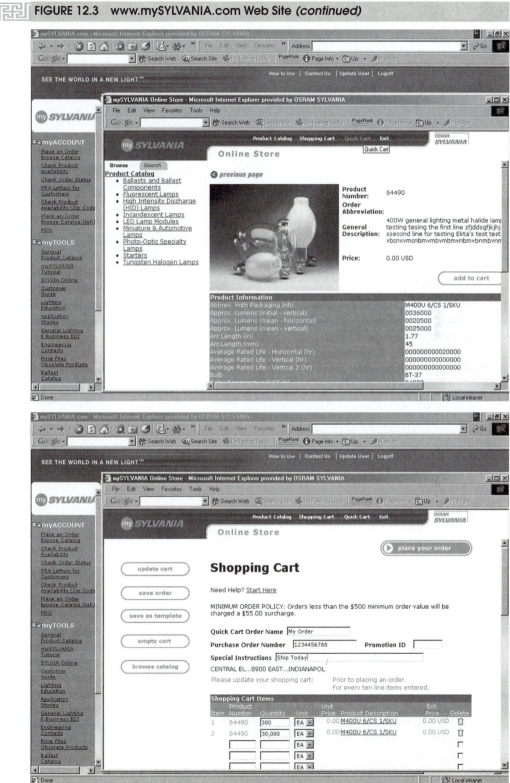

FIGURE 12.3 www.mySYLVANIA.com Web Site *(continued)*

SAP's mySAP.com CRM solution allows the customers of OSRAM Sylvania to place orders, pay for them, and track them on-line. Customers and company personnel can access information on orders and track order status. SAP solutions automatically track inventory and place and track orders. The solution handles each customer's particular discount, payment terms, and other contract conditions. Everything is Web based and Web accessible, so customers and partners can do business anywhere, anytime.

Using SAP, OSRAM Sylvania has integrated all its existing back-end data on suppliers, customers, and partners with front-office applications that those partners can access (see this chapter's appendix for more background on SAP).

Adoption Issues for mySYLVANIA.com

Although the concept of mySLYVANIA.com was well planned, it still faced obstacles to adoption, both externally and internally. Customers needed to be convinced to use the Web as a channel, and that meant assuaging concerns about security. Internally, the company faced some pushback from the ultimate users and benefactors of the site.

External Concerns: Security

The first major challenge was customers' concerns about security. Customers wanted a high level of security and were unwilling to hook up to OSRAM Sylvania's site without some guarantees of security. Moreover, different customers demanded different levels of security. In addition, the customers wanted the company to provide distributed security. This meant offering different levels of security access for different classes of employees at the customer site. For example, a customer's purchasing administrator could access the customer-specific pricing and specifications but could not authorize a transaction, while the customer's purchasing manager would be authorized to do everything. Essentially, OSRAM Sylvania needed to take the level of access and security down to the individual business level and personalize the experience differently for different employee roles at the customer site. This was admittedly the "less glamorous" part of the project and indeed was "arduous" to implement for all customers. It was, however, a prerequisite to building trust between the company and its customers and to achieving the critical mass of site-using customers required to make the site a success.

Internal Obstacles to Adoption

The second major challenge was internal adoption of the new on-line customer interface. OSRAM Sylvania needed buy-in from its internal sales force because they would be the people introducing the system to customers. If the sales force did not believe in mySYLVANIA.com, how could they convince customers to use the Web site? Mehrdad Laghaeian recalls the start of the project: "At the beginning there were a lot of nonbelievers." People didn't think the system would work or that customers would be interested. Some employees were uncomfortable changing the established ways of doing business. Others worried that a system that gave more control to customers would reduce the influence of the salespeople."

In order to get buy-in, Greg Schmidt explained, "We used a traditional 'carrot and stick' approach." Eventually, as internal users got on board, the first results came in, and the adoption began to grow on its own. Laghaeian recalled,

> We pushed in the beginning to get the initiative going, but now it is an organic movement. On the IT side, we are now trying to cover our bases. We don't have to have as strong an involvement in the next steps. The businesses are pulling IT instead of being pushed by IT. Requirements are now coming out of the installed base. In fact, they are jumping way ahead and are asking for things like virtual packaging and 3D capability. I call it the "slingshot effect." We are now trying to manage this "digital euphoria" to make sure costs don't get too high and we focus on real business needs.

First Successes

Given the hundreds of requests for price quotes received per week, it used to take OSRAM Sylvania around three weeks to resolve each one in the off-line world—from customer request to the issuance of a price quote. The new system reduced this cycle time to less than two days in most cases, including the management decision process. In addition, salespeople have begun to understand they can shift their time from administrative tasks to more value-added tasks.

Changes in the Marketing and Sales Organization

mySYLVANIA.com is driving a number of changes to the company's approach to marketing. First, the site affected the organization of the marketing and sales departments and OSRAM Sylvania's relationship with smaller customers. Early on, the marketing department segmented its customer base and considered shifting its very small customers to master distributors—outboarding small direct customers to an indirect-sales channel. "They were 80 percent of our customers in terms of number but made up only 20 percent of sales and were very costly to serve with a sales force," said Denise champagne, the company's marketing manager. Fortunately, the advent of the mySYLVANIA.com Web site changed all of that, bringing down the costs of doing business with these small customers. Marketing changed its strategy from one of outboarding these customers to one of serving them exclusively through the Web channel. A special channel under mySYLVANIA.com was set up for this group and developed new marketing material and promotions exclusively for the small customers. Although web-based service would be promoted, small customers could access support from a customer service call center staffed by inside sales representatives. Some were worried that these customers would be upset that a salesperson was no longer visiting them, but, as Champagne explained, "with their own Web site, dedicated newsletter, and targeted promotions, the small customers were getting more attention now than ever before."

In addition, the system offers new ways to maintain contact with customers, but it also creates new burdens on marketing. One challenge for Champagne and her group is to keep the customer base visiting the Web site. To keep customers interested, Champagne said, "the content must be valuable and fresh." Currently, Schmidt's group tracks visits by customers, and if they have not visited the site in 120 days, the system automatically sends an e-mail that highlights the newest information and promotions on the Web to get the customer to revisit the site. This e-mail campaign has created a positive response in terms of click-through rates, but the group also wonders about the optimum frequency of e-mail reminders—too many reminders might be annoying rather than helpful.

Finally, mySYLVANIA.com offers new opportunities for segmenting the market and personalizing the company's marketing messages. Champagne explained that the marketing strategy for the web is to add value to the customer relationship by offering an organized library of information for people throughout the value chain who need information. The information is tailored to the needs of each of the channels in the mySYLVANIA.com portal and is dubbed the "Sales Resource Center." The data are personalized down to the role of the person accessing within a channel. The channel structure within the portal allows Champagne to subsegment within customer segments and offer tailored marketing materials and promotions to these fine-grained channels. Personalizing down to the customer level and achieving true one-to-one marketing is OSRAM Sylvania's ultimate goal.

Future Plans

mySYLVANIA.com lays the groundwork for future efforts to improve understanding of customers, expand marketing efforts, create greater personalization, and implement a full-featured suite of CRM tools. Marketing is considering how to use the information generated by the site to learn more about customers and to fine-tune its campaigns. The company is collecting "oceans" of clickstream data and transaction data. Through the site, the company can track what customers are viewing on the site, what transactions are used most, the date of last sign-on, dollar amount purchased, and products purchased per session. From this information, the company has developed profiles for a first level of user categories (e.g., customers or specifiers/influencers). Further use of such data will help the company understand what pages are being clicked on most, which on-line promotions have the best success rates, and which channels have the highest usage of the Web site. Rigorous data on what works and what does not work will serve as benchmarks for future marketing efforts.

With the channel-based mySLYVANIA.com up and running, OSRAM Sylvania has the opportunity to expand its marketing efforts to span a greater part of the value chain. For example, Champagne is now looking at major end-customer segments to begin more personalized interaction with indirect customers. Her first task will be to develop a marketing plan for the contractor segment of the end-user customer base. Her goal is to better understand how this segment makes its purchasing decisions and to be able to directly market OSRAM Sylvania's products to this segment without creating channel conflict with current distribution channels. mySYLVANIA.com is the first step in a planned CRM system for OSRAM Sylvania. The main functionality of the system to date includes personalized information at a broad channel level as well as order entry and look-up. The IT and marketing groups have plans to expand the CRM system to allow on-line contact management, sales force automation, and greater personalization using the data mined from the site.

Issues

After successfully implementing the first steps in OSRAM Sylvania's CRM system, both Greg Schmidt and Denise Champagne see the following issues facing the company:

- What should OSRAM Sylvania do with the "ocean" of data that has now been generated through the system? How to use the vast amounts of data in an intelligent way?
- How can the company use the CRM system to create a barrier to competitors and to "lock in" accounts?
- How can the Web add value to the customer relationship beyond reducing the cost of service?
- How can OSRAM Sylvania target end-customer segments without disintermediating current distribution channels and endangering its relationship with these crucial partners?

QUESTIONS

In addition to thinking about the previously listed issues, be prepared to discuss the following:

1. Why was this implementation successful?
2. What user requirements should be given priority? Security? Others?
3. Given the new Web site, how should Denise Champagne realign her selling strategy to get more customers? Should she revise her existing advertising, promotion, and channel strategy?
4. What should the IT and marketing groups do with the data coming out of the initial system?
5. What next steps would you recommend to further develop OSRAM Sylvania's CRM system?

SAP Products

Background

SAP began in 1972 as a spin-off of IBM when five systems analysts left IBM to create a new company that would provide standard enterprise software to integrate all business processes. The idea came to them through their work as systems consultants for IBM when they noticed that client after client was developing the same or very similar computer programs. The second part of their vision was that data should be processed interactively in real time and that the computer screen should become the focal point of data processing.

Products

SAP's first system was called R/1 and began with a Financial Accounting module, a Materials Management, module and an Asset Accounting module. All modules could be integrated, and this integration has become the hallmark of SAP's systems. In 1979, SAP introduced R/2, which was SAP's mainframe solution, and in 1992 the now famous client-server system R/3 was introduced. With the introduction of its R/3 enterprise resource planning (ERP) software, what began as a small regional software company quickly grew into a global software solutions provider. Headquartered in Walldorf, Germany, with U.S. operations headquarters located in Newtown Square, Pennsylvania, SAP is the world's largest intraenterprise software company and the world's third largest independent software supplier overall. With 2.5 billion Euros in sales, SAP employs over 27,800 people in more than 50 countries. Customers include Microsoft, IBM, Hewlett-Packard, Siemens, Volkswagen, Dow Corning, and Ericsson.

Recognizing the future importance of collaborative systems spurred by the Internet, SAP introduced an Internet-enabled version of SAP in 1996 and then in 1999 introduced mySAP.com, a collaborative e-business platform that allows employees, customers, and business partners to work together anywhere, anytime. mySAP.com is open and flexible, supporting databases, applications, operating systems, and hardware from almost every major vendor. mySAP.com offers the following solutions:

mySAP.com Solutions

- Industry Solutions
- mySAP Enterprise Portals
- mySAP Supply Chain Management
- mySAP Customer Relationship Management
- mySAP E-Procurement
- mySAP Product Lifecycle Management
- mySAP Business Intelligence
- mySAP Financials
- mySAP Human Resources
- mySAP Mobile Business
- mySAP Exchanges
- mySAP Hosted Solutions
- mySAP Technology

CRM Product

mySAP CRM creates an Interaction Center for a company that allows them to interact with their customers by telephone, fax, e-mail, and Web site and with mobile devices such as laptops, cell phones, and personal digital assistants. The software enables interaction with a customer through all phases of the customer life cycle, from customer acquisition and multichannel sales to order processing and customer service. In addition, Operational CRM manages and synchronizes customer interactions in marketing, sales, and service. Analytical CRM helps optimize information sources for a better understanding of customer behavior. Collaborative CRM allows for collaboration with suppliers, partners, and customers to improve processes and meet customer needs.

CHAPTER

13

Pricing and Distribution

Introduction

In addition to communicating your product to your target audience, you must price and distribute effectively. We have talked about pricing in new product design (chapter 9) because price is part of the total product package of benefits. In consumer response, (chapter 3), pricing is a decision variable. In chapter 15, we will see price as an issue for deal-prone customers as it encourages push marketing. In this chapter, we emphasize the impact of digital technologies on pricing.

Pricing Strategies

First, let us look at several methods for selecting a price for a product. The price of a product must lie between the cost of the product to the company and the value of the product to the customer. If the price is below the cost, the company loses money. If the price is above the value, the customers will refuse to buy it. In theory, the price of the new product is set by considerations of maximizing total profitability—finding a trade-off between a high-price strategy (high profits per sale but few sales) and low-price strategy (low profits per sale but much greater volume). Understanding the demand curve (sales vs. price) and supply curve (required sales for profitability at a given price) helps the company pick the best price.

Because a company can easily compute the cost of a product, many companies use cost-based pricing. A common approach, called *cost plus,* is to mark up costs by some amount. Another approach is to calculate a price that results in a break-even return for a conservative sales estimate. These are simple methods to implement, but they may underprice or overprice a product.

A better approach is to understand the level of sales volume as a function of price level—recalling the importance of understanding customer behavior from chapter 3. Thus, another common approach is to set prices at a level slightly below competitive products. The presumption is that competitive pricing will bring high market share.

Setting the price involves more than just selecting the price that is best for short-term profits. For example, one might consider *penetration pricing,* which is a pricing strategy designed to build a market. This strategy involves setting a low price initially in order to build sales volume and loyalty (such as when the value of the product is unknown or unproven) (see Narashim, 1989, for an analytical approach to pricing and the diffusion of innovation). Such penetration pricing scenarios make the most sense if the firms use their production experience over time to lower costs and improve the engineering design. Such experience solidifies the firm's competitive capabilities and leads to long-run profitability. Another reason for penetration pricing is to stimulate word-of-mouth recommendations or acceptance by the channel of distribution (recall word of mouth from chapter 3). A disadvantage of penetration pricing is that if the market does not grow at the expected rate, the product may never be profitable.

Incentive Sites

One of the new marketing tools available to companies is the use of the Internet to provide incentives to attract new customers and introduce them to the company's products. For example, companies such as Wal-Mart, Barnes & Noble, and Office Depot use programs such as MyPoints.com to attract new shoppers. MyPoints.com is a Web site that offers customers points and discounts when they read e-mails, view ads, or buy products. Customers register minimal information (name, ZIP code, and e-mail address) and check off their areas of interest (such as apparel, books, automobiles, finance, or home and family, see figure 13.1). Providing additional information (address, income level, education level, or profession) entitles the consumer to additional points. Once registered, consumers earn points for each purchase they make through MyPoints.com. The advantage for participating companies is that they can test promotions and attract potential new buyers.

Other companies, such as JC Penney and IBM, run their own incentive and promotion sites. JC Penney, for example, has an opt-in e-mail newsletter that currently has over five million people who have signed up to receive the e-mails. JC Penney uses the e-mail channel to promote new products or offer special deals to members.

Business-to-Business Exchanges

Business-to-business exchanges were originally viewed as *the* killer application of the Internet, and hundreds were created in the dot-com heyday. Almost all these exchanges have failed, and the example of SemiSales shows why this was so.

Semisales

SemiSales is an example of a marketplace exchange that tried to revolutionize the semiconductor supply industry's distribution process by using the Internet. SemiSales was founded in January 2000 on a plan to provide an exchange for semiconductor manufacturers and their suppliers. A key function of the exchange was to prequalify suppliers for the buyers. On paper, the plan looked promising because the industry was so fragmented (over 3,000 existing suppliers to the semiconductor manufacturers and Original Equipment Manufacturers) and the exchange could significantly reduce transaction costs during the prequalification process.

The problem SemiSales faced in July 2000 was that despite having several key charter supplier tenants on the exchange and signing up 30 more paying tenants, buyers were

FIGURE 13.1   Screenshot of MyPoints.com

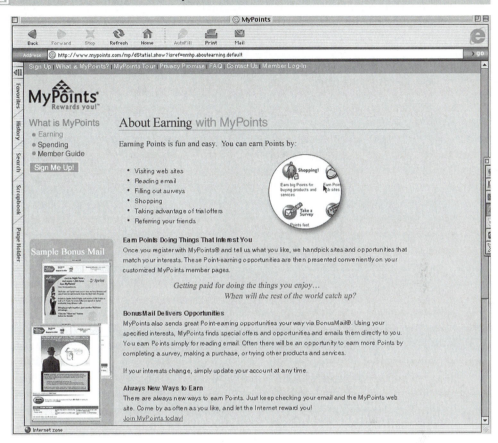

reluctant to use the site. On analysis, SemiSales discovered that approximately 90 percent of the transactions between suppliers and buyers in the semiconductor space are under long-term contracts. Digging a bit deeper, the company realized that many buyers take the relationship that they have with their suppliers very seriously. Many buyers partner with their suppliers and ask them to customize their supplies to give the manufacturer a competitive edge. This becomes part of the intellectual property of the manufacturer, and manufacturers are very sensitive about allowing any third party to intrude on that relationship. Intel, for example, views this as a competitive advantage and does not even want its competitors to know the names of the suppliers it is using. SemiSales realized its mistake too late, and the company was forced to close. The lesson to learn is that existing relationships and business practices play a role in the formation of an on-line exchange.

SemiSales' fatal flaw was in not understanding the purchasing process of one of their key customers—the semiconductor manufacturer. If SemiSales founders had interviewed one or two of the main buyers, mapping out their purchasing process, they would have realized the flaw in its strategy and could have reevaluated its business model sooner.

It is vital to understand your customers, to segment accurately, and to meet the needs of your customers. Exchanges that take these steps flourish, as the Tele Flower Auction example illustrates.

Tele Flower Auction

The Tele Flower Auction (TFA) is an electronic market for trading flowers. The market began when Dutch flower markets began to implement restrictions on imported flowers, excluding imported flowers (because the lower prices of those imports were depressing Holland's domestic flower prices). In response to this exclusion, flower growers from East Africa created the TFA. The TFA succeeded because it provided an effective way for growers to participate in the Dutch flower industry. The TFA included all the necessary support services, and its strict quality controls and efficient distribution of flowers from its warehouses enabled buyers to purchase flowers without seeing them in person.

Reverse Auctions

Reverse auctions are an example of customer power related to pricing. Reverse auctions and information exchange between companies' proprietary information systems are prevalent. Such end-to-end systems include price bidding, procurement, and distribution. In a reverse auction, suppliers bid to supply a specified product or service, with the lowest-price bidder typically getting the business (unlike traditional auctions, in which buyers bid upward on the price they will pay for a product, with the highest bidder typically getting the business). FreeMarkets is an on-line reverse-auction marketplace. When originally founded, FreeMarkets focused on price-based auctions, but since that time it has expanded its services. FreeMarkets services now include multilanguage auctions, multicurrency auctions (bidders see the auction price in their own currencies), net-present-value auctions (auctions that include complex multiyear bid packages), rank-only auctions (bidders only see their rank so that they cannot collude by encoding messages in their numerical price bids), and multi-attribute auctions (where the value of an offer is a complex function of price and other variables).

FreeMarkets not only runs the on-line auction but also prequalifies suppliers and helps clients prepare and send out requests for proposals. Most important, FreeMarkets maintains a depth of expertise in specific areas and uses that knowledge to help its clients. For example, whereas a given company might bid out for metal stampings only a few times each year, FreeMarkets has a dedicated team of professionals who handle 75 auctions for metal stampings each year. This means that FreeMarkets has a better understanding of that (and other) vertical segments than would the purchasing department of a company. Unlike SemiSales, FreeMarkets continues to thrive because it provides such a wide range of services that create an attractive core business proposition for companies.

eBay

eBay originally began as an on-line marketplace where individuals could buy and sell collectibles. eBay provided a price-finding option by auction, letting consumers themselves decide the value of an item by deciding what they were willing to bid on it. Since its founding in 1995, the company has expanded beyond collectibles, into computers, furniture, sporting goods, and even automobiles. eBay creates value by linking small buyers and sellers. The fact that 50 million members are registered at the site proves its success. eBay has now expanded beyond individuals, allowing businesses to set up storefronts on the site. The idea attracted 18,000 businesses, making it one of the largest on-line shopping malls. eBay also implemented a "buy it now" feature that lets people bypass the auction process and simply buy the product for a fixed cost. Companies now use eBay for liquidation of excess inventory. In 2002, eBay facilitated over $15 billion in gross merchandise sales—a 52 percent increase over the previous year. They even sold $2.5 billion dollars worth of used cars!

Distribution

Distribution involves *physical distribution* (transport and storage) and *channels of distribution* (such as wholesalers and retailers). Distribution channels are intermediaries that facilitate getting the product or service to the consumer. The Internet became a new distribution channel, allowing manufacturers to sell their products directly to the end customer rather than selling products through wholesalers and retailers. In the early days of the Internet, pundits predicted the death of intermediaries, believing that manufacturers would use the Internet to reach consumers directly. In fact, this expected disintermediation did not occur. Ironically, the Internet has brought the rise of even more intermediaries. Intermediaries on the Internet are flourishing because they create value in three ways:

Matching buyers and sellers (intermediaries provide data about buyers, data about sellers, and data about products)

Requisitioning (intermediaries provide economies of scale, economies of scope, and time-and-place utility)

Problem solving (providing quality assurance, preserving anonymity, and tailoring goods and services)

Manufacturers that sell direct to the customer must take precautions not to arouse *channel conflict,* that is, taking business away from channel partners such as retailers by making the product available through the Internet at a lower price than the retailer. When Palm decided to sell its personal digital assistants direct to consumers, it charged the same price on-line as in retail channels.

Maytag Avoids Channel Conflict

When Maytag wanted to set up direct on-line sales of Maytag appliances in 1999, its retailers and distributors balked, saying that their businesses would suffer. Maytag put its plans on hold until it devised an e-commerce strategy that would not alienate its channel partners. In January 2001, Maytag launched a Web site that lets customers choose the appliance they want. Customers place their order on-line, and then software automatically transfers the customers to a local retailer's site. Here is how it works: Customers go to the Maytag site, review information about Maytag products, select the product that best meets their needs, and then type in their ZIP code to get pricing and delivery. (The pricing is set by the local dealer, but the experience is seamless for the customer, and the customer does not leave the Maytag Web site.) The retailer then fulfills the order, meaning that Maytag does not need to handle the shipping and fulfillment.

Both manufacturer and retailer win in this scenario: Maytag adds an on-line sales channel without angering retailers, and retailers get new sales (half of on-line orders come during nonbusiness hours) and lower cost per sale (no salesperson is needed, and the average sale is over $1,000).

End-to-End Systems Integration

Digital technologies are enabling tighter integration between companies to promote distribution. Companies are linking their information systems from procurement and planning to inventory and replenishment. These new end-to-end systems are a competitive weapon. Wal-Mart, for example, sees its distribution system as a competitive weapon. Here is how digital technology makes it work: Wal-Mart's Inventory Management System assists in automatically calculating and placing replenishment orders. The Inventory Management System is tied to Wal-Mart's Point-of-Sale (POS) System, which has up-to-the-minute sales scanning data from all Wal-Mart stores and Sam's Clubs. These sales data are complemented by a Perpetual Inventory System, which uses portable handheld terminals that allow store associates to adjust on-hand counts and system parameters for shelf capacities. Finally, Wal-Mart uses a Back Room Receiving System to automatically add newly received merchandise to the store's on-hand counts. The Inventory Management System calculates the selling rate of each item at each store by using the POS data. It also adds changes to weekly and daily selling rate variables to adjust for product seasonality and promotional activity. The inventory system places orders to distribution centers and vendor partners on a daily basis. With access to accurate, up-to-date information, this digital process helps ensure that the right products are on store shelves at the right time.

Introduction to Logistics.com Case

Logistics.com is an example of the new mechanisms for service distribution and innovative pricing opportunities offered by the Internet. Logistics.com is a new company that offers software optimization tools. The case describes how a company can grow and survive in the face of giants entering the E2E space. "Logistics.com, Part A," deals with the issues that faced the company in 2000–2001 and asks you to formulate a growth plan for the company for 2001. "Logistics.com, Part B," is set in September 2001, when it was clear that growth was no longer the issue. Rather, consolidation and increased competition from integrated supply chain providers now dominate the horizon. You are asked to develop a strategy for 2002 given this new environment.

REFERENCES

Anderson, Philip, and Erin Anderson. 2002. "The New E-Commerce Intermediaries." *Sloan Management Review* 43, no. 4: 53–62.

Fein, Adam J., and Sandy Jap. 1999. "Manage Consolidation in the Distribution Channel." *Sloan Management Review* 41, no. 1: 61–72.

Jap, Sandy. 2000. "Going, Going, Gone." *Harvard Business Review* 78, no. 6: 30.

Kambill, Ajit, and Eric van Heck. 2001. *Making Markets.* Boston: Harvard Business School Press.

Narashim, C. 1989. "Incorporation Consumer Price Expectations in Diffusion Models." *Marketing Science* 8, no. 4: 342–57.

CHAPTER 14

Logistics.com

Part A

Introduction

Yossi Sheffi, founder of Logistics.com, knows that the biggest issue facing the company today is how to grow the company. Sheffi feels that his company has a strong base of rigorous appropriate technology, deep industry experience, and good relations with current industry players. He is wondering how to leverage these strengths to expand in one of four directions: expand internationally, expand to cover more modes of freight transportation beyond trucking, expand to cover related business areas such as warehousing and supply chain, or expand to hosting more varied logistics software.

Sheffi, a Professor at the Massachusetts Institute of Technology and director of the Center of Transportation Studies, Sheffi formally founded Logistics.com in 2000, although the core of the company had begun nearly 15 years earlier. As the market for transportation services and logistics software grew during this period, so grew Logistics.com, from a founding team of four to its current size of 180 employees. During 2000, the firm moved from a software sales model to its current application service provider (ASP) model. Through its various incarnations, Logistics.com expanded its market focus from the trucking industry to encompass transportation services and logistics. It has also expanded its products from optimization to shipping management, procurement of transportation services, and yield management. With the growth of both the firm and the field, Logistics.com is poised to become a world-leading firm in this market.

The Market and Opportunity

To understand the products and services of Logistics.com, it is important to understand the nature of the company's customer base and competition. The transportation and shipping industry, which Logistics.com supports, is both large and complex. The transportation and shipping industry is one of the largest industries in the United States, accounting for about one-tenth of the gross domestic product. Analysts estimate the total industry size to be over $3 trillion globally, with the United States accounting for about one-third of this figure.[1] Land-based freight comprises about $600 billion annually in the United States, and trucking in particular accounts for about 80 percent of the land-based freight. In Europe, trucking makes up an even larger percentage of the land-based freight industry. As a company whose products and services can boost the efficiency of this massive industry, Logistics.com enjoys a concomitantly large opportunity.

Participants

Although the shipping and logistics industry features a panoply of players, shippers and carriers are the two primary categories of participants. *Shippers* are those firms that have freight to be moved. This includes nearly every manufacturer or distributor in the supply chain. Examples include Nestlé, General Motors, and Levi Strauss. For shippers, the term "logistics" typically refers to the shipper's operational needs and encompasses shipping, inventory management, and warehousing, or "the management of inventory in motion and rest."[2] Although shippers worry about costs, they need confidence that their freight will arrive on time and in good shape. Logisitics.com supports shippers with software products and services that help shippers develop and execute optimal transportation strategies.

The second category of players is carriers. *Carriers* possess the transportation assets and staff to move the freight of the shippers. Examples include Yellow Transportation and J.B. Hunt. For carriers, "transportation services" refers to the services intended to improve management of carrier resources. Again, although cost is a critical component of any carrier's value proposition, the assurance of properly delivered freight is also critical. The carrier is the last party a shipper sees as products leave the place of business, and the first party the recipient (generally the downstream customer) sees. When one considers the volumes of freight moved in a single truck shipment and its value (hundreds of thousands or even millions of dollars), the need for trust among shippers and carriers is evident. Logistics.com supports carriers with decision support products and services that help carriers better manage their transportation assets to increase utilization and profitability.

In addition to the two primary participants, brokers, software vendors, and third-party logistics providers also participate in the transportation services and logistics space. *Brokers* act as matchmakers between shippers and carriers in the spot market (essentially the one-time engagement market). The shipping industry is highly fragmented with large numbers of shippers and large numbers of carriers. For the numerous small, independent trucking firms (sometimes nothing more than a single owner-operated truck), the broker not only finds freight for them but also guarantees payment.

The intricacies of managing inventory, orders, shipments, routes, trucks, and so on drove both shippers and carriers to create or buy software. Although some companies

---

[1] *Logistics in the Digital Economy: A Comprehensive Overview of Outsourced Logistics,* Credit Suisse First Boston Corporation, September 25, 2000.
[2] *A Review of the Commercial Transportation and Logistics Economy,* A.G. Edwards, March 26, 2001.

created homegrown applications, others have looked to a wide range of software providers for sophisticated applications without the cost of development. *Software vendors* include a range of niche market providers, supply chain software providers, and enterprise software providers. Shippers and carriers use software to handle both the day-to-day operational details and the longer-term optimization and management of logistics. With the rise of the Internet, some software vendors have moved to the ASP model that rents the use of the software over a Web-based connection. Logistics.com is one of these software vendors, offering powerful logistics software through an ASP model.

Despite all the available software, the sheer complexity of (and the associated cost of managing) logistics drives some shippers to outsource this function to a third-party logistics provider (referred to as a 3PL). *Third-party logistics providers* take over some or all of the activities related to inventory management, warehousing, order management, fulfillment, and selection and management of carriers. Rather than simply provide software to assist in logistics management or one-time consulting advice, 3PLs actually perform the services on a day-to-day basis. When run properly, 3PLs offer firms without the resources or interest in developing logistics expertise the option to take advantage of some of the learning, technical advances, and economies of scale and scope of a larger firm.

Growing Opportunity: Transportation Industry

The transportation industry, and the trucking industry in particular, is a relatively mature, cyclical industry. On a macrolevel, industrywide financial performance is largely a function of capacity relative to demand, fuel prices, labor costs, asset costs, and the performance of the economy in general. Despite the industry's maturity, Logistics.com sees an opportunity for effective transportation solutions that is attractive for five reasons.

First, the industry is sufficiently large. In the United States, as a $1 trillion industry, shipping is larger than either health care or defense. Second, applications and/or services that increase efficiency or productivity in mature industries with high fixed costs are particularly valuable. Indeed, the ability to increase efficiency becomes more valuable during difficult economic periods. Thus, the market for Logistics.com's services may be countercyclical. Third, the freight industry is sufficiently complex to benefit greatly from optimization and other efficiency-enhancing services. Fourth, the amount of information available to and recorded by shippers and carriers continues to increase. Technologies such as the Internet, wireless, Global Positioning System (GPS), and others provide richer data to related parties. As the data become more robust, optimization in the freight industry becomes more effective. Finally, despite popular perception, the trucking industry is highly advanced technologically. Many transportation companies have assimilated advanced information technology into their business processes.

Growing Opportunity: Logistics

In recent years, firms began to recognize that effective logistics management was not merely a source of cost containment but a source of competitive advantage as well. For example, firms such as Dell and Wal-Mart dominated their industries through adept management of their entire supply chain and specifically their ability to compete effectively through logistics-intensive strategies. With this evidence, other firms recognized that logistics can be a core competency or source of competitive advantage. The growth of the 3PL industry is indicative of the greater awareness that shippers have for the role of logistics in success. According to a BB&T analyst report, the worldwide 3PL space grew about 19 percent annually since 1996, reaching today's $175 billion. The United States accounts for about 22 percent of this market, or $38.5 billion. Expectations are for 15 to 20 percent annual growth over the next five years. As explanations for this growth, the report cites outsourcing trends, the development of total solution-oriented 3PLs, and growth in the overall transportation and logistics space.[3]

Company Overview

Logistics.com provides both services and software products designed to improve efficiency and reduce costs in a variety of shipping-related and logistics activities. As its Web site suggests, Logistics.com empowers "shippers and transport providers with the technology to buy, sell, manage, and optimize transportation services." Specifically, the products and services optimize freight in a variety of transportation modes (air, land, rail, and trucking for shippers), automate work flow, and provide decision support. On the shipper side, the company's clients include Procter & Gamble, Kraft, Colgate-Palmolive, Ford, and Wal-Mart. Seven of the top 10 trucking firms in the United States use Logistics.com's carrier solutions.

History

Logistics.com began as Princeton Transportation Consulting Group (PTCG) in 1987 when Professor Sheffi and three former graduate students founded the company. The business grew slowly and was purchased outright by Sheffi in 1991. Under Sheffi's ownership, PTCG grew to 60 employees, established itself as a leader in the trucking (carrier) market, and began to leverage its accumulated knowledge for developing new logistics solutions for shippers. In 1996, PTCG's solid reputation led the Sabre Group (a subsidiary of AMR Corp., the parent company of American Airlines) to purchase the company from Sheffi. Despite what appeared to be strong synergies between PTCG and Sabre, Sheffi believed that the company that he had begun nearly 10 years earlier was not prospering under Sabre's ownership. In 2000, with the help of Internet Capital Group, Sheffi bought back his former company and renamed it Logistics.com. Then, in June 2000, Logistics.com acquired Quoteship.com. This acquisition provided Logistics.com with technological expertise as well as logistics experience in air- and water-based freight—modes of transport traditionally outside Logistics.com's realm of expertise. Under Sheffi, the company grew again, reaching 180 employees.

Logistics.com has four lines of business within the transportation procurement space: (1) carrier solutions, (2) shipper solutions, (3) multiattribute transportation auctions, and (4) digital transportation marketplace.

Products: Software Solutions for Carriers and Shippers

Logistics.com offers software products for both shippers and carriers, and each product suite has multiple modules. The following sections discuss Logistics.com's three product suites.

---

[3] *Airfreight/Logistics: Shipper Survey Results,* BB&T Capital Markets Equity Research, April 5, 2001.

OptiManage

OptiManage is a suite of products that helps shippers manage their day-to-day transportation, essentially transforming their myriad orders into actual loads for specific consignees. A press release from Logistics.com describes OptiManage as "a comprehensive transportation management solution that gives shippers unsurpassed control over the transportation resources in their supply chain" and creates "efficiencies into a shipper's transportation management process in the form of reduced transaction times and costs through automation, optimization and integration."[4]

OptiBid

The OptiBid suite simplifies the Request For Proposal/Request For Quote process for transportation services, managing the relationship between carriers and shippers. It helps shippers execute an overall freight/transportation strategy, and it includes the ability to manage exceptions (incidents or needs not covered contractually) on a real-time basis. Transportation procurement is fundamentally different from other types of buying. Economies of scope, or contracting for a variety of routes (rather than scale, or sending several trucks along the same route), are critical to achieving efficiencies for carriers. When negotiating contracts with shippers, carriers strive to create these efficiencies or else to make shippers pay for routes that prevent efficient use of the transportation assets. The optimal bid for any given route or shipment is a function of the carrier's other routes and shipments. As an example, imagine a highly efficient trucking route with three legs that returns to its origin on the last leg. When bidding for a shipping contract, a carrier may need to bid for each leg separately but would prefer to bid on the total combination of legs (each leg is expensive in isolation but inexpensive in combination). Adding more trucks and more routes compounds the interdependencies between routes. Often, carriers submit artificially high bids on particular routes in order to ensure a reasonable overall deal. OptiBid creates transparency in this process by allowing shippers to see the impact various routes have on the total contract value and by encouraging carriers to bid their true price. The result is lower total contract prices for shippers and more efficient use of resources by carriers.

OptiYield

OptiYield is a carrier-oriented suite of products with the overall goal of providing decision support. Logistics.com describes it as a "management and analysis solution for transport providers that helps them maximize profits while solving their most challenging business problems."[5] OptiYield is designed for truckload, less-than-truckload, rail, air, parcel, and ocean transport providers. An example of an application of OptiYield is fuel minimization. For a truck moving across the country, OptiYield draws on a database of real-time fuel prices, including contract fuel prices for the particular carrier. The result is instructions given to the truck driver that may advise refueling in states with more favorable fuel taxes, changing routes on the

---

[4] Logistics.com press release, www.logistics.com/news/pressreleases/pressrelease29.asp, February 1, 2001.
[5] Logistics.com press release, www.logistics.com/news/pressreleases/pressrelease29.asp, February 1, 2001.

basis of proximity to cheaper fuel, or partially filling the tank in anticipation of cheaper fuel availability. Such decision support can save trucking firms 6 to 7 percent on fuel costs, which is significant given the fact that fuel costs make up about 25 percent of total costs. In such a low-margin business, the impact on the bottom line is substantial.

For example, under carrier solutions, Logistics.com offers the MicroMap tool. MicroMap assigns drivers to routes, taking into consideration many factors simultaneously, such as minimizing deadhead miles, bringing drivers home when they request, and so on. This optimization runs in real time to support the day-to-day operations of carriers. Similarly, software tools like OptiYield minimize the cost of fuel by telling drivers where to fill up on the basis of their location (tracked via satellite in the truck cab). This real-time optimization and multiattribute decision support system is being used by over 120 carriers, with 50,000 trucks optimized daily for customers such as Yellow Transportation, J.B. Hunt, RPS, and Daiichi.

Competition for Logistics.com's Software Solutions

Logistics.com's competition varies from product to product. OptiYield is Logistics.com's strongest product suite, derived from the deep domain expertise in both the trucking industry and the optimization field. Logistics.com's software dominates in the transportation services (carrier) segment, serving 7 of the 10 largest trucking firms. This product historically accounted for a large portion of the firm's revenues. In this segment, Logistics.com considers itself the clear market leader.

The company encountered competition as it leveraged its transportation services (carrier) expertise and migrated into the logistics (shipper) segment. For the shipper-oriented packages (OptiManage and OptiBid), competition comes from other supply chain management software and more general purpose optimization packages, such as i2 and Manugistics. Despite this competition, Sheffi expects OptiBid to account for a large portion of the firm's revenue by the end of 2001 and for OptiManage to be the firm's biggest revenue generator by 2003.

A recent Morgan Stanley report analyzing carrier-bidding processes describes the competition to the OptiBid suite. Among the competition are other software providers, industry/bidding experts, outsourced solutions from 3PLs, and the shipper's own internal logistics-related departments. Each of the software providers (i2 and FreeMarkets) has moved into the carrier-bidding segment from different vantage points. FreeMarkets began in the business-to-business reverse-auction space and extended its depth to other markets, such as carrier procurement. In contrast, i2 offers general supply chain management and optimization software, and it created a product specifically for the carrier-bidding process. In the Morgan Stanley report, OptiBid was rated more highly on seven of eight criteria than the other software providers, and it was rated more highly than all competition (excluding internal processes) on six of eight criteria.[6] Thus far, deep domain knowledge appears to be more advantageous than breadth.

---

[6] *Week 14: Trucking Snapshot,* Morgan Stanley Dean Witter, April 4, 2001.

Internet-Based Transportation Exchanges: Dream versus Reality

As Internet adoption rose in the late 1990s, nearly every industry seemed poised for a revolution through this disruptive technology.[7] Transportation was no exception. In fact, transportation seemed an ideal candidate for such transformation. The intuition was that freight carriers should never have less than a full load. Surely, the Internet could help connect the hundreds of thousands of carrier trucks to the millions of shipments created by the shippers, and deadheading (returning with an empty truck after a delivery) would be a relic of the past. No freight-carrying vehicle would ever move with a partial load. The Internet would help shippers get a good deal on every shipment, and carriers would see asset utilization climb to unheard-of levels. By some estimates, as many as 19 percent of the trucks on the roads are less than full (Sheffi believes the figure may be as high as 30 percent). The resulting inefficiency creates an annual $30 billion loss for U.S. firms.[8] Cyberspace would help consolidate and streamline the entire transportation sector.

In theory, Internet-based exchanges or marketplaces would drive transportation industry consolidation by allowing shippers and carriers to bid in a reverse-auction format for particular freight and routes. Shippers would enjoy better prices, cost-competitive carriers would enjoy more business, and the exchange provider would thrive on the flow of nominal transaction fees. Moreover, exchanges would offer additional services, such as work flow automation, creating value for both parties.

Despite what appears to be a huge opportunity and a good use of business-to-business exchange technology, few if any of the firms came close to realizing the efficiencies promised. Indeed, many have shut down, while those that have survived often made dramatic changes in their business models. FreightWise, a reverse-auction exchange for trucking and rail freight, shut down in February 2001 despite strong venture backing. Originally founded as a venture out of Burlington Northern Santa Fe Railway Corporation, FreightWise also received an investment from General Electric.[9] Nonetheless, industry knowledge from the parent firm and backing from one of the world's most respected companies was not enough.

Reality: Role of Relationships and Trust

What explains this failure? First, the exchange model assumes that the products or services being auctioned are commodities. Under this assumption, the services of different carriers are interchangeable so that price is the only differentiating attribute. Yet Sheffi contends that trust is a major factor in the shipping decision, making a single-attribute auction unattractive for all but a few shippers. Farid Daibachi, chief executive

---

[7] While Logistics.com operates a private exchange, it is a very small part of its business. This section is provided for general discussion purposes.

[8] Computerworld.com, "Online Exchange Helps Trim Shipping Costs," www.computerworld.com/cwi/story/0,1199,NAV47_STO55263,00.html.

[9] e-businessworld.com, "Transportation Exchange FreightWise Closes," www.e-businessworld.com/english/crd_ebiz_415907.html.

officer of a transportation software provider, confirms that "the mistake most companies made was treating transportation as a commodity."[10] Second, the freight market (among others) can be divided into two categories: spot markets and contract markets. Spot markets cover single or one-time purchases, while contract markets cover long-term relationships. The spot market, which is more appropriate for exchanges, accounts for only 10 to 15 percent of the total trucking market. Confirming this notion, Gregg Runyan of the Yankee Group suggested that "in the logistics space, marketplaces that are pure intermediaries [those that bring buyers and sellers together] have had a tough go of it" because of this lack of contract transactions.[11] Sheffi agreed, noting that big shippers and carriers rarely operate in the spot market. Third, the counterargument that even the spot market is large enough to support exchanges fails to consider the composition of the spot market. The spot market is often composed of small firms and independents, making it difficult for the exchange to create a critical mass of participants. Worse, shippers enter this market looking for low prices, and carriers enter it looking for high prices. This mismatch of expectations means that Internet-based exchanges have a difficult time creating matches. Finally, exchanges failed to realize that they must also provide payment guarantee if they were to compete with the large freight brokers that have traditionally served the function of matching shippers and carriers.

Reality: Simple Technology Solution versus Complex Industry-Specific Problem

The real reason for the failure of so many transportation auction sites is that many of them put forward a simplistic technological solution without a true understanding of the complexities of transportation procurement. In traditional single-attribute auctions, carriers had to bid for each traffic lane separately, submitting lane rates per mile or per move. Shippers then picked the low bid for each lane or move. But this "low bid" outcome was not optimized for the potential efficiencies for round-trip combinations of routes.

In reality, the interdependencies among routes make auctions for transportation much more complicated. Carriers can minimize their costs (and reduce their bid price) only when they can assemble a network of interconnected routes that maximize asset utilization (filling as many trucks for as many miles as possible). Bidding on individual routes forces the carrier to bid high, meaning that simplistic route-by-route auctions lead to unfavorable prices for the shipper. Yet the most efficient package of routes varies between carriers, depending on each carrier's existing contracts, base of operations, and asset composition. For the shipper that is trying to hold the auction, the bids packages can become a complex mess of overlapping, disjointed sets of routes.

---

[10] redherring.com, "Web-Based Logistics Can't Sell Space," www.redherring.com/index.asp?layout=story_generic&doc_id=RH550018055.
[11] e-businessworld.com, "Transportation Exchange FreightWise Closes," www.e-businessworld.com/english/crd_ebiz_415907.html.

Better Solution: Combinatorial, Multiattribute Auction Technology

Logistics.com created more sophisticated auction software and services that help both the carrier and the shipper deal with two realities of the transportation space. First, the tools support the reality that multiple attributes, beyond just price, affect the desirability of a carrier's bid and influence a shipper's decisions. For example, shippers can specify attributes such as having 15 percent of their business go to minority-owned carriers, having no more than five carriers but no less than three, and so on. The software calculates the "what if" costs that shippers will incur under these different scenarios. Multiple attributes cover more than just the needs of shippers. Carriers can submit their capacity constraints so that the software can take those constraints into account (e.g., a carrier could submit bids for East Coast routes and for West Coast routes but not have the capacity to service both sets of routes).

Second, the tools support the combinatorial reality of how cost (and thus bid price) must vary as a function of different combinations of routes. Logistics.com supports conditional bidding, which lets carriers bid one price for a single route and a different price if that route is combined with another route. Thus, carriers can submit multiple overlapping bids with different combinations (thus bidding for efficient route combinations that have round-trips, have closed tours, or mesh well with that carrier's other routes). As a result, the auction might receive tens of millions of bids. Logistics.com's tools help carriers construct sensible bid packages that conditionally price routes for efficiency. The tools automate the evaluation of large numbers of bid packages to find a combination of bids that covers all the routes, minimizes total cost, satisfies other constraints, and optimizes other attributes.

The result is that combinatorial, multiattribute auctions achieve economies of scope and density for the benefit of both carriers and shippers. Combinatorial bidding removes the need for carriers to hedge prices to cover worst-case inefficiencies (i.e., bidding high in case they do not win the bid for the back-haul route). With this type of auction, carriers can set prices on the basis of the efficiency of the routes, giving discounts on the basis of economies of scope and density. Logistics.com handles auctions for transportation by giving carriers free access to software that lets them optimize their routes. Shippers benefit by getting lower prices.

In the multiattribute transportation auctions space, Logistics.com offers QuickBid, which is an Internet-based bidding auction for service contracts. The tool has been live since 1997 and has handled over $5 billion in transportation service contracts for shippers like Wal-Mart, Nestlé, Colgate-Palmolive, and Lucent Technologies.

Expansion Issues

Since early 2000, Logisitics.com has been shifting and expanding its market focus. From its roots as PTCG, the firm has used its knowledge of the trucking industry to establish market-leading software. It then leveraged this knowledge to develop software to manage the relationships between carriers and shippers and to develop logistics solutions for shippers. But the company desires further growth.

Sheffi identified four potential areas for expansion: (1) international expansion, (2) carrier solutions for additional modes of transportation other than trucking, (3) horizontal integration into other areas of supply chain management, and

(4) hosting an increased range of logistics solutions. To some degree, the company has moved in each of these directions, although the firm's deepest knowledge and strongest product offerings are still based in the trucking industry.

Option 1: International Expansion

Logistics.com could leverage its relationships with large multinational customers and perform transportation services procurement and management across borders and overseas. The firm already performs worldwide procurement for some of its clients, but it is not yet managing overseas operations with its applications. For carriers, the firm would apply its deep industry expertise in the U.S. trucking industry to other international areas (it already has trucking clients in Europe and Japan). Europe accounts for about 28 percent of the $3 trillion logistics and transportation market, while Asia accounts for about 18 percent.[12] In Europe, trucking accounts for an even larger percentage of the total freight business than in the United States. Moreover, the move to a European Union and the Euro should create increasing opportunities for providers of transportation services on the Continent. However, Logistics.com fears that its current relationships with major industry players may not have the same value abroad.

Option 2: New Modes of Transportation

While the company's shipper solutions serve its customers across all modes of transportation, Logistics.com currently provides carrier decision support systems for only the trucking industry and a few rail clients. In the future, the firm could apply its optimization and general transportation expertise to develop new carrier solutions for air freight and ocean carriers. Expanding to cover all modes for both shippers and carriers meets the company's long-term goal of creating a set of automated processes between shippers and carriers. If Logistics.com is to reach this goal, it must get "inside" other modes of transportation.

Option 3: Horizontal Integration

Currently, Logistics.com operates in the vertical market of shipping and transportation. But the company could expand horizontally to cover associated markets for software and services in supply chain management. The potential markets in this horizontal expansion include more general purpose supply management applications and services and expanding the existing applications further into existing distribution networks. To this end, Logistics.com recently partnered with J.D. Edwards (provider of enterprise resource planning [ERP] software) to bring transportation procurement and management capabilities and direct on-line connectivity to thousands of transportation-focused trading partners.[13] Rather than simply help existing clients optimize their freight and shipping operations, Logistics.com might provide applications to support warehouse management. Or Logistics.com might leverage its multiattribute, combinatorial auction

---

[12] *Logistics in the Digital Economy: A Comprehensive Overview of Outsourced Logistics,* Credit Suisse First Boston Corporation, September 25, 2000.
[13] "Logistics.com and J.D. Edwards Announce Strategic Alliance to Provide Global Transportation Procurement and Management Solutions," www.logistics.com/news/pressreleases/pressrelease31.asp, February 6, 2001.

technology for the procurement of a wide range of goods and services, not just for transportation-related ones.

While the opportunity is big, the competition is certainly more intense. Entrenched supply chain software vendors such as i2 and Manugistics already provide sophisticated general purpose optimization technology, and competitors with deep market knowledge exist in nearly every specialized sector (e.g., warehouse management). ERP vendors (e.g., SAP, Oracle, and J.D. Edwards) also lay claim to large tracts of the market for software in this space. In services, Logistics.com might encounter giants like United Parcel Service (UPS), which is moving beyond transactional package delivery to more diverse logistics and supply chain services. Although UPS may not have the depth of expertise in traditional trucking, it does have a massive asset base and a $1 billion new ventures fund.

Option 4: Hosting Logistics Solutions

Logistics.com currently operates as an ASP. By hosting the application, Logistics.com makes it easier for customers to tightly integrate their software with other logistics and supply chain management packages despite complex or old legacy systems. Tight integration makes the product more valuable for Logistics.com's clients. To meet its expansion goals, the company is considering hosting entire outsourced logistics solutions. In other words, Logistics.com would host other firms' software, such as warehouse management, in addition to its own. Essentially, customer companies could outsource their entire information technology function related to logistics management to Logistics.com. This would allow Logistics.com to move closer to the 3PL market without actually providing decision personnel or transportation services. To this end, Logistics.com is also considering providing a complete outsourcing of trucking ERP solutions, including all back-office functions. Moving into the broader enterprise-to-enterprise space will bring Logistics.com into competition with entrenched enterprise software firms (e.g., Oracle and IBM) as well as information technology services firms (e.g., EDS and Accenture). Although these potential competitors lack deep experience in transportation, they excel in general enterprise software and outsourced information technology services, respectively.

QUESTIONS

1. Given the particular expertise of Logistics.com, competition, opportunities for the logistics field, and any specific knowledge you may have, provide a recommendation for a specific area of expansion for Logistics.com.
2. Do you think there is any value in Web-based exchanges in this field? Despite some well-documented missteps from some of the early entrants, is there a sufficiently large opportunity for someone who understands the freight industry?
3. Operating as an ASP gives Logistics.com many advantages, including simpler integration, greater reliability, and the ability to make consistent upgrades to its customers' software. Still, many firms prefer to own their software, citing security and control issues. How can Logistics.com resolve these issues? Should it also offer its products as traditional software?
4. What new alternatives should be considered for growth, and what do you recommend for a growth strategy?

Part B

Current Situation

In September 2001, Logistics.com was sold to Internet Capital Group and Sheffi retired from his position as chairman.

The 300 percent growth projection that the company had forecasted never materialized. The company grew 50 percent from 2000 to 2001 and hired aggressively in anticipation of higher growth. When the economic downturn came, Logistics.com was forced to trim the workforce by one-third, down to 120 people. Logistics.com's current goal is to be cash positive by early 2003, and company management feels that the company has a good chance of achieving this goal.

Logistics Software Market

The logistics software market is part of the larger supply chain management market (SCM). The SCM solutions market is predicted to increase 41 percent annually from $6.9 billion in 2000 to $39 billion in 2005, according to IDC. Of this market, the logistics software market was $1.1 billion in 2000, and research firm AMR predicts that the market will grow slightly slower than the overall SCM market at 36 percent per annum, reaching $5.1 billion in 2005.

Merrill Lynch divides the logistics market into six main segments: transportation management systems, warehouse management systems, logistics optimization software, visibility software, connectivity and messaging services, and international trade logistics software. The market for these segments is described in table 14.1.

TABLE 14.1   E-Logistics Total Revenue Forecast by Application Revenue, 2000–2005 ($ millions)

Segment	2000	2001	2002	2003	2004	2005	Compound Annual Growth Rate
Transportation management systems	150	203	273	383	536	750	38%
Warehouse management systems	339	424	594	831	1,164	1,629	37%
Logistics optimization software	52	70	98	138	193	270	39%
Visibility software	200	310	450	600	740	850	34%
Connectivity and messaging services	215	280	363	491	662	894	33%
International trade logistics software	140	203	294	412	556	723	39%
Total	1,096	1,489	2,073	2,854	3,851	5,116	36%

Note: Figures include license and maintenance revenues only.

Source: AMR Research (2000), ARC Advisory Group (2000), Forrester Research (November 2000), and Merrill Lynch & Co.

Successes and Failures of Logistics.com

Despite the 300 percent expected growth, Logistics.com faced a much slower adoption of the ASP software delivery model in the market. While the ASP model has worked well for analysis and planning software applications, when it comes to software that helps companies run their everyday business, two main barriers seem to slow down adoption. First, big corporations are not prepared to have mission-critical information leave their firewalls and in some way be out of their control. Second, and more recently, there is pressure created by the possibility that some software providers might not be able to survive the current crisis.

However, Logistics.com has meanwhile established its position in the physical transportation management area and has established working relationships with several Fortune 500 companies.

Changing Competitive Environment

Now that many corporations have successfully implemented ERP and SCM software systems, they are looking for new areas to optimize. E-logistics provides the new opportunity. Merrill Lynch believes that the first companies to use e-logistics will be companies from the high-tech, telecommunications equipment, consumer electronics, and retail industries. As demand grows, competition in the e-logistics space will increase. The growing market size will attract larger software providers that previously saw the SCM market as too small to enter. These larger competitors include SCM players such as Manugistics and i2 as well as logistics pure-play firms such as Descartes. Furthermore, the large ERP powerhouses like SAP and PeopleSoft are unlikely to stay on the sidelines and can easily integrate SCM functionality into their product offerings. Finally, 3PLs like UPS and FedEx are already offering outsourced logistics solutions. They can provide their own software as part of their outsourced service offering, thereby cutting into the software market. Prudential Financial forecasts that "as larger companies continue to broaden their product depth and deepen their module functionality, niche providers may have difficulty remaining viable." Smaller niche players may be overwhelmed or acquired by larger competitors.

Besides the threat from larger competitors, logistics pure-play competitor Descartes is offering a new business model in the market. Rather than the traditional license revenue model or the newer ASP model (which Logistics.com offers), Descartes has created the Global Logistics Network to facilitate collaborative, Internet-based commerce between the providers (carriers) and users (shippers) of logistics services. By using an Internet-based architecture, participants can join the network at a low cost. Because the cost of participation is negligible, Descartes has been able to get carrier participation. Network services revenue consists of transaction and subscription revenue generated when customers utilize applications and services over the Global Logistics Network. Salomon Smith Barney believes that the Global Logistics Network is currently the largest logistics network with over $20 million in pure network revenue and significantly improved gross margins over the license-revenue model.

A Trend Toward Consolidation

The market for SCM solutions is still very fragmented. For some companies, supply chain decisions are made everyday based on more or less sophisticated manual calculations or spreadsheet models. Some prefer to use solutions provided by large software providers such as i2 or Manugistics while others opt by smaller local software houses. More recently, SAP and other ERP software providers started to offer SCM solutions, which might not be as sophisticated as the products developed by other specialist companies, but offer the advantage of integrating easily with other parts of the company.

Software solutions like warehouse management and transportation management are fairly developed at this point, but software that is able to handle international transportation as an end-to-end tool is still far from being a reality. This leaves open big opportunities for market development.

The economic downturn, together with a slower-than-expected adoption of technologies such as those developed by Logistics.com and its competitors, has left several companies struggling in this space. On the other hand, a few bigger players see these companies as an opportunity to naturally expand their businesses. Established SCM software companies such as Manhattan Associates could expand from the warehouse management to transportation or logistics optimization, while ERP software providers could add functionality to their enterprise software offer. In the build-versus-buy trade-off, companies such as PeopleSoft and J.D. Edwards are traditionally seen in the market more as possible buyers, while SAP is seen more as a builder of its own solution.

This consolidation trend would also open the opportunity for a smaller company to roll up some of its competitors or for a group of small companies to merge. However, not many investors seem to be willing to start such a risky endeavor against more established competitors.

The biggest issue facing Logistics.com today is survival. Given the increased competitive environment and the worsening economy, Logistics.com needs to find a way to become cash positive by mid-2002.

QUESTIONS

1. Given the particular expertise of Logistics.com, the competition, the opportunities for the logistics field, and any specific knowledge you may have, provide a recommendation for a strategy for Logistics.com in this difficult market.
2. How (if at all) should Logistics.com react to the new "network" business model being offered successfully by competitor Descartes?
3. In your opinion, can Logistics.com survive in the logistics software space given the increased interest in this segment by larger software systems companies and 3PLs? What alternatives do you see for Logistics.com?

CHAPTER

15

Build a Trusting Relationship with Customers

Introduction

After understanding customer needs, designing a marketing strategy, and implementing the strategy, the final step is building an enduring relationship with customers based on trust. If you have implemented a trust-based marketing strategy, the step toward building a trusting relationship with customers will be natural. If you have followed a push-based strategy, a trusting relationship will be difficult to build because push-based strategies create a more adversarial relationship, forcing companies to resell the value proposition based on price each time.

Trust Is a Process

Trust is a process. Issues such as fulfillment of the core value proposition are critical. To build a trusting relationship with customers does not require perfection, but it does require honesty. For example, if your company makes a mistake on quality or service, the action to take is to admit the mistake and explain to the customer what you are doing to fix the problem. Trying to cover up the problem will breed distrust.

The issue of trust and of creating trust is distinctly different between the two main phases of the customer-company relationship: the initial acquisition of a new customer and the long-term retention of an existing customer. Creating trust that creates new customers is all about creating expectations that resonate with the potential customer. Branding, brochureware, and trusted advisor systems tell prospective customers what they are going to get and why it is right for them. If what the company promises meshes with what the customer wants, then the customer will more seriously consider the products and services of that company.

But prospective customers (who by definition have no direct experience with the company) will also want some assurance that the company will deliver on its promises. Guarantees, product return policies, and legal contracts all help the company ensure that some level of satisfaction (or redress) is guaranteed to the customer. Third-party ratings, trade magazine articles on the company, product reviews, and customer testimonials provide semi-independent evidence that the company will deliver on its promises. If the

157

prospective customer is satisfied with the promised features and is satisfied that the company will meet expectations, then the prospect will become a customer.

By contrast, customer retention implies following through on all the expectations that the company created during customer acquisition. Creating and sustaining trust in existing customers requires competent fulfillment and good customer service if things go wrong. It also requires having good products and services. After the sale, branding messages mean little except as a reminder of the expectations that the company created. Loyal customers are less concerned with third-party ratings or the testimonials of others and more concerned with the company's fulfillment of its promises. After the sale, the customer's direct experience with the company supplants indirect experience as a major source of trust building.

The Web plays a major role in customer acquisition, but it also plays a role in customer retention. On-line tools that help customers track their orders, manage their accounts, and get after-sale support are all part of the Web's role in creating trust and customer retention. The Web can help customers get the most out of their purchases. Customers who have bought a bread maker can go to the company's Web site for recipes for the bread maker. Customers who have bought a PC can go the company's Web site for the latest software upgrades for that PC. Customers managing financial accounts can be e-mailed investment alerts.

The Web presents an extraordinary opportunity to connect with new and existing customers. Done well, a Web site deepens a company's relationship with the customer. Consider the example of Dell Computer Corp., which uses the Web to strengthen its relationship with customers.

Dell Computer Corp.

Dell Computer Corp. has created customized Web pages for its customers through its Premier Dell.com service. Each organization that uses Premier Dell.com sees a custom-configured Web site with features, products, and prices that are tailored specifically to that organization. For example, the page shows only those computers that match the information technology compatibility needs of that particular company. Each company also sees the list of prices that the company has negotiated with Dell. Premier Dell.com also includes tools to help its customers manage purchase approvals, purchase orders, invoices, and payments. The customized pages give customers a strong reason to buy more exclusively from Dell. Dell then further deepens the relationship by offering exclusive on-line tools, such as asset management and technical support tools, that again are customized to each organization.

Customer Relationship Management

Creating profitable, loyal customers is the ultimate goal of customer relationship management (CRM). CRM is a business strategy that provides a company with a complete view of its customer base. Technology supports the strategy: A CRM system brings together many of the pieces of information about customers, sales, market trends, marketing effectiveness, and responsiveness. CRM helps companies improve the profitability of their interactions with customers while making those interactions appear friendlier through individualization. Companies use CRM tools to help in continuing communication with their customers. For more information on CRM, see the MarketSoft Corporation case (chapter 10) and its appendix on Siebel and the OSRAM Sylvania case (chapter 12), which details OSRAM's implementation of SAP's CRM system.

Cross Sell and Grow the Relationship

Customer Loyalty

One of the biggest benefits of trusting relationships is loyalty. Customers who trust a company stay loyal to that company. Tesco, now the largest supermarket chain in the United Kingdom, provides a valuable model of a company that built a trusting relationship with customers and then expanded that relationship beyond grocery stores.

In its early days, Tesco was known as the low-price grocery store. "Pile it high and sell it cheap" was the chain's motto. But Tesco realized that low cost alone was not a sustainable strategy. Tesco had little idea whether its customers were young or old, rich or poor, or how far they drove to get to a Tesco store. In order to learn more about its customers and what they truly want, Tesco created a loyalty card program. The program, called ClubCard, gives customers coupons and discounts in exchange for providing demographic information about themselves. Members receive a ClubCard, which they present with each purchase. The ClubCard entitles them to discounts, and in turn the card links each customer's purchase with his or her demographic information, giving Tesco insight into the buying patterns and preferences of its customers. Since the launch of the program in 1995, 10 million people (one out of every three households in the United Kingdom) have joined the program. With the in-depth knowledge about its customers the program brings Tesco, Tesco can offer a host of new products and services to its customers. Indeed, Tesco has expanded to providing savings accounts, banking services, credit card services, gas station services, and new categories in its stores (such as books, CDs, and even clothing).

Tesco's results have been impressive. Tesco has outpaced its major competitors on sales growth and has achieved more than double the profit before tax and double the customer satisfaction of its closest competitor.

MarketSoft.com

MarketSoft has created a new "cross-sell" product. It uses the same software engine as its lead management product (see the Marketsoft case in Chapter 10). It uses CRM data in a way that generates profits by allowing line marketing managers to easily enter their own promotion rules. For example, if a marketing manager knows that you recently had a child and have a $25,000 balance in your savings account, the manager will direct a wealth management planner to call you and explain the advantages of a Roth IRA and other college saving instruments and include a special incentive of no-service charge on the IRA set up. The marketing manager can also coordinate a series of information mailings on college planning and insurance in case of death. If you call the company for service, the CRM system can flash a message to the service representative to ask how you are feeling about college savings for your new child. Such an easy-to-use system leverages line marketing managers and is being successfully used at firms such as Fidelity to design implement and evaluate cross-sell and up-sell opportunities.

Constant Innovation

Deep customer relationships also require constant innovation, responding to customers' changing needs and moving with the customer in directions the customer wants to go. As we saw in chapter 9, this involves understanding the product life cycle, extending the product line, and rejuvenating products. The following GE Aircraft example shows how GE Aircraft expanded its offering from engine and engine parts to engine services. The example shows GE's willingness to innovate and create service bundles that meet customers' specific needs. The example also shows how GE further deepens its relationships with customers by offering them free consulting services. Many of GE Aircraft's customers were hard hit by the events of September 11, 2001. By sharing its Six Sigma knowledge with customers, GE helps their customers lower their internal costs and stay in business.

Example: GE Aircraft Engines

GE Aircraft Engines is an $11.4 billion division of $126 billion dollar giant General Electric Company. In 1996, the revenue contribution of services to the GE Aircraft division was $1 billion. In 2001, it was $5 billion, indicating the growing importance of services to GE. GE's business model is no longer to simply sell an engine at a low price and then sell 30 years' worth of spare parts for the engine at inflated prices. Rather, GE is partnering with its customers to reduce their total cost of ownership of the engine, maximizing engine performance and uptime at minimum cost.

GE's philosophy is to meet customer needs by tailoring different solutions to different customer needs. For example, some companies want to overhaul aircraft engines themselves, while others want to outsource the service. GE therefore offers a range of products and services that will meet these different needs. For example, GE sells new parts, renewed parts, and spare parts individually or in kits that assemble all the parts needed for an engine overhaul. This service offering is called "Material by the Hour," in which the customer (such as Northwest Airlines) does its own maintenance but buys all the needed parts for a fixed price from GE. For customers that do not want to do their own maintenance, such as Southwest Airlines, GE offers "Power by the Hour," in which Southwest pays GE a fixed fee each time it runs an engine. In return, GE performs all the maintenance and guarantees the reliability of the engine. In both cases, GE's goal is to provide customers with a lower cost of owning the GE aircraft engine.

The GE example shows GE's willingness to innovate and create service bundles that meet customers' specific needs. Furthermore, GE recently started a new program that shows its willingness to go even further to build a trusting relationship with its customers. The program, called "At the Customer, For the Customer," involves GE's sending some of its own staff to a company to provide consulting services to the company. The program centers on the Six Sigma quality and process improvement initiative, which GE has been practicing internally for seven years. In the program, GE employees are trained in quality processes and eliminating variation out of processes. The company has trained leaders ("blackbelts") who pursue improvement programs within GE. Because of the success that GE was having with

Six Sigma programs within its own company, GE decided to offer the programs free of charge to its top customers. In the program, GE sends a blackbelt to the customer site. The blackbelt works with a team of the customer's employees on a project designed to improve the customer's processes. The program does not even have to relate to GE in any way—the goal is mainly to transfer best practices and help GE customers remain profitable. Example blackbelt projects include an investigation into why items get held up in customs (which delays the repair of engines) or exhaust gas analysis to improve engine performance. Other projects focus on billing or finance or warehouse management. GE's "At the Customer, For the Customer" is designed to help GE's customers by sharing GE knowledge and experience with them, strengthening the relationship and building a trusting relationship with customers.

> **The First Tech Credit Union Story**
> Credit unions are one of the most trusted financial institutions. In the United States, 80 million people are members of credit unions and regularly deposit their salary with credit unions. They go to credit unions for financial services such as auto loans. First Tech is the credit union for Microsoft, Intel, and many other companies. First Tech is viewed as a leader in the industry. It uses on-line trusted advisors to help widen its service to customers in adjacent financial products like mortgages, IRAs, and equities. For example, the advisors on the First Tech Web site help members "select the perfect mortgage" with a system that allows the selection of attributes and information about each feature (see figure 15.1). This system has received rave reviews from customers (92 percent would recommend the advisor to a friend) and has increased the mortgage volume by 60 percent. The same site supports loan officers, branch representatives, and teleresponse personnel to give a coherent trust face to customers. First Tech is now expanding the advisor to all loans, credit card, deposits, and wealth management. Digital technology helps First Tech leverage its staff and supply the customer with information and education. With digital technology, First Tech can grow from being a credit union to providing a broad range of financial management services that can compete with large banks based on trust and enduring customer relationships.

Introduction to Travelocity Case

The Travelocity case discusses Travelocity's strategic options in creating a loyalty program for frequent buyers of travel services. Travelocity uses the loyalty program to differentiate itself from the competition. The loyalty program also provider Travelocity with valuable data that help it identify new areas of innovation that its customers would value.

FIGURE 15.1 Screenshots from 1sttech.com

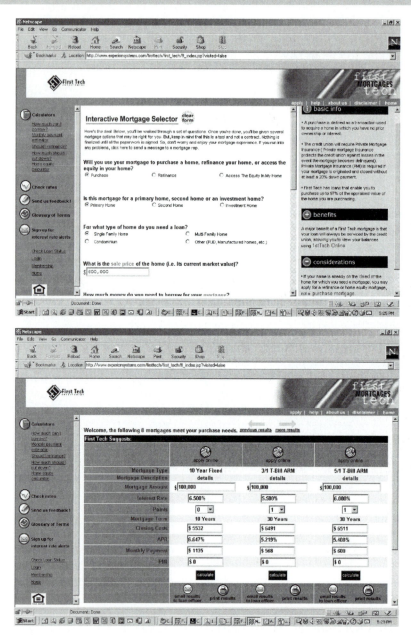

REFERENCES

Reichheld, Frederick. 1996. *The Loyalty Effect.* Boston: Harvard Business School Press.

Urban, Glen L., Fareena Sultan, and William Qualls. 2000. "Placing Trust at the Center of Your Internet Strategy." *MIT Sloan Management Review* 42, no. 1: 39–48.

Zikmund, William G. 2003. *Customer Relationship Management: Integrating Marketing Strategy and Information Technology.* New York: Wiley.

CHAPTER

Travelocity

Introduction

Online pioneer Travelocity is facing new competitive pressures. Travelocity is one of the leading providers of travel services on the Internet, particularly for leisure and small-business travelers. Travelocity.com provides customers with one-stop travel shopping and reservation services, including real-time access to schedule, pricing, and availability information for over 500 airlines, 13,000 hotels, and all major rental car companies. In addition, Travelocity offers vacation packages, promotional fares, travel news, and destination information.

In early 2002, Travelocity faced increased competition from new entrants (such as Orbitz.com) and more aggressive on-line activities from the airlines themselves. To respond to this competition, Travelocity is considering launching a loyalty program. Mike Stacy, vice president of marketing, believes that a loyalty program can help respond to competitive pressures, but he faces a number of questions. How should the loyalty program be structured? What loyalty programs have worked in other industries? Will Travelocity's program generate enough repeat purchases among its customers to keep Travelocity profitable?

Travel Industry Background[1]

Travel agents fill the value-added role of providing information to the traveling public and connecting consumers with the myriad of travel suppliers (e.g., airlines, cruise lines, hotels, rental cars, and tour operators). Traditional agencies also provide a physical location for handling paperwork and a personal point of contact for travelers. Travel agents work with travelers to help them learn about destinations and to decipher the timetables, fare structures, and the "fine print" of travel offers. Using specialized computer terminals and proprietary applications, travel agents tap into electronic global distribution

---

[1] Bear Stearns Travel Industry Report, April 2000.

systems (GDSs), such as SABRE, Apollo Galileo, and Worldspan. These systems let the travel agent search for flights, compute fares, check availability, and make reservations.

Thus, travel agents are a crucial distribution channel for travel suppliers because they create a point of presence for suppliers. Distribution (in the form of ticketing, sales, and promotions) accounts for 20 percent of an airline's operating costs. Because no supplier could afford to have its own direct-sales outlet in every town, suppliers willingly enlisted the aid of travel agents. For many years, travel agents were a major distribution channel. Suppliers actively marketed themselves to travel agents to enlist the agent's help in influencing the end consumer. In return for these services, suppliers paid commissions to the agent.

The Rise of On-Line Travel Agents

Travelocity.com and other on-line travel sites shook the travel industry by giving customers significantly more choice and more power in making their travel plans. Consumers could now easily do their own searches, create their own travel itineraries, and book their own flights from the comfort of their homes. On-line travel agents benefited from a confluence of trends, including the following:

- The rise of a computer- and travel-literate populace
- The advent of low-cost public Internet access that can perform the same function as the proprietary connections used by travel agents
- Airline adoption of paperless ticketing systems and the widespread penetration of credit cards

The result is that on-line travel is a substantive and growing business. Consumers now spend more than $1 billion per month at travel sites—one-third of all money spent on-line, according to Nielsen/Net ratings. And an increasing number of customers use the Internet to make their travel plans. Currently, 75 percent of American households have used the Internet to research travel, but only 20 percent of those researchers have actually purchased travel on-line. Analysts expect the number of on-line travel buyers to triple between 1998 and 2003, reaching almost 72 million. What's more, customers want to buy travel on-line more than any other product. The research firm Forrester estimates that 18.9 million households will spend $16.7 billion in 2001 on leisure travel, compared with 14.9 million households that spent $12.3 billion in 2000.

Travel Agents Face Shifting Conditions

The shift to on-line booking has changed the power structure of the travel industry. In the past, travel agents enjoyed a 10 percent commission on ticket sales. Now the Internet lets customers book tickets on-line directly. As a result, suppliers (airlines) can reduce their costs significantly (reducing the costs of call centers, travel agent commissions, and costs from handling paper tickets). Airlines have started disintermediating travel agents by reducing or eliminating the commissions that they are willing to pay agents (cutting the commission to 5 percent and lowering the cap of the commission to $20 in some cases and reducing the commission to zero in others).[2] While airlines were initially fearful that cutting commissions would anger

---

[2] Christopher Calnan, "Travel Agents Finding Economic Trip Bumpy," *Florida Times Union,* January 14, 2002.

agents, airlines have since realized that they can cut commissions with impunity. The shift to on-line booking and reductions in commissions have decimated the ranks of traditional travel agents. In the first half of 1999, nearly 1,800 traditional travel agencies (out of 25,000 in North America) went out of business. The American Society of Travel Agents reports that 8 percent of its members are closing their agencies and that another 18 percent are selling the business or merging with another agency.[3]

Consumer travel bookings on-line would be impossible without GDSs. Currently, GDSs account for 70 percent of all airline tickets booked (down from 80 percent a few years ago).[4] GDSs compile data for airlines, hotels, car rental companies, and cruise lines. On-line sites and travel agencies use GDSs (for a fee) to access information and book tickets. As commission prices are driven down, however, on-line agencies are realizing how important it is to obtain their own higher-margin inventory contracted directly from the supplier.

The Agent Model versus the Merchant Model

Some travel agents, Travelocity included, are considering shifting from the traditional agent model of commission sales to a merchant model of reselling travel services. Under the traditional agent model, the agent sells airline tickets at the airline's published fare in return for a contractually agreed-on commission from the airline. But airlines have been whittling away at commissions for agents. Finally, on October 24, 2001, Continental Airlines announced elimination of commissions on travel booked through the Internet. Although all travel agencies will lose the percentage of revenue that came from commissions, the move may prove positive for on-line agencies. Because of the dual blows of recession and terrorism, airlines are struggling. The result is that airlines face extreme pressures to both reduce costs and fill empty seats.

Thus, agents like Travelocity could move to a merchant model—buying airline ticket and hotel inventory at a wholesale price and reselling it at another, higher retail price. If on-line agencies can purchase blocks of excess inventory from the airlines directly and then sell them on their sites at a higher price, they can in effect extract a "fee" on the sale of the ticket. For example, Travelocity.com could purchase 10 seats (excess airline inventory) from an airline at $250 each and then sell them at $270, netting a $20 gross profit. Tickets not sold could be bought back by the supplier. This revenue model, called the merchant model, benefits travel agencies and suppliers alike. Travel agencies are able to purchase inventory at lower cost, and suppliers can sell excess inventory to gain additional revenue. Analysts predict that airlines will increasingly rely on on-line agencies to move excess inventory despite their move to eliminate commissions. In addition, as an interim step, some agents (including traditional agents and Orbitz) have moved to a service-fee model. These agents sell airline tickets at the airline's published price but charge a modest service fee to cover the agent's costs and replace diminished commission revenues.

Will on-line travel sites be needed in the future? If airlines can sell tickets directly to customers, then perhaps they will not need either traditional or on-line travel agencies.

[3] Ibid.
[4] Jennifer Michels, "Online Travel Experts See More Mergers and Zero Commissions," *Travel Agent,* November 5, 2001.

Research, however, indicates that this is an unlikely scenario. Suppliers want to maximize their profits; having multiple distribution channels allows them to do this. What *will* change is the amount of business that travel agencies do. Industry analysts estimate that by 2003, supplier sites will capture 60 percent of the travel bookings compared with 40 percent by on-line agencies.

Travelocity.com Background

Travelocity.com is headquartered in Fort Worth, Texas, and caters primarily to leisure travel. In fact, the leisure customer segment accounts for 70 percent of Travelocity's on-line bookings. In just under five years of business, Travelocity has moved from being the 33,000th largest U.S. travel agency to the sixth largest in terms of gross travel bookings. Despite a concern about converting on-line travel browsers into buyers, Travelocity consistently converts more customers than any other on-line travel Web site. To keep up with the growing business and to meet service demands, Travelocity is hiring 25 customer service representatives each week. Currently, Travelocity's customer service area handles more than 14,000 calls and 3,000 e-mails per day.

In 2001, Travelocity demonstrated that it is one of the few on-line businesses that can make money. The company has gross margins of about 67 percent (calculated as [Revenues – Cost of Goods Sold]/Revenues). Travelocity earns revenue from travel commissions, advertising, and a cut of SABRE's booking fees.

Competitors

Travelocity faces two sources of competition: other on-line travel agencies and the direct-sales efforts of suppliers (e.g., airlines and hotels). Although suppliers value the indirect channel provided by travel agents, they prefer to create direct relationships with loyal customers.

The three major players in the on-line travel agency space are Travelocity, Expedia, and Orbitz. Other competitors include Priceline.com, Hotwire.com, and Lowestfare.com. As of 2000, Travelocity and Expedia led the on-line travel market with 35 and 25 percent, res, of gross on-line bookings. Expedia, like Travelocity, has turned a profit.

	June Growth			July Growth			August Growth			September Growth			October Growth		
Company	Seq.	Y-o-Y	Visitors (millions)	Seq.	Y-o-Y	Visitors (millions)	Seq.	Y-o-Y	Visitors (millions)	Seq.	Y-o-Y	Visitors (millions)	Seq.	Y-o-Y	Visitors (millions)
Travelocity	5%	19%	7.8	12%	20%	8.8	−4%	22%	8.5	−14%	13%	7.3	14%	20%	8.3
Expedia	1%	−2%	7.9	21%	42%	9.5	−2%	38%	9.3	2%	64%	9.4	3%	64%	9.7
Orbitz	NA	NA	3.8	40%	NA	5.3	31%	NA	6.9	−25%	NA	5.2	51%	NA	7.8

Note: "Seq." = month to month, "Y-o-Y" = year to year, NA = not available.
Source: C. E. Unterberg, Towbin, Expedia Company Report, December 2001.

Expedia.com

Expedia is the number two on-line agent behind Travelocity, as measured by gross travel bookings. Expedia, however, has been gaining market share. On July 16, 2001, Expedia announced that USA Networks agreed to purchase all of Microsoft's interest in Expedia.com. This could be a profitable and threatening alliance. USA Networks could potentially copromote its complementary travel products, including cruise packages, its upcoming Travel Channel, and its Ticketmaster/CitySearch properties, to establish a larger on-line travel group. Already, Expedia has been making strides in moving to a merchant model through its acquisition of Travelscape. Acquiring Travelscape has allowed Expedia to generate higher margin revenue in the hotel space. The USA Networks deal may propel Expedia farther along the merchant model track, leaving it less vulnerable to competition by new players such as Orbitz.

Orbitz.com

In June 2001, Orbitz appeared on the scene. Orbitz is operated by five major carriers: American, Delta, United, Northwest, and Continental Airlines. It is the first on-line site owned and operated by major carriers. (This collaboration by five major competitors brought scrutiny from the U.S. Department of Justice's antitrust division.) Orbitz provides information on two billion flight fare options, 200 hotel chains, 42 rental car companies, 18 cruise lines, and 30 vacation package providers. On-line travel agencies are concerned about the impact Orbitz will have on their business. Fueled by one of the largest advertising campaigns of a dot-com since 1999, Orbitz recorded $100 million in ticket sales and attracted 3.7 million visitors in the first month of operation. Orbitz has already gained a significant market share of 10 percent. Orbitz poses a sizable threat to its competitors, especially those who rely primarily on airline ticket sales for revenues, including competitors like Travelocity.com. Interestingly, Orbitz also has a link to another on-line travel site called Hotwire.com. On the Orbitz site, customers who have flexible travel times are directed to Hotwire. Using Hotwire, customers enter their departure and return dates and their airport origination and destination. Hotwire displays the price, and customers have one hour to purchase the ticket. The Hotwire price is lower than the typical Orbitz price because customer flexibility reduces the price. At the time of purchase, Hotwire displays the airline name and the specific flight times.

Priceline.com

Priceline epitomizes a new business model made possible by the Web. The site is geared to flexible, price-sensitive travelers. Rather than search for flights and fares, customers on Priceline submit bids for flights to their desired destination. Customers "name their own price" and input their credit card information. If the customer's bid is accepted, his or her credit card is automatically charged for the airline ticket. Customers do not know which airline they will be flying until after the bid is accepted. When entering a bid, customers can select their flight date and set the maximum number of connections they are willing to accept. Customers who use this site must be flexible because customers do not know their departure times or the duration of connections until after the ticket has been purchased.

Although Priceline is known primarily as a site on which to buy airline tickets, Priceline has expanded into additional product offerings, including rental cars, hotel rooms, new cars, and home financing. Although Priceline's attempt to expand the concept to groceries and gasoline was an abject failure, the travel division continues to do well. Currently, Priceline does not offer vacation packages.

Lowestfare.com

Lowestfare is not a particularly big threat to Travelocity, but the site is representative of the many travel sites available on the Web. Lowestfare.com offers discounted rates on air, hotels, cars, cruises, and vacation packages. The prevalence of travel sites means that consumers can easily check all these various travel sites in search of the lowest airfare.

Positioning for Two Types of Customers: The Loyal and the Cheap

Airlines have identified two groups of customers. The first are brand-loyal customers who tend to use one airline exclusively. Such customers are motivated by some combination of the frequent-flier programs of the chosen airline, corporate contracts with the airline, perceptions of the quality of that airline, and the dominance of that airline at the local airport. Such customers tend to buy tickets directly from that one airline instead of shopping around. For the loyal customer segment, airlines do not have an incentive to provide a service that allows customers to compare airline ticket prices, as this would conflict with their goals of extracting the surplus from this segment. The second group of customers consists of price-sensitive customers who seek the lowest-priced flight to the chosen destination.

Finding the Lowest Price: A Commodity Service

Although Travelocity offers a wide array of vacation packages, rental cars, and cruises, the bulk of its sales are airline tickets. Unfortunately, customers perceive the service of acquiring airline tickets to be a commodity product. With a commodity product, customers are driven primarily by price. The Internet makes it easy for customers to compare competitors' prices. For Travelocity, this convenience can negatively impact the bottom line. If a customer wants to book a flight from Boston to Chicago, he or she can search all the major on-line travel and airline sites in just a matter of minutes to identify the lowest fare. Travelocity understands that its customers are price sensitive and that often it is not able to offer the lowest fare in certain markets.

Fortunately, airlines' emphasis on loyal customers means that most airlines' direct channels are weakly positioned to compete with on-line travel agencies, such as Travelocity and Expedia, for the price-sensitive customers. Unfortunately, with the creation of Orbitz, airlines can compete semidirectly for the price-sensitive customer segment and also be in a position to gain access to valuable customer preferences and trends through Orbitz.

Orbitz is a serious threat to independent on-line travel agents, such as Travelocity, because Orbitz is owned by the very same airlines that supply tickets through on-line travel agents. The fear is that Orbitz will have preferential access to the best fares that these airlines provide. Some analysts on Wall Street feel that although the travel pie is large, Orbitz may represent a greater threat to Travelocity than some other potential entrants, given its more than $100 million advertising investment and the participation of most major airlines. Interestingly, however, agencies such as Travelocity and Expedia generate revenues through advertising, travel commissions, and a cut of the GDSs' booking fees. Because Orbitz is the "owner" of its own inventory, it does not generate revenue through booking fees or commissions. Orbitz also cannot sustain the levels of advertising and marketing expenditures to build brand awareness that it had made prior to its launch. How will Orbitz generate revenue? On December 2, 2001, Orbitz announced that customers would now pay a fee on top of the ticket price when purchasing from Orbitz. This fee is similar to the fee imposed by some traditional travel agents who saw their revenues cut when airlines reduced commissions paid to travel agents. Imposition of this fee is good news for other on-line agencies, such as Expedia and Travelocity.

Travelocity's Competitive Response

To keep pace with its competitors, Travelocity increased its advertising expenditures, improved its technology infrastructure, expanded its products, and entered into cobranding agreements.

Technology Infrastructure Improvements

Although on-line travel customers are concerned primarily with price, Travelocity also believes that customers are looking for the "right" price, not necessarily the "lowest" price. Travelocity believes that other aspects of the on-line experience, such as a good shopping experience and an easily navigable and reliable site, affect purchase. As a result, Travelocity invests heavily in its technological infrastructure and its customer service to ensure that its site is working and functional at all times.

Product Diversification

Travelocity, like Expedia, recognizes the need to diversify its product line in order to compete with incoming entrants such as Orbitz. Because it is difficult to compete with the supplier itself, Travelocity is pushing its nonair bookings more aggressively. Results include the following:

Hotel reservation revenues increased 132 percent over 2000.
Car rental revenues increased 98 percent over 2000.
Vacation/cruise sales nearly quadrupled since 2000.

As a result, nonair revenues accounted for 29 percent of Travelocity's revenues during the second quarter of 2001 compared with 20 percent in 2001.

Cobranding

Travelocity entered into partnership agreements with America Online, Yahoo!, Excite, Lycos, and Time Warner's Road Runner, among others. Most of these agreements are exclusive; Travelocity runs the travel section of the portals. In exchange for being able to reach a larger audience, Travelocity must share revenues with the portals for tickets sold through each site. Apart from some minor differences in formatting and features, the service and "experience" sold by Travelocity through the portals is the same as what appears on the Travelocity Web site. While it is advantageous to sell its service through cobranded sites because of economies of scale, Travelocity extracts a lower margin from these transactions because revenue is shared.

Loyalty and Competitive Impact

Despite these competitive moves, Travelocity still faces a fundamental threat. Consumers perceive Travelocity's primary product, airline tickets, as a commodity product, meaning that purchase decisions regarding the product are price driven. To combat this, Travelocity is launching several loyalty programs. These programs could play a significant role in helping Travelocity, given that 40 percent of on-line visitors who visited Travelocity also visited Expedia and vice versa.[5] The same is true for visitors to airline sites—30 percent of people visiting American and United Airlines sites cross between the two, with 55 to 60 percent also visiting other major airline sites.[6]

Examples of Successful Loyalty Programs

Across industries, loyalty programs reward customers for their continuing frequency and volume of business. Loyalty programs differ from mere discounting in that the customer generally must make repeated purchases over time in order to accrue the benefit—yesterday's purchases plus today's purchases lead to tomorrow's benefits. Example programs include the following:

- "buy-10-get-1-free cards" at local coffee shops
- airline frequent flyer programs
- cash-back bonus on credit cards
- bonus gifts for cereal box tops
- combined programs like airline miles for calling card usage
- branded credit card rebate programs (the rebate applies to the purchase of particular brands of items).

Types of Bonuses: In-Kind and Fungible

Loyalty programs can be divided into two categories, defined by the nature of the benefits. The first category offers an in-kind bonus, such as free airline travel as a reward for paid airline travel. The second category offers a fungible bonus in which the customer uses accumulated loyalty "points" to buy a "free gift" from a catalog. An example of a fungible benefits loyalty program is that of Hiltons. For each hotel stay, Hilton gives members "points" that can be used not only on future hotel stays but also on completely unrelated products, from flowers to Disneyland tickets.

---

[5] David, Newkirk, Brad Corrodi, and Alison James, "Catching Travelers on the Fly," *Strategy and Business,* Fourth Quarter 2001.
[6] Ibid.

In-kind loyalty programs are better at generating loyalty and additional revenue because the customer must stay with the company to redeem the bonus (e.g., use United Airlines award miles on a United flight). Even better, in redeeming the benefit, the customer may do additional paid business with the firm (e.g., paying for one airline ticket while redeeming miles for a companion ticket, ordering room service on a free hotel stay, or buying a muffin with free coffee). In contrast, fungible benefits programs are most useful when in-kind benefits would be too expensive to offer within a reasonable span of customer business, such as when it would take years for the average customer to earn a useful number of loyalty points.

Nonlinear Loyalty Programs

Although some loyalty programs offer benefits that are linearly proportional to the customer's volume of business, examining successful airline loyalty programs reveals that airlines award disproportionate benefits to their most valuable customers (their most frequent flyers). For example, United's loyalty program, Mileage Plus, gives members reward miles that equal the number of miles flown on a flight. But "Premier" customers (those who fly more than 25,000 miles per year on United) receive 125 percent reward miles, that is, instead of only 1,000 reward miles for a 1,000-mile fight, they get 1,250 reward miles. The most loyal customers (those who fly over 100,000 miles with United) get double the number of miles they fly (2,000 reward miles for a 1,000-mile flight). Likewise, customers who purchase first-class tickets receive a 50 percent bonus on their flight miles.

Loyal, high-mileage customers also enjoy other benefits, such as free upgrades, priority service, and discounted membership at the airline's lounge. Other airlines and hoteliers offer similar, nonlinear, tiered benefits programs that induce customers to reach particular volumes of business with the company each calendar year.

Using Loyalty Programs to Deepen the Relationship

Other industries have used loyalty programs to learn about their customers in an effort to sell them additional products and services. For example, U.K. supermarket chain Tesco launched a loyalty program in 1995. The loyalty program gives customers coupons and discounts when they buy groceries. But to participate in the loyalty program and receive the discounts, customers must give extensive demographic information about themselves. And each time customers check out at the cash register, they must give their loyalty card number. This means that Tesco knows exactly what customers buy, and Tesco can match with demographic data on the customer. Tesco's loyalty program gives it unprecedented information about its customers' buying habits and preferences, which Tesco uses to offer targeted promotions, new products, and new services. The program has been successful, growing to 10 million members in three years.

Retaining and Rewarding High Profit Margin Customers

Discount brokerage firm Charles Schwab offers a reward to customers who do a high volume of business with Schwab, inducing those customers to do even more business with the company. Specifically, Schwab offers Signature Services, through which high-net-worth individuals and active traders receive better, more personal service (such as dedicated account representatives, waived fees, reduced trading costs, and access to extensive research). In setting up an account, these customers must either open the account with $100,000 or prove their trading activity via statements from their existing broker. Segregating high-volume and low-volume customers lets Schwab conserve limited customer service resources while retaining high-profitability customers—in short, improving the loyalty of the customers who are worth keeping. Schwab can afford to give Signature Services customers more services because many brokerage costs (e.g., administration, monthly statements, and prospectus materials) cost the same for both small and large clients. Large-volume clients have higher profit margins, especially if they actively use additional services that create additional revenue. Moreover, active experienced customers often have lower support costs because they already know what they are doing. Finally, like Tesco, Schwab is diversifying its product base to include insurance and mortgage services (through a partnership with eLoan). Building a solid relationship with its loyal members makes it easier for Schwab to cross-sell additional services to them.

Using Loyalty Programs to Modify Customer Behavior

Airlines use their loyalty programs to influence customer behavior beyond simply encouraging repeat business. For example, they may offer customers double miles if they fly certain routes at certain times or give a special bonus for taking three more flights by a certain deadline. Airlines even use their loyalty programs to further disintermediate travel agents of both the traditional and the on-line variety. For example, United has offered up to 4,000 reward miles to customers when they booked their flight on-line at United.com for the first time. And customers receive ongoing bonuses of 500 miles each time they purchase a ticket directly from the airline. United has also used a mileage bonus to induce customers to fill out a questionnaire about their travel behavior, similar to Tesco's efforts to use a loyalty program to gather more information on customers.

Turning Loyalty Programs into Profit Centers

In general, a loyalty program is a cost center—a source of new costs in the form of administrative expenses, promotional costs, and the cost of the benefit itself. But many of the larger airlines have converted their loyalty programs into profit centers, selling "miles" to other companies for the other company's loyalty programs. Examples include the various travel partner programs (e.g., airline miles for staying with a partner hotel or for renting a car). Examples from other industries include Ameritrade's offer of up to 25,000 American Airlines miles for new accounts, American Express' offer of Delta Airlines miles for credit card purchases, and MCI's offer of five Continental Airlines miles for every dollar spent on MCI's calling card. Consumers' insatiable appetite for airline miles lets airlines sell loyalty program miles for about two cents a mile of up-front revenue. Such revenue brings a very high profit margin because (1) some consumers wait years before redeeming award miles, (2) some consumers never redeem their miles, and (3) airlines manage to restrict award travel to seats that would be empty anyway.

Travelocity's Targeted Loyalty Programs

Travelocity intends to both retain existing customers and encourage additional purchases from those customers. To accomplish this, Travelocity has developed a number of programs to build loyalty. (As of early 2002, none of Travelocity's on-line travel agent competitors offered loyalty programs.)

First, Travelocity launched a Travelocity credit card through Citibank. With this card, customers earn points on all modes of travel and face no blackout dates. For every 8,000 points earned on the card, the customer receives a $100 credit toward his or her travel purchase. To date, the card has been marketed through direct mail. Travelocity is working to develop more creative ways of marketing the card in an effort to increase response rates.

Second, Travelocity introduced a preferred traveler program called "Travelocity Preferred" to improve customer loyalty. For $29.95, customers receive Travelocity Preferred Benefits, and for $79.95 they receive Preferred Elite Benefits. The benefits for the Preferred Program include the following:

- Two category upgrades on Carnival Cruise Lines
- 15 percent savings at 4,000 nationwide restaurants
- Global assistance

For the $79.95 fee, customers receive the following:

- 5 percent cash back on specially marked Travelocity fares
- Airline club lounge passes (two per airline per year)
- 20 percent savings at 7,000 restaurants nationwide
- Personal concierge service

The Travelocity Web site states that as a Preferred Elite Member, customers can receive day passes to both the American Admirals Club and the US Airways Club. After booking a flight on either of these airlines using Travelocity, Elite Member must fill out a request form. Each Elite Member can request two passes per year for each airline club. Currently, Travelocity has 100,000 subscribers in this program, but the company is hoping to increase the impact of this program and has a yet-undisclosed plan to do this. Rather than relying solely on fee revenue from this program, Travelocity is hoping to develop programs and incentives that reward loyalty even more.

Travelocity faces challenges ahead, but it believes that its multifaceted strategy will allow the company to attract and retain current and future customers.

QUESTIONS

1. What are the strong and weak points of the current proposals for the loyalty program?
2. How does the increased competitive intensity with Orbitz and the airline sites affect the loyalty strategy?
3. What alternative program(s) would you propose to create value and help build a trusting relationship?

The Future of Digital Marketing

Introduction

Although the Internet's early burst of youthful exuberance is over, the steady march to maturity is only beginning. The Internet and digital technology will continue their inexorable penetration into all aspects of life and business. Business will adopt and leverage enterprise and supply chain technologies for an increasing percentage of business operations. Companies will connect digitally to their customers with increasing frequency.

Interconnectivity will increase in both depth and reach. Broadband will increase in penetration as companies slowly figure out what to do with that bandwidth and consumers learn to enjoy the natural advantages of instant access to a wide range of media. Wireless will also grow as a combination of 3G cellular and wireless network technologies advance along their natural adoption curves. More people will be able to access more digital services from more places than ever before.

As we learned from the initial slow rate of adoption of broadband, it is not just the existence of the technology that counts—it must be offered at an attractive price/value. Technology adoption is fueled by the continuing improvement in the price–performance ratio of electronic devices and services. The $3,000 corporate desktop computer of 10 years ago becomes the $300 portable consumer gadget of today, which becomes the $30 children's toy of 10 years from now. Telecommunication services that were priced in dollars per minute become priced in pennies per minute even as they increase in bandwidth. And software has the most powerful cost curve of all the technologies—once the development costs are covered, the marginal cost of creating another copy can be effectively zero. In many cases, the costs of hardware, software, and service are so low that companies can offer an inexpensive subscription-based package deal with virtually unlimited usage and no up-front investment on the customer's part.

At the same time that the costs of technology are dropping, the value is increasing. The drive toward standardization leads to network effects in the value proposition. Network effects mean that each new bit of digital technology increases the value of every other existing bit of digital technology. When anything can plug into anything and communicate with everything, the value of technology grows, and the range of applications expands.

〔〕 Marketing Structural Changes

More Information

The rise of digital technology is forcing marketers to create new depth to their content. As we saw in chapter 12, a 30-second ad, a pithy slogan, or a magazine ad needs to be backed by on-line information that covers dozens or hundreds of pages. Customers now expect to be able to find out anything on any product. Companies will be measured by whether they satisfy customers' curiosity and maintain a trustworthy level of transparency. Customers also want education to help them understand how to get the most out of new products, especially the complex digitally enhanced products that are becoming increasingly common. New infomericals and do-it-yourself segments will help customers buy and use products—if they are honest and complete. And with their busy lives, consumers will want 24/7 access to this information. Media advertising will be increasingly used to generate excitement and curiosity, driving customers to the Internet for in-depth information.

Industrial customers are especially demanding of good content before, during, and after the sale. In designing new products and considering a potential supplier's components, industrial customers need engineering and manufacturing support to ensure that the components they buy meet the exacting needs of their application. Industrial customers also need ongoing support to maintain a smooth flow of parts. That is, they need accurate information on availability and shipments. Companies that cannot provide reliable, in-depth information on a timely basis will not survive.

More Channels

More customers and more companies will see that multichannel operations are the way to go. Neither traditional channels nor the Internet suffice to cover every interaction between a company and its customers. Consumers will demand on-line access to everything—checking their bank balance on their cell phone before making a big purchase or checking whether a shirt bought at one retailer matches the pants found at another retailer. Yet the on-line channel will not cover everything. Sometimes, browsing the aisles, "kicking the tires," or talking to an informed salesperson is a crucial part of the purchase process. Moreover, the labor costs of the last mile of delivery will mean that many people will prefer to pick up purchases themselves rather than pay for delivery.

And retailers will come to encourage those pickups, preferring to have customers see the store and browse other products while picking up a purchase made on-line. Even service companies, which have recently tried to push people to low-cost self-service channels, will seek out personal contact with their most valued customers. Their goal is to up-sell, cross-sell, or just understand their customers a little better. Overall, the result will be much more intensive coordination among a growing number of channels, creating "one face to the customer" regardless of how the customer chooses to interact with the company.

More Innovation

On the broader stage, digital technology is a powerful innovation accelerator. Digital technology provides the tools to design, simulate, test, and implement the rollout of new innovations. Digital technology accelerates new product development. And new digitally augmented marketing strategies accelerate the roll out and adoption of new products. Digital innovation is self-amplifying, meaning that digital technology helps create new digital technologies. Innovation will therefore continue to accelerate.

Accelerated innovation, development, and adoption curves mean that more high-growth markets will appear in the future. The continued adoption of digital technology is a threat to the slow and an opportunity for the innovators. Existing forward-thinking companies and new start-ups will find exciting new opportunities, while laggards will face an unprecedented erosion of market share.

All Marketing Is Digital Marketing

In the early days of the Internet, companies created separate e-business units that focused on digital activities. Now, however, companies have come to realize that all functions are impacted by digital marketing strategies, so the separate organizational structures will become less prominent. For example, General Motors (GM) created eGM as a separate organization in 1998, but in 2001 it absorbed eGM back into the GM organization, recognizing that digital activities were integral to the organization as a whole.

The Rise of Customer Power

Customer power will only increase as more people use digital technology for more activities. The ability of both consumers and business customers to uncover the truth, share stories about products, or search for alternative suppliers means that companies will need to improve quality and create win-win relationships with customers. People will use multiple channels—entering an order over the Internet, choosing a pickup time on a cell phone on the way to the mall, inspecting the goods and making impulse purchases in the store, and paying for the purchase with an on-line payment transfer to the retailer. Customer with busy lives will seek to control the relationship.

Digital technology will have an even more profound impact on companies with business customers than on those targeting consumers. End-to-end integration will grow in prominence. As the technology becomes cheaper and more standardized, companies will connect with even their smallest business partners (both suppliers and customers). The result will be both tighter relationships with business partners and more efficient operations. Paradoxically, the same tools that let companies inexpensively create deeper connections will let them switch suppliers, too. To satisfy tough customers (both businesses and consumers), companies will need to create true value-added relationships.

The Rise of Trust, the Fall of the Untrustworthy

The rise of customer power, with its increasing demand for information, and the reduction in the cost of maintaining relationships will lead more companies toward selected or fully trust-based marketing approaches. Push marketing will provide less traction than in the past as customers become increasingly jaded to hype or repelled by low-value products and services. Fortunately, enterprise digital technologies will make it easier for companies to create the level of operational excellence and transparency required by a trust-based strategy.

To support relationship-based and trust-based marketing, companies will create more software for their own use as well as for sale. New tools that help advise and inform customers will be combined with readily accessible content about products to help customers make the right purchase. Trust-based advisors, deep product content, and sophisticated product selection aids will help companies earn the trust of customers.

Trust is an inextricably linked concept. When a company pursues a trust-based strategy, it needs to seek out trustworthy suppliers, business partners, and distributors. If an unreliable supplier or dishonest distributor can destroy your reputation, it behooves your company to certify the excellence and trustworthiness of strategic partners. Thus, more companies will expect more from their partners, thereby pulling those partners toward trust-based strategies, too.

Industries that provide critical products and services are the most likely to move toward trust-based strategies. These industries include key component and raw material suppliers to large manufacturers, financial services companies, and pharmaceuticals manufacturers. In addition, industries that provide truly valued, value-added products and services are likely to join the ranks of the trustworthy (i.e., luxury goods companies). Industries that depend on long-term repeat buying are also likely to go the way of trust-based strategies because they realize that retaining customer loyalty is more profitable than acquiring new customers. On the other hand, industries that are subject to brutal price competition, that have excess capacity, that suffer a fundamental inability to control quality, or that have undifferentiated commodity services are less likely to move toward trust-based strategies. Deal-prone customers will drive some firms and industries toward traditional push marketing, but this will be in a decreasing share of markets.

The technological resources and brand power of big companies will give them an initial advantage in crafting coordinated trust-based strategies. Large companies will have the muscle to insist that suppliers, partners, distributors, and retailers adhere to trustworthy codes of conduct and maintain operations excellence. But, as with all technology, trust-enabling technologies (relationship management systems and operational excellence enablers) will grow in availability and drop in cost. Software companies will create trust-enabling software for use at modest price points. Eventually, even the smallest companies will be able to implement a coherent trust-based marketing strategy.

Implications for Marketing Managers

Managers will find many opportunities in this rapid-growth world to leverage technology in support of marketing. Digital technology will change what people look for, how they look for it, and what they buy. Skilled marketing managers will watch for these shifts and leverage the technology to either proactively create new marketing strategies or reactively adapt to a dynamic marketplace. The new tools offer managers the opportunity to really create new value for their customers and for their companies because the better a company can connect to the customer, the greater the opportunity.

The use of digital technology to automate many routine interactions will shift the emphasis of marketing and sales from operational minutia of media placements, orders, and volume discounts to more knowledge-intensive relationship-based connections with customers. Marketing and sales will become more strategic and less operational. Underlying all this will be increased demand for highly coordinated information systems that put all employees on the same page to provide a seamless, high-quality service experience for the customer.

Unanswered Questions

Marketing managers should be aware that the future is not so much a technological utopia as it is the evolving application of digital technologies to more facets of personal and business life. With these new applications will come new challenges to individuals, businesses, and governments. Issues of continued adoption, privacy, security, reliability, and payments raise many questions. A wide-ranging number of questions about the future impact digital marketing:

- How far down the economic ladder will digital technologies penetrate, and will government encourage or mandate some form of universal service or broadband digital dial tone?
- How will other countries and other cultures (with their different viewpoints on intellectual property rights, personal freedom, data privacy, trust levels, business regulations, and so on) pursue the adoption of digital technologies and benefit from them?
- What will happen as the likes of Microsoft, America Online, Dell, T-Mobile, Sony, and Visa jockey for a greater slice of the digital economic pie and insert themselves into a greater percentage of on-line interactions?
- Will regulators, entertainment producers, entertainment distributors, and consumer electronics makers agree on mechanisms for distributing music and video in a way that respects fair use, provides equitable payments to copyright owners, is economically viable for distributors, and is easy to use by consumers?
- Will government impose regulations to preserve privacy and security of personal data?
- What will happen if the U.S. Postal Service implements its proposed plan to provide an e-mail address for every physical address in the country?
- Will cagey consumers seek ever more powerful methods of blocking spam, banner ads, cookies, television commercials, and sales calls through some combination of technology and government regulation?
- Will stockholders evaluate long-run customer relationships positively and pay more for their stock?

The answers to these open questions and many others will shape the details of digital marketing, creating some opportunities while destroying others. Marketing managers need to be ready to adapt to the different digital futures implied by questions such as these.

Methodology Supersedes the Details

Ultimately, the answer to the previous questions and the accuracy of specific prognostications about the digital future is not very critical. It does not matter very much whether customers use a cell phone implanted on their wrist or surf the Web on a six-foot-tall home theater screen; whether the future is dominated by Microsoft or some unknown start-up in a dorm; whether technology helps big companies vertically integrate and dominate or helps small companies craft agile, seamless alliances; or whether the future of digital technology is shaped by paternalistic government regulation or the street fights of monopolistic corporations.

What does matter, in a brave new world of uncertain and unpredictable new technologies and trends, is that the basics of marketing strategy remain unchanged. Managers still need to understand customers, create strategy, implement well, and build relationships with customers. The job of the marketing manager is to leverage all that the new digital technologies offer in service of these four steps. Managers must be sensitive to change, adapt quickly to it, and innovate in the face of uncertainty and rapid change. In summary, digital technologies augment the four steps in the following ways:

1. Understand customer needs and behavior
   - New feedback and data-gathering channels to uncover customers' needs
   - Reduced costs for high-volume data warehousing
   - New data analysis methods and software tools to spot developing trends
   - New on-line tools to test concepts and query customers
2. Formulate a strategy to fill needs
   - New knowledge work tools to coordinate strategy internally
   - New simulation and modeling tools to forecast response
   - New reach to leverage the products and services of business partners
3. Implement effectively and efficiently
   - Multiple media for connecting with and delivering service to customers
   - New enterprise tools for internal operation excellence
   - Supply chain coordination tools to aid in promotions and fulfillment
   - Multiple channels for distribution and reaching customers
4. Build trusting relationship with customers
   - New tools to customize products and services
   - Trust-based advisors to help customers make the right decisions
   - Increased transparency
   - Reduced costs for deeper long-run relationships with customers

Although the specific details are unpredictable and unimportant, digital technology will inevitably accelerate, intensify, and reduce the cost of marketing activities. What is important is that marketing managers use a sound methodology to understand their customers and guide their companies toward serving those customers better. At the same time, marketing managers will help guide the company's customers toward better utilization of the company's products and services. Throughout all the change, the issues of digital marketing are the same: how companies can create value for their customers that, in turn, creates value for their shareholders.

We think that a paradigm shift is taking place that will move more and more companies to trust-based strategies. The Internet and the information it brings to customers is unstoppable. Companies that stake out the trust territory will gain a big first-mover advantage. Companies that maintain collaborative relationships with customers will flourish.

卐卐 Introduction to Citibank Online Case

This case illustrates the impact of digital technologies by describing the efforts of Citibank to capitalize on digital technology while leveraging its existing multichannel assets.

CHAPTER 18

Citibank Online

Introduction

Mark Parsells, president and chief operating officer of Citibank Online, is responsible for Citigroup's on-line retail banking strategy and implementation. Prior to his arrival at Citibank, the company had pursued several different on-line strategies and launched multiple Internet-based products over the previous two years. Citibank was committed to developing an effective Internet presence and was willing to experiment with Internet strategy. Yet Parsells knew that the bank would soon expect positive and demonstrable returns on the large investments made thus far. In addition, his strategy and its subsequent execution needed to prepare Citibank for long-term competition with an increasing number of entrants with novel business models and strategies, many of whom lacked short-term profit expectations. The following questions direct his efforts:

- What is the right mix of price, service, on-line access, and physical presence?
- What is the right positioning for the on-line service, and on what terms or features would it compete?
- In what ways is a large and profitable bank with millions of accounts helpful to establishing a competitive on-line service in this space, and to what extent is it a liability? What assets can be leveraged, and what legacies need to be overcome?
- Is Citibank Online evaluating its success with appropriate metrics?

Why On-Line Banking?

Long before the Internet appeared in consumers' homes, banks were trying to interest people in banking from home via personal computers. Banks desperately wanted to replace the costly handling of paper checks and walk-up retail services with low-cost-of-service computer-based services. Indeed, this low cost of service for on-line banking drove the business models and marketing messages of early on-line banks. On-line banks parlayed their lean cost structure into price-advantageous service offerings.

While traditional banks were levying a litany of fees on retail customers, on-line banks were touting no fees and higher interest rates on accounts.

Aside from the bottom-line efficiencies of electronic banking, banks saw the Internet as an immense opportunity for top-line growth for two reasons. First, on-line banking would help banks compete for the accounts of affluent professionals. Households that had PCs and Internet access had a very attractive demographic: young college-educated professionals in need of a wide range of financial services (checking and savings accounts, mortgages, car loans, credit cards, savings accounts for children's education, and so on) Second, the Internet would help banks exploit the ongoing relaxation of the Depression-era Glass-Steagall Act rules, letting banks offer new financial services, such as insurance and brokerage services. The Internet promised the potential to create financial supermarkets at which consumers could access a comprehensive range of financial services. Banks hoped that offering more services to customers would both create new earnings streams and increase customer loyalty.

Against this backdrop of the fundamental price and service advantages of on-line banking was the rising exuberance for all things Internet related. Analysts' projections for exponential growth, hot IPOs, and a gush of venture capital drove the formation of a wide range of dot-com ventures in every sector of the economy, including banking and financial services. Internet proponents argued that a new economy would arise that would replace the old economy. Meanwhile, old-economy firms like Citibank were not about to sit idle.

History of Citibank's Early On-Line Efforts

Citibank's initial on-line consumer products took two forms: Direct Access and Citi F/I. Direct Access was a Web-based retrofit of Citibank's old dial-up PC banking service. The primary purpose of Direct Access was simply to provide account holders with basic information regarding their accounts. Direct Access was the latest incarnation of Citibank's long-running effort to move customers toward electronic banking. Citibank positioned Direct Access as a value-added service for traditional retail banking.

Citi F/I: Competing with Yourself

In contrast with Direct Access, Citi F/I was a newly formed, stand-alone, Internet-only banking unit. It was a separate organization within Citibank with the expressed purpose of competing directly with Citibank's own traditional banking business. Citi F/I would displace Citibank because the old brick-and-mortar division was thought to be too slow, too big, and too burdened with existing systems and processes to offer a competitive and compelling on-line offering. Instead, Citi F/I would operate with a lean Internet-only operation without the costs of bank buildings, impressive lobbies, or tellers. Moreover, research firms such as Jupiter predicted 400 percent annual growth in on-line banking, meaning that Internet pure-play banks would attract large amounts of capital and enjoy huge valuations. With these advantages and assuming that Internet-only banks were the future of the banking industry, Citi F/I hoped to ultimately put the traditional bank out of business.

John Reed, Citigroup's chairman and co–chief executive officer at the time, championed the creation of Citi F/I in June 1997. He and others argued that Citi F/I should cannibalize Citibank's accounts before another on-line entrant did so. After more than two years of development, Citibank debuted its Citi F/I to the public. In comparison, BankOne (a traditional bank competitor to Citibank) launched its Wingspan.com pure-play on-line banking unit after only five months of development. Initial public reception for Citi F/I was lukewarm, and other on-line banks also discovered the excessive optimism of initial market predictions and the exorbitant costs of attracting account holders.

Citi F/I Gains a COO but Loses Its Champion

In an effort to improve Citi F/I, Citibank hired one of Wingspan.com's key personnel, Mark Parsells. Parsells was the head of strategic planning and business development and general manager of the Wingspan Marketplace, the Wingspan group that sold loan and insurance products. Like Citi F/I's relationship with Citibank, Wingspan.com was a pure-play greenfield effort by BankOne. Like Citi F/I, Wingspan.com was a separate entity from its parent firm, for many of the same reasons cited for Citi F/I's separation. Both Citibank and BankOne believed that existing processes, metrics, incentives, and personnel would make it difficult for an existing traditional bank to implement an effective on-line strategy at "Internet speed." Parsells became head of Citi F/I in February 2000 after interviewing with CitiGroup's top Internet management, including Reed.

Arriving for his first day at Citibank on February 28, 2000, Parsells faced a difficult situation: Reed, the spiritual leader of the Internet vision, which had attracted Parsells to Citibank, announced his resignation on that same day. Clearly, big changes were likely for Citibank's on-line consumer division. In addition to Reed's resignation, the performance of Citi F/I product was trailing expectations. The general consensus was that the Citi F/I project had taken too long, cost too much money, and generated too little in return. Worse, others on the traditional side of Citibank resented Reed's efforts to create an on-line bank to supplant the traditional bank. Bereft of its champion and facing detractors from the traditional side of Citibank, Parsells would need to craft a new strategy for Citibank's on-line efforts.

Competitive Environment during the Early Efforts

At the same time that Citibank was crafting its on-line banking initiatives, others were launching their efforts. At the time that Parsells joined Citibank in February 2000, the on-line banking industry took two forms: traditional banks offering Web access to existing retail accounts (e.g., Citibank's Direct Access) and pure-play, or Internet-only, banks (e.g., E-Trade Bank and NetBank)[1]. In some cases, traditional banks spawned ostensibly separate pure-play Internet banking units (e.g., Citibank's Citi F/I, and BankOne's Winspan.com).[2]

Traditional Banks

The traditional banking sector is comprised of banks that provide at least some access to account information and services over the Internet. Included in this segment are Citibank's Direct Access, Fleet Bank, Bank of America, and Wells Fargo Bank. Some

---

[1] Piper Jaffrey 1999 Online Banking Report.
[2] Karen Epper Hoffman, "Fuming Customers and Whistling Bells," *Bank Technology News,* June 2001.

advantages inherent to these traditional banks are a large established base of existing account holders, a wide variety of financial products, and a well-established brick-and-mortar presence. As a result of their longer business histories, traditional banks also tend to generate greater trust among their banking clients. A Deloitte Consulting survey recently reported that about two-thirds of the respondents are not interested in Internet banking and will require education and better on-line service to overcome this stated lack of interest. Jupiter research, by contrast, predicted that about 40 percent of U.S. households will conduct some banking transactions on the Web by 2005.[3] Some of the larger banks in this space had successfully enrolled several million account holders in their on-line services.

Internet-Only Banks

Banks in this sector included NetBank, Wingspan, directbanking.com, and BankDirect. Without a brick-and-mortar presence, account holders use existing ATM networks for physical transactions, and they often use such services as direct deposits and on-line bill payment to conduct other business. The key selling points of Internet-only banks were few (if any) fees, generous interest-bearing checking accounts, and cutting-edge, technology-based services, such as access to accounts through cell phones and personal digital assistants (PDAs).

In late 2000, the largest Internet-only bank, E-Trade Bank, had approximately 290,000 accounts. Despite touted advantages, such banks held only about 5 percent of the U.S. Internet banking market[4] and considerably less of the overall consumer banking market. While Wingspan.com was more effective at developing and launching its service than was Citi F/I, it too was unable to attract the volume of new accounts that its market research had suggested were possible. Growth at Wingspan.com was sluggish, signing up only 107,000 customers in its first six months since its 1999 launch despite having spent $150 million. Internationally, Internet-only banks were a bit more successful. Egg, a British Internet-only bank, had over 1.2 million customers.[5]

On-Line Banking's Fatal Flaw: Early Adopters versus Late Adopters

Through his experience at Wingspan.com and with the help of new and revised research, Parsells concluded that the price-based Internet-only model was fatally flawed. The Internet-only banks were based on research of on-line users in 1997 and 1998. These early adopters rarely doubted the Internet's security, despised going into branches, disliked old-economy brand names, and made choices primarily by price. Such priced-based customers are not the best customers. "Price-based customers are only looking for the best deal. You will never be able to keep those customers or make money off of them," Parsells said. Early adopters were also technophiles who were comfortable with their ability to handle a technology product. In early 1999, only 4.4 million U.S. households were banking on-line—a fraction of the mainstream 80 million banking households by any measure of the total market.[6]

---

[3] The Red Herring, www.redherring.com/industries/2000/1005/ind-webfinance100500.html.
[4] The Industry Standard, www.thestandard.com/article/display/0,1151,19581,00.html.
[5] The Red Herring, www.redherring.com/companies/2000/1020/com-egg102000.html.
[6] Piper Jaffrey 1999 Online Banking Report.

The customers who came on-line in 1999 and 2000, however, were very different from the early adopters. These new on-line customers wanted a trusted, traditional brand that would keep their personal information secure, remain financially solvent, protect their assets, and deliver great customer service. They were less comfortable with technology and less tolerant of glitches. A 2001 study by Jupiter Media Metrix found that mainstream customers were more risk averse than early adopters—more focused on usability and security.[7] "They will wait until something has become an established standard, and even then they will want to see lots of support and tend to buy, therefore, from large-well-established companies," said Geoffrey Moore, author of *Crossing the Chasm: Marketing and Selling High-Tech Products to Mainstream Consumers.* Mainstream consumers also wanted access to their accounts across multiple channels, including the Internet, phone, branches, ATM, and interactive voice response. A 2001 TowerGroup study found that 85 percent of Americans who have signed up for on-line services still regularly visit a branch bank. This shows that Americans are taking advantage of new technologies and multiple channels even though those new channels have not supplanted the old. "A lot of people are more comfortable doing specific types of activities with branch staff, such as opening an account or discussing a problem," said Michael Weill, managing director of primary market research at TowerGroup. Convenience and value—defined as easy access to all accounts in one place and services like free electronic bill payment—were more important to these customers than price alone.

Citibank Online: Citibank's Reformulated On-Line Strategy

In early 2000, Citibank knew that pure-play Internet banking was not playing well, yet the promise of on-line banking was too tempting to abandon completely. In late May 2000, a few months after Reed's departure, Parsells was tapped to implement the new on-line strategy for Citigroup (the parent of Citibank). By the end of June, Parsells got approval to scrap the pure-play Citi F/I in favor of a new "bricks-and-clicks" strategy. Rather than exist as a separate entity, Citibank Online would work within the traditional bank. The new strategy was to offer a "personal financial portal," which offered a view into each account holder's financial world. Specifically, Citibank Online provided access to banking and brokerage accounts and additional services, such as on-line bill payment, fund transfers, and integration with Citibank's other on-line products. Furthermore, in creating the personal financial portal, it also offered robust planning tools, real-time market information, portfolio trackers, and other services.

The new improved Citibank Online would merge the existing on-line services: Citi F/I and Direct Access. Parsells's team committed to design, develop, and launch the product in only 12 weeks. If successful, Parsells would earn a "quick win" for the demoralized team. More important, a successful launch of Citibank Online would prove Citigroup's ability to execute an effective Internet strategy in the post-Reed era.

---

[7] Karen Epper Hoffman, "Fuming Customers and Whistling Bells," *Bank Technology News,* June 2001.

Citibank Online launched on October 1, 2000. According to plan, the time from inception to development and launch was 12 weeks. Citibank Online was a major success in its initial form, exceeding initial goals. The site skyrocketed in the rankings, operated under more favorable economics, had significantly better business results, raised morale through the timely launch, and, most important, proved that old-economy Citigroup could deliver on the new-economy Internet.

The Service Offering

Citibank Online was now the most content-rich, fully integrated site in the industry. Account holders had access to checking and saving accounts, brokerage accounts, credit card information, retirement products, and personal loans. Citibank Online users could use services like free on-line bill payment, investment information for brokerage account holders, a "financial health check" for general evaluation of users' financial situations, and "smart deals," which were tailored special offers for account holders, such as incentives for enrolling in direct-deposit programs. In addition, customers could personalize their home page with market news, up-to-the-minute portfolio trackers, account information, and links to favorite sites. With the exception of brokerage services, these features were available to existing Citibank account holders without additional fees.

Performance Metrics

Citibank also wanted to set performance goals for its on-line operations, ensuring that Citibank Online contributed to the bottom line. But whereas measuring the performance of a stand-alone business such as Citi F/I is easy, measuring the performance of an adjunct service, such as Citibank Online for traditional Citibank customers, is harder. Citibank chose to evaluate its on-line efforts in two ways. First, Citibank would judge Citibank Online by its ratings from an independent rating service—judging Citibank Online's relative performance against competing on-line banking efforts. Second, Citibank would measure Citibank Online's contribution to return on the invested capital by assessing how Citibank Online customers differed from Citibank's non–on-line customers.

Industry Ratings

While there are a number of rating services, Citibank Online's goal was to rank number 3 in the Gomez rankings by the end of 2001. Gomez.com is a popular rating service that evaluates and compares on-line products and services in a variety of industries. Gomez rates on-line services on a number of dimensions, such as breadth of services, site performance, fees, availability and quality of customer service, and the experiences of several consumer segments. Gomez describes itself as follows:

> Gomez is the leading provider of e-commerce customer experience measurement, benchmarking, and customer acquisition services to help firms build successful e-businesses and guide consumers in transacting online. Gomez provides an unparalleled view of online customer experience by combining industry specific expertise, a thoroughly objective and extensive Internet evaluation methodology, and high-quality community ratings and reviews of online businesses.[8]

---

[8] Gomez.com, www.gomezadvisors.com/

At the time of Parsells's hiring, Citibank's Direct Access was ranked an unimpressive number 9, and Citi F/I held the dismal number 17 spot. By November 2000, after only five weeks in the market and 14 months ahead of schedule, Citibank Online had vaulted up the rating scale. Gomez ranked Citibank Online as the number 1 Internet banking service—the first time a traditional bank had held that coveted position. Citibank Online beat a number of other competitors, including both Internet-only banks (e.g., NetBank and Wingspan) and other clicks-and-mortar banks (e.g., Key Bank, Bank of America, and Wells Fargo). In their review of Citibank Online, Gomez stated, "Citibank Online is beginning to make the financial supermarket concept a reality," and praised the service for access to a variety of accounts, excellent bill payment services, and easy-to-understand disclosure about the cost and features of Citibank's many available financial products.[9] In December, Citibank Online received other accolades in the form of a number one rating from Forrester Research and being voted "Best of the Web" by Forbes.

Return on Investment

By combining the Direct Access and Citi F/I businesses, operating expenses were reduced by over 50 percent. Despite the cost reduction, new account acquisition in the first quarter of 2000 was up over 50 percent compared to the first quarter of 1999. Return on the invested capital, or the financial benefit to the firm as a whole, was measured using the following four metrics:

- **Improvement in Attrition Rates:**   Users of Citibank Online tended to have lower attrition (account cancellation) rates than account holders who used only Citibank's traditional services. During their first year, on-line users tended to average 5 percent attrition, while 20 percent of traditional, off-line-only customers tended to cancel their accounts. Attrition rates were less than 1 percent for on-line users in the following years. To maintain these lower attrition rates, Citibank Online offered services to make the site "stickier" and provided disincentives for customers to cancel their accounts. On-line bill payment and portfolio trackers were examples of such services.
- **Higher Balances:**   Account holders who made use of the Internet channel tended to have higher balances and more accounts than those who used only the traditional channel.
- **New Customers and Activations:**   Citibank Online provided a new way to attract new customers in addition to traditional or off-line marketing efforts. The company also focused on activating existing off-line account holders or having them use Citibank Online. To make the process simple, off-line customers simply had to enter their ATM card number and PIN to activate the service.
- **Cross-Sell Opportunities:**   Increased information about customers combined with Citibank's wide variety of financial products afforded Citibank Online many cross-selling opportunities. Specifically, through the offering of "Smart Deals," which are incentives for users to expand their on-line usage, Citibank Online tailors offers to individuals. For example, users are offered $50 to enroll in on-line bill payment, direct deposit, and other services.

---

[9] Gomez.com, www.gomezadvisors.com/scorecards/

Emerging Competition: "Hybrid" Banks and Others

Simultaneous with the launch of Citibank Online, a new form of competition emerged in the on-line banking space: hybrid banks. Typically, hybrid banks are new banks with a strong Internet presence that respond to customer demand for physical presence, providing nontraditional branches or locations to conduct simple transactions. Juniper Bank launched with the suite of technologically advanced features commonly associated with Internet-only banks, including wireless and PDA access. Through a cooperative relationship with Mail Boxes Etc., customers can make deposits at some Mail Boxes Etc. locations. Richard Vague and James Stewart, former Wingspan.com executives who believed strongly in the future of on-line banks despite the lack of demonstrated commercial feasibility, founded Juniper. Using ATMs as a historical example, they predicted that Internet-only banks would soon enjoy similar popularity despite slow initial adoption. Despite difficulties for all Internet-only banks, Juniper was able to raise over $150 million venture capital from some of Silicon Valley's most prestigious firms.[10] ING, a Dutch bank with an international presence, launched its INGDirect service in the United States. To create a physical presence, INGDirect constructed cafes in a few major U.S. cities to provide some of the services available at bank branches. Specifically, the cafes accept deposits, are staffed by representatives who provide sales and customer service assistance, and offer ATMs and computer terminals for account holders to make transactions or surf the Web. The U.S. president and chief executive officer of INGDirect, Arkadi Kuhlmann, believes that INGDirect will have 500,000 customers in two years.[11] Other traditional banks also pursued the hybrid bricks-and-clicks approach of bringing on-line banking features to their traditional banking masses. For example, FleetBoston doubled its on-line banking enrollment to 1.4 million by July 2001, and Bank of America Corp's enrollment increased 64 percent during the same one-year period, reaching 3.3 million by July 2001.[12] Meanwhile, the pure Internet-only banking concept faded. By the end of 2001, it was evident that the Internet-only business model was not working. BankOne dissolved Wingspan.com in June 2001 and brought the accounts into its own operations. NetBank acquired rival Internet-only bank Compubank (which had signed up only 6,000 customers from its launch in 1998 to April 2000). Two weeks after acquiring Compubank, NetBank acquired Market Street Mortgage, a brick-and-mortar operation that would add physical locations to the bank for the first time.[13]

Opening Doors Leads to Opening Accounts

One of the reasons for the emergence of hybrid banks is that research showed that about 80 percent of the new products and services sold by banks are done in person. Once a service is purchased, customers can migrate on-line to do routine transactions,

---

[10] The Industry Standard, www.thestandard.com/article/display/0,1151,19581,00.html.
[11] The Red Herring, www.redherring.com/industries/2000/0728/ind-onlinebank072800.html.
[12] Bill Stoneman, "Expectations in Changes for Online Banking and Brokerage," *American Banker,* July 2001.
[13] David Roundtree, "NetBank Marks Fifth Anniversary," *Bank Technology News,* June 2001.

but the physical contact remains important. As a case in point, Internet-only bank directbanking.com opened a physical location in Boston, and during its first four and a half months, walk-in customers increased the bank's assets by $22 million, compared to the $20 million during the same time on-line. "We're a customer-driven organization, and customers told us that they like the convenience of the Internet, but they also want to know they have the access to a location," said senior vice president Janis Dodge. "People want to know there is someone they can deal with, that there's a substance behind it. They can picture it, and it gives them confidence."[14]

In addition to Internet pure plays and hybrid banks, other players have also become interested in the Internet banking market. Recall Citibank Online's strategy of providing a "personal financial portal," giving users access not only to traditional bank services but also to other financial services and personalized information. Today, there are other firms that might be able to move into similar territory, particularly brokerage firms, insurance companies, and credit card issuers. Such firms possess some of the assets that appear to be a requirement for success, such as a trusted brand and large numbers of account holders. In addition, the technical barriers to entry are relatively low. While some of the potential entrants might not be able to become (or interested in becoming) a replacement for a full-service bank, the ability to offer products like CDs and money market accounts may lure some consumer funds away from full-service banks. Because high-transaction accounts such as checking and savings are more costly than CDs and money market accounts, these firms are happy to attract only the low-transaction accounts from traditional banks.

Citibank Online Today

As of August 2001, Citibank had signed up nine million user accounts through its Web portal, Citibank.com.[15] In 2000, Citibank became the first financial institution to offer aggregated account services, letting consumers consolidate services for banking, credit card payment, insurance, and brokerage services through one sign-on. For example, consumers can pay credit card bills or make loan payments from their on-line checking accounts. They can get quotes and information on life, auto, and home owners insurance (through Travelers Insurance Co., Citigroup's 1998 acquisition) or track their portfolios at Salomon Smith Barney.

Citibank continued to enjoy its top-ranked position from Gomez, which praised the site's easy-to-use menus and good customization capabilities. For example, customers can choose what their account home pages display, including content from other sites, such as other credit cards or frequent-flyer accounts. The site also lets customers set up recurring payments, access financial news and research, apply for student loans or home equity loans or mortgages, use financial tools, or e-mail money to other people through Citibank's C2it person-to-person payment service.

Pooling information about a customer from across the customer's relationships with different areas of Citigroup (such as Travelers or Salomon) also lets Citibank

---

[14] Janet Bigham Bernstel, "Online Pay-Off?," *Bank Marketing,* July 2001.
[15] Christopher Huen, and Alorie Gilbert, "Websites That Work," *InformationWeek,* August 27, 2001.

make smarter decisions about how to serve the customer. For example, a customer who has a large account with the Salomon Smith Barney brokerage unit and a Citibank credit card is not the ideal target for a late fee if their payment arrives a few days late.

QUESTIONS

Although Citibank Online has been successful thus far, maintaining its leadership position will be far more difficult given the potential competition and improvement among direct competitors. In light of Citibank's objectives, how do you recommend that Parsells proceed in order to maintain the company's leadership position? In constructing your proposal, bear in mind the following issues:

- **Value versus Price:** Citibank Online considers itself a value play as opposed to a low-cost provider (in the form of low fees and interest-bearing checking accounts) offered by Internet-only banks. What is the appropriate mix of features, service, and cost for Citibank Online?
- **Trust:** What specifically creates trust in consumers? Physical presence? Operating history? Do you believe that, like ATMs, on-line banking will soon have the full confidence of the majority of consumers? Are there other nonbanks that may have created ample trust in their existing customer base to move into banking?
- **Emerging Models:** How effective will hybrid banks be at offering the benefits of both Internet-only and traditional banks? How successful do you think that the on-line banking industry will ultimately be? What other threats do you perceive?
- **Innovation:** Now that Citibank Online has successfully integrated clicks and mortar and exploited the multichannel link, what should its next innovation be? What should Citibank do to keep growing?

Name Index

Subject Index

193